THE
CARDBOARD
CLASSROOM

A **DESIGN-THINKING GUIDE** FOR ELEMENTARY TEACHERS

DOUG ROBERTSON | JENNIFER BORGIOLI BINIS

Solution Tree | Press *a division of* Solution Tree

555 North Morton Street
Bloomington, IN 47404
800.733.6786 (toll free) / 812.336.7700
FAX: 812.336.7790

email: info@SolutionTree.com
SolutionTree.com

Visit **go.SolutionTree.com/instruction** to download the free reproducibles in this book.

Printed in the United States of America

Library of Congress Cataloging-in-Publication Data

Names: Robertson, Doug, 1981- author. | Borgioli Binis, Jennifer, author.
Title: The cardboard classroom : a design-thinking guide for elementary
    teachers / Doug Robertson, Jennifer Borgioli Binis.
Description: Bloomington, IN : Solution Tree Press, 2022. | Includes
    bibliographical references and index.
Identifiers: LCCN 2021054251 (print) | LCCN 2021054252 (ebook) | ISBN
    9781952812552 (paperback) | ISBN 9781952812569 (ebook)
Subjects: LCSH: Elementary school teaching. | Instructional
    systems--Design. | Critical thinking--Study and teaching (Elementary) |
    Classroom environment.
Classification: LCC LB1555 .R64 2022 (print) | LCC LB1555 (ebook) | DDC
    372.1102--dc23/eng/20211213
LC record available at https://lccn.loc.gov/2021054251
LC ebook record available at https://lccn.loc.gov/2021054252

Solution Tree
Jeffrey C. Jones, CEO
Edmund M. Ackerman, President

Solution Tree Press
President and Publisher: Douglas M. Rife
Associate Publisher: Sarah Payne-Mills
Managing Production Editor: Kendra Slayton
Editorial Director: Todd Brakke
Art Director: Rian Anderson
Copy Chief: Jessi Finn
Production Editor: Gabriella Jones-Monserrate
Content Development Specialist: Amy Rubenstein
Acquisitions Editor: Sarah Jubar
Copy Editor: Jessi Finn
Proofreader: Elijah Oates
Text and Cover Designer: Abigail Bowen
Associate Editor: Sarah Ludwig
Editorial Assistants: Charlotte Jones and Elijah Oates

ACKNOWLEDGMENTS

From Doug Robertson:

Thank you first and foremost to my incredible wife, Angela, who did more than I'll ever know to make sure I could write this, and to my three children for being wonderful and crazy and finally falling asleep so Daddy could work. Thank you to the friends who listened to me talk endlessly about this and encouraged me. A million thanks to my coauthor, Jenn, without whom this book never would have been possible, as well as to Sarah Jubar, who would not take no as an answer from me, and Gabriella Jones-Monserrate, who guided the book's creation with a steady and sure hand. Thanks also to the rest of the Solution Tree team.

The most thanks go to every student in every class I've been lucky enough to teach and so many of the teachers I've had and worked alongside. Teaching is all I've ever wanted to do, and you renew that in me every day.

And to everyone above the administrator level: pay us better and treat us like the professionals we are. We deserve it.

From Jennifer Borgioli Binis:

I was deeply amused to discover writing the acknowledgments was the hardest part of this book for me. The hardest part wasn't figuring out how to help Doug tell his story—that part was easy. Thanks, Doug, for being a delightful writing partner. It was a chaotic adventure, and I learned a whole bunch, much like your students! The hardest part wasn't figuring out how to blend our voices. All the gratitude to the reviewers who volunteered their time to read early drafts and affirmed that we found a good mix. The hardest part wasn't figuring out how to work on a book during a global pandemic and a career change. That came about because of new and old friends of the heart and mind. Many thanks to the brilliant Amanda, Angela L., Angela S., Diane, Giselle, Heather, Joanne, Jonelle, Julie, Linda, Lisa, Marianne, Nora, Patti, Reshma, and almost all of EduTwitter, plus the generous souls at Buffalo Mutual Aid Network and the awesome nerds at r/AskHistorians who provided me a way to be useful and a sense of purpose when everything felt untethered. Finding the time wasn't hard. The best chef and human being I know, my husband Paul, made that possible, despite the efforts of the hufflelumps, Steve! and Kevin, who demanded all the pets and *fud* whenever they sensed an opportunity. The hardest part wasn't staying on track—all the gratitude to Solution Tree for assigning Sarah and Gabriella our project, as they were delightful to work with and ready with an extra oar when we found ourselves heading for a shoal. And the hardest part surely wasn't finding inspiration or motivation to work on the book. That came in infinite forms from teachers past, present, and future—the women, men, and nonbinary adults who, of all the professions in all the world, picked the messiest, most embattled, least understood one available to them. Teachers rock. You, dear readers, rock. I hope you all get the chance to tell your stories.

And just like that, I did the hardest part of this book. I think there's a life lesson here.

Solution Tree Press would like to thank the following reviewers:

Larissa Bailey
Second-Grade Teacher
Pleasant Valley School District
Bettendorf, Iowa

Cassie Hetzel
Fifth-Grade Teacher
Thermopolis Middle School
Thermopolis, Wyoming

Jennifer Carr
Instructional Coach
La Mirada Academy K–8
San Marcos, California

Katie Saunders
Middle Level Teacher
Anglophone School District West
Woodstock, New Brunswick

Charles Ames Fischer
Education Consultant
Decatur, Tennessee

Ericka Sutherland
Classroom Teacher K–2
Halifax, Nova Scotia

Natalie Fish
Kindergarten Teacher
Welchester Elementary School
Golden, Colorado

Natalie Vardabasso
Assessment Instructional Design Lead
Calgary Academy
Calgary, Alberta

Nathalie Fournier
K–5 French Immersion Teacher
Prairie South School Division
Moose Jaw, Saskatchewan

Visit **go.SolutionTree.com/instruction** to download the free reproducibles in this book.

TABLE OF CONTENTS

Reproducible pages are in italics.

CHAPTER 3
Design: How Can We Solve the Problem? 37

CHAPTER 4
Build: How Do We Create a Solution? 53

CHAPTER 5
Test and Revise: What Happens When We Try Out the
Solution and Respond to Data? 71

CHAPTER 6
Reflect: What Did We Learn? 87

CHAPTER 7
Put It Into Practice **103**

PART 2

Becoming a Design-Minded Teacher **117**

CHAPTER 8
Specific Designs. **119**

ABOUT THE AUTHORS

 **Doug Robertson** (he/him) is a fifth-grade teacher in the Gresham-Barlow School District of Gresham, Oregon. He received his bachelor of arts in multi-subject education from the University of the Pacific in Stockton, California (go Tigers!), in 2003 and has been teaching ever since. Over his years of teaching, he has taught fourth grade in northern Oregon; third and fourth grades in southern Oregon; third, fourth, and sixth grades in Hawaii on the island of Oahu; and third grade in Southern California. These schools include predominantly low-income neighborhoods, military populations, multiple-language households and classrooms, and a wide range of diverse student backgrounds.

Doug has run districtwide professional development on using technology and creativity in the classroom, as well as keynoted and presented at the IntegratED PDX conference in 2017, 2018, and 2019. He has also presented at multiple Computer-Using Educators (CUE) conferences on using the Google Workspace in the classroom and being the best weird teacher you can be. He also presented on making and using puppets in the classroom at the International Society for Technology in Education (ISTE) conference in 2015.

Doug has written three previous education books—*He's the Weird Teacher*, *THE Teaching Text (You're Welcome)*, and *A Classroom of One*—and one novel, *The Unforgiving Road*.

To learn more about Doug's work, follow him on Twitter and Instagram at @TheWeirdTeacher, and on TikTok at @WeirdTeacher.

Jennifer Borgioli Binis (she/her) is president of Schoolmarm Advisors, a freelance editing, fact-checking, and research service for education authors and publishers. A former middle school special education teacher and professional development provider, Jennifer facilitated large- and small-scale audit and design projects with and for schools, districts, and states. After almost twenty years of giving teachers words, she now helps teachers put their own words out into the world. She is published in gifted, special, and middle-level education and is a member of the Editorial Freelancers Association, the History of Education Society, and the Association for Supervision and Curriculum Development (ASCD).

Jennifer received her bachelor's degree in education from the State University of New York (SUNY) at Fredonia and her master's degree from Peabody College at Vanderbilt University.

To learn more about Jennifer's work, follow her on Twitter at @JennBinis. Visit her freelance editing and fact-checking service website at www.schoolmarmadvisors.com.

Please visit www.cardboardclassroom.com to access extra materials beyond this book. To book Doug Robertson for professional development, contact pd@SolutionTree.com.

PREFACE

We wrote large chunks of this book during the Great Stay Home of 2020–2021 while everyone was figuring out emergency schooling and what it meant to be a citizen of the world during a global pandemic. We wrote between bouts of panic over current events and our concerns for our and other people's families. We pulled on our lived experiences as educators, researchers, writers, builders, and designers to find words to describe a particular approach to teaching we know is joyful, messy, and adventurous—everything we hope students experience when they return to full-time in-person schooling.

Being *design minded* is about being open to inspiration and recognizing how big and small moments can lead to something unexpected and wonderful. It's not about having the perfect project or ticking off all of a checklist's boxes in a certain order by a certain time. It's less "Do this" and more "Have you considered this?" This book is the result of one teacher adopting a design mindset in the classroom and wanting to share the lessons he learned with the wider world. It provides a candid exploration of what it means to find the line between control and chaos in the classroom. We look across grade levels, standards, school district policies, budget constraints, the "big tests at the end," and everything else educators deal with and, we hope, offer a clear view of what's possible.

Our thanks to those who took the time out of teaching during a pandemic to share their thinking about design in their classrooms, especially Erin Quinn, Krystle Merchant, Beth Crawford, Trevor Aleo, Sherien Sultan, Scott Cody, M. David López, Justin Jackson, and Eliza Statile. Let this book be the lightning rod to invite students to bring their thunder.

This book is for our fellow designers, be they big or small.

—Doug and Jenn

INTRODUCTION
Lightning and Thunder

Thought precedes action as lightning precedes thunder.

—*Heinrich Heine*

If you are used to quiet and orderly schools, your first visit to an elementary classroom led by a design-minded teacher can be disconcerting. The noise usually registers first, the air full of words related to learning as well as those seemingly unrelated to the subjects listed on the class schedule. Once your ears adjust, you'll notice the mess. Odds are good there will be stacks of stuff—just *stuff*, everywhere. You might even find yourself wondering why and how exactly one goes about accumulating so much cardboard.

You'll likely have questions. Why is the teacher's desk buried under piles of papers? Is that student thinking, staring off into space, or counting tiles on the ceiling? Is another student doing the work of learning or doodling? One student group's entire project just collapsed into a pile of mush, and rather than bemoan their misfortune, they appear to be celebrating. Another group of students has been making last-minute changes to whatever they're working on and taking copious notes. What could they possibly be writing? In the few minutes you've been observing them, they've filled several blank sheets with notes and calculations, and there seems to be no end in sight.

Inevitably, your eyes will start to wander the room, looking for the teacher. We're used to the teacher being the tallest person in the elementary classroom, so you start there. When you don't see anyone who is a head taller than everyone else in the room, you lower your gaze to scan the groups of students. You find the teacher just as you begin to fear this roomful of students is somehow unsupervised. They're on the floor beside a student, transcribing as the student uses a variety of props and emotive gestures to talk through their process, their words coming at a faster pace than they themselves could write.

If this visit was planned so you could learn more about the concept of design in the classroom, you likely did research to prepare and came across resources such as IDEO's (2012) white paper *Design Thinking for Educators* or books like John Spencer and A. J. Juliani's (2016) *Launch: Using Design Thinking to Boost Creativity and Bring Out the Maker in Every Student* and Ann Kaiser's (2020) *Designing the Future: How Engineering Builds Creative Critical Thinkers in the Classroom*. You would have come across graphics and visuals describing a process that made you think you would hear things like *iterate* or *prototype* or *stage 3* when you positioned yourself next to a group "doing" design. Instead, when you ask a group what they're working on, a student carefully sets aside their clipboard, puts their hands on their hips, and proclaims, "Well, this is what happened. We tried this thing." They gesture toward a pile of stuff. "And it didn't work. So now we're gonna try this." And they make another gesture at a different pile of stuff. "And if that doesn't work, we're going to try this other thing. Or maybe we'll notice an easier way to make it work. Hopefully. And we're writing down what we learned here." They proudly hold up their clipboard, and there it is: their successes, failures, designs, and evidence of their learning.

This messy and imprecise space for iteration, failure, and learning is a cardboard classroom. Instead of a textbook-worthy explanation of a clear procedure, you see enthusiasm, vision, engagement, and learning. Instead of clean delineations between phases, you see jagged edges and rough-hewn solutions. It feels disorganized but hums along like a well-oiled machine. It looks frenetic but there's a clear sense of structure. Standards and goals are written in students' writing instead of put on the whiteboard by a teacher. The class likely sounds nothing like what your childhood classrooms sounded like, but you can't deny the joy and light filling the room. This book is about the process of getting from *students as participants in design* to *students as designers*, and from design as an add-on to design as a mindset. It's about the mistakes an elementary teacher made as he developed his identity as a design-minded teacher, going from nothing to all and then dialing it back to find the balance that works for him, his school community, his students' families, and most importantly, his students and their learning.

A column that learning scientist Daniel T. Willingham (2021) wrote on a viral Twitter thread concerning a father, his daughter, a can opener, and learning serves as a useful reminder about the importance of the balance we'll explore in this book. In the thread, the father explains that his daughter wanted to open a can of beans. His approach was to hand her the can opener and basically refuse to help. According to the thread, it took her six hours to open the can. The general response on Twitter was along the lines of "Why not teach her how to use the can opener?" The father, in effect, made the same mistake that Doug made as he was developing the structures for a design-minded classroom: the father leaned too far into expecting a learner to find her own solution. Turning *all* learning over to students isn't good for anyone, as they need guidance, grace, structure, and space. Yet just opening the can for the daughter would have leaned too far in the other direction; she wanted to learn how to open the can, not have someone do it for her. *The Cardboard Classroom: A Design-Thinking Guide for Elementary Teachers* details how educators can find the balance between opening the can and handing a student the can opener.

In the remainder of this introduction, you will learn what it means to be a design-minded teacher, who this book is for, and what you'll get from this book, and you will review a quick note about the citation practices used in this book.

What It Means to Be a Design-Minded Teacher

Teachers' mindsets and philosophies shape their classrooms in ways big and small. Boundaries aren't cut and dry, and it's impossible to simplify an individual teacher's entire philosophy into a single term. However, teachers often connect with a particular construct or organizing idea. For example, someone who is most comfortable with pedagogical practices that position them as a "sage on the stage," or someone who provides direct instruction, could be described as a *traditionalist*. A *progressive* teacher is likely one who has adopted a pedagogical approach that centers their students so they can act as a "guide on the side." Other teachers connect more with the idea of being a "meddler in the middle" and are uncomfortable with single-word labels because their pedagogy combines several different approaches. There are teachers who chafe at the idea of a scope and sequence and those who seek out scripted curricula to minimize the number of decisions they need to make. Meanwhile, teachers' pedagogical identities sit alongside or on top of their personal or political identities. Teachers of all pedagogical persuasions may identify as *conservative* or *anti-racist* or *trauma informed*. There might even be traditionalist teachers who are politically progressive and progressive teachers who are politically conservative reading this book right now. All these identities shape the experiences students have in the classroom, but practicing classroom teachers rarely explain how they got to their preferred construct or explain to other teachers what it means once they're there. Unfortunately, all too often, the people investing energy and words in trying to figure out and describe what's happening between teachers' ears are non-teachers.

Every generation of teachers has been scrutinized by non-teachers with varying degrees of insight. In 1938, Frances R. Donovan published an almost-four-hundred-page treatise on the inner workings of the American teacher, called *The Schoolma'am*. She broke teachers into categories (unmarried, married, widow, and the like) and provided, in excruciating detail, her observations on teachers' thinking (Donovan, 1938). When Dan C. Lortie published the first edition of his book *Schoolteacher* in 1975, he coined the phrase *apprenticeship of observation* to describe the decades-long process teachers go through observing teachers do their job before becoming teachers themselves, and the impact that process has on their identity. Some have even taken a philosophical approach, as Lee S. Shulman (2004) did in his foundational book *The Wisdom of Practice: Essays on Teaching, Learning, and Learning to Teach*, a collection of observations on the professional paradoxes teachers negotiate from autonomy and obligation and the mixed messages of teacher preparation and independent practice. More recently, Robert J. Marzano and Jana S. Marzano (2015) went all in for their book *Managing the Inner World of Teaching*, offering advice on how teachers can best think about their practice. Thinking and pontificating about teachers' thinking is a popular topic and sometimes a spectator sport.

Dozens more books look to explore, explain, extrapolate, or otherwise study from afar what happens between a teachers' ears, but this book isn't one of them. This book aims to show, not tell, and to advocate for how elementary teachers can overlay a design-minded approach on whatever mental models they hold regarding their relationships with students and pedagogy or with society and politics. This book describes, up close and personal, what it looks like to make decisions that create a classroom where the teacher and students are comfortable with being uncomfortable.

Artfully put, being design minded is about learning to predict the lightning of thought to control the thunder of action. By embracing a design-centered worldview, teachers and their students become like Doc Brown of the *Back to the Future* (Zemeckis, 1985) films, standing atop the clock tower of their minds, calling to the storm with the hope of changing someone's life. Pragmatically speaking, being design minded is about breaking bad habits related to the "game of school." Historians of education use the phrase *grammar of schooling* (Tyack & Cuban, 1995) to describe the things that happen in a school that distinguish it as a school; the grammar includes things like apple motifs, bulletin boards, and the calling of adults by a gender identifier and their last name. It also includes grades, the archetype of a teacher standing at the front of the room with students sitting at desks, and the idea that teachers have planned every second of the school day and carefully managed behavior. A classroom led by a design-minded teacher breaks many of those rules and challenges norms.

The design-thinking mindset involves being present with students and not flinching from inspiration. We want to help you trust yourself and your students in the moment. In effect, we want to model how possibility (the lightning) can power and create. We want to show you how you can use design (the thunder), in whatever form it takes for you, to explore the limits of what's possible in the elementary classroom.

Who This Book Is For

It would be swell if teachers from early childhood to higher education adopted a design-minded approach. But for us to be able to speak from a place of confidence and state firmly that every idea, activity, and practice in the book can work (and has worked) with students, we're focusing on grades 3–5 teachers with recommendations embedded throughout for K–2 teachers. This isn't to say middle and high school teachers couldn't adopt a design-minded approach. When we first put out a call to connect with other design-minded teachers on social media, most responses came from high school teachers. It made perfect sense, as there are many resources for high school teachers to do design with their students or incorporate design into their single-subject classrooms. However, we can only confidently speak to what a design-minded approach looks like in an elementary classroom, and frankly, a lot of adults think elementary students can't handle that approach. This book, we hope, disproves that.

We have both done professional development with teachers and have heard well-founded concerns from participants essentially saying, "This is great, but I don't have time to add one more thing to my classroom." This book isn't about adding. It's about thinking differently about the thousands of decisions you're already making. As a way to help you put that into practice, we'll periodically ask you questions about your thinking. You'll reflect on your decision-making process, how you became the teacher you are, and the kind of teacher (or administrator) you want to be.

The reason we focus on mindset is we know a teacher's thinking about their students, pedagogy, curriculum, and instruction impacts classroom dynamics (Martin-Kniep & Picone-Zocchia, 2009; Marzano & Marzano, 2015; Stitzlein, 2008). Meanwhile, the average teacher in the United States is a forty-something, nondisabled, cisgender white woman, a fact that serves as a reminder: being design minded cannot be a teacher's entire identity (Will, 2020). Attending to culturally responsive practices and engaging students in active citizenship, dissent, and content-specific instructional pedagogy are also part of a teacher's daily cognitive considerations (Hammond, 2015; Stitzlein, 2012). Adopting a design-minded approach to the classroom is a way to resolve some of the tensions emerging from competing pressures about all the various things teachers are asked (or told) to attend to. It's our hope that this book sits in conversation with other resources on how to teach.

We wrote this book with the goal of showing the politically progressive traditionalists and the politically conservative progressives who read this book that design thinking has a place in their classroom. This book is here to show them what makes a teacher design minded isn't a specific sequence or observable traits that a classroom visitor can cross off a checklist. Among the many lessons he learned about design in the classroom, Doug discovered that his classroom ran the smoothest and his students were most successful when his head was in the right space. He learned to welcome cumulonimbus clouds because they meant a storm was on its way; they meant he could put away his umbrella and start singing and dancing in the rain. At the risk of spoiling the ending, adopting a design-minded approach is about seeing the turbulence in the daily routines of school life as a chance for everyone, especially the adults, to create, learn, grow, and adapt.

What You'll Get From This Book

One of the most challenging things about writing an education book is ensuring it offers something different to the field. There are many books about the concept of design, and we'll gladly sing their praises. Few of those books, though, get into the gooey bits: the in-the-moment complexities of consistently leading a group of students through a successful design process, embedding design in daily routines, and ensuring students are learning the content teachers are tasked with teaching.

We get into those gooey bits. We set the stage with chapter 1 by laying a foundation and offering up our arguments in an Overview of Design-Minded Teaching. Basically, we pull out all the stops to explain the design-minded approach in the hope you'll be amenable to it. Consider this your orientation to design-minded thinking.

Then part 1 of this book, aptly titled "Putting Design-Minded Teaching Into Practice," explores how a design-minded teacher moves through the five-step design process. Doug breaks down his unique design process and provides practical advice, anecdotes, and research supporting different claims. The final chapter in this section puts all these steps together to give you a step-by-step review of how the design process works together. Doug's design process contains the following steps in order, each with its own dedicated chapter.

- **Chapter 2: Define.** Here, we ask, "What's the problem? What's the goal?"
- **Chapter 3: Design.** Here, we ask, "How can we solve the problem?"
- **Chapter 4: Build.** Here, we ask, "How do we create a solution?"
- **Chapter 5: Test and Revise.** Here, we ask, "What happens when we try out the solution and respond to data?"
- **Chapter 6: Reflect.** Here, we ask, "What did we learn?"
- **Chapter 7: Put It Into Practice.** Here, we ask, "What does the design process look like when all the steps work together?" (And we answer that question with example projects.)

Each chapter in part 1 includes special sections to help guide readers through the design mindset. Look out for the following features throughout the chapters.

- **Vox Magister (Voice of the Teacher):** There are a surprising number of design-minded teachers out there. We reached out to dozens of teachers who have adopted a design mindset and use design in their classroom. Descriptions of their experiences appear in these feature boxes throughout the book, and the experiences they relate shaped this book's content in ways big and small. Some teachers, like Doug, worked their way into a routine after years of iterations. Others went through formal training around project- or problem-based learning and were part of schoolwide adoptions (and all related complications). A few reported feeling like design dropouts. Others raved about their students' success and offered to share movie-length videos of their students talking about what they learned. The teachers shared their successes and their failures. They discussed what always works and what never does. Teachers have a way of adopting superstitions they feel help their teaching along, so they shared what might work if the moon isn't full and it's a Tuesday or Thursday and it hasn't been windy.

- **Thinking Like a Designer:** Sometimes, it's helpful for a design-minded teacher to stop and say, "This is me thinking like a designer." Exercising self-awareness when developing a new teaching style helps the process along. These elements explore just what it means to think like a designer when solving a particular pedagogical problem or classroom conundrum.

▸ **Redesigning for K–2:** We use Doug's experience and expertise as a classroom teacher to inform this book. However, that experience only includes teaching grades 3–6. We know some things in a K–2 classroom don't translate directly to a grades 3–5 one. In these elements, Doug uses his knowledge to help those who teach younger students, but with the understanding that this advice, while within his expertise, lies outside his personal experience.

▸ **Reflection questions:** At the end of each chapter, reflection prompts invite you to think about who you are as a teacher, reflect on what Doug offers through his experiences, and imagine the classroom you want to design for yourself and your students.

Part 2, "Becoming a Design-Minded Teacher," specifies successful and unsuccessful design projects using Doug's classroom as the setting for anecdotal observation. This part focuses on the nitty-gritty, minute-by-minute details of what being a design-minded teacher means. Some examples include a review of why borrowing and sharing each other's design plans is a good thing and how people can find inspiration in other's work. We start by offering some specific designs in chapter 8 (page 119). Teachers can implement the projects in this chapter directly into the classroom. Or, based on an individual classroom and context, they can break Doug's plans down for parts and use what works best for them and their classroom. Chapter 9 (page 153) is all about assessment in the design-minded classroom, from teacher evaluation to grades. We even explore how to reconcile design-minded teaching with large-scale, state-mandated tests. Then, in chapter 10 (page 171), we consider the role of cure-alls, the concept of buy-in, and trust. In this chapter, we lean fully into failure by candidly exploring the ways a teacher, class, and school can struggle to stay in a design-minded headspace. We aim to be transparent and avoid any implications of ease; design mindedness won't solve all of a classroom's woes. This part offers ways to mitigate the struggles and supply a common language supporting lasting relationships and learning habits. It includes recommendations on how to engage wary students and even warier adults and explores how to evaluate projects created via the design process by reviewing grading and state tests.

We end the book by addressing common questions about how this process can be slow and untraditional and again highlighting why we believe it's all worth it.

A Note About Citation Practices

Every author surely sits down with the best of intentions when writing their manuscript. From the start, we intended to ensure the cited research includes a diverse and rich collection of voices from inside and outside the classroom. Our good intentions, though, were no match for the way information often gets disseminated in education. There are a few reasons for this, including the consequences of writing a book in 2020 during the global COVID-19 pandemic. However, that was just a short-term (albeit massive) disruption. Historical patterns play a much larger role in deciding who is an "expert" in education. Even though teaching is a field dominated by women, we frequently assume men outside the classroom are more likely to hold the title of expert. At the same time, the person behind high-profile or well-respected research in education is most likely white. This, too, is part of the grammar of schooling.

Following the profession's feminization during the rise of common (later, public) schools beginning in the 1830s, a new class of educators emerged. Known as *schoolmen*, these principals, superintendents, college professors, and consultants wrote many words and had many opinions on how schools should operate. The rise of the schoolmen resulted in what sociologist Christine L. Williams (2013) calls the *glass escalator*. This term refers to the way straight men racialized as white in women-dominated professions are more likely to fall into positions of leadership. In other words, if Doug had a nickel for every time someone asked him when he was leaving the classroom to become a full-time consultant, he could pay to fly any teacher interested in observing his classroom out for a visit. As they often recommended each other as school experts, schoolmen created a cultural norm where those who teach are mostly women and those who lead, advise, or critique education are mostly men (Borgioli Binis, 2016, 2019). Add to that a long history of white parents enacting laws and policies to keep the public education resources away from children of color, and we end up with a world of design in the classroom that is exceptionally white. Harvard Graduate School of Education professor Jal Mehta (2014) noticed the pattern in an article titled "Deeper Learning Has a Race Problem." As a response to his essay, Gia Truong (2014), chief executive officer at Envision Education, offered:

> Educators have the power in a classroom. They have the ability to shape their students' experiences of school and their identities as learners. Because of this, they need to understand their privileged position, and then they need to understand the people on the other side of the biggest desk in the room.

These words are a reminder: we need to be conscious of who we cite and how we engage with the literature. We need to actively seek out expertise and inspiration from educators who've often been historically muted or minimized. We are grateful to Christen A. Smith, who is the founder of Cite Black Women, and Sara Ahmed (2017), who reminds us all, "Citation is how we acknowledge our debt to those who came before; those who helped us find our way when the way was obscured because we deviated from the paths we were told to follow" (p. 17).

Throughout this book, we've done our best to heed that advice and cite a diverse range of experts on deeper learning, learning sciences, design in the classroom, pedagogy, assessment, and more. We know we fell short. Like any good designers, though, we're going to keep iterating. On our website, https://cardboardclassroom.com, we'll update our reference list with connections to social media accounts, blog posts, YouTube channels, and more as they cross our radar with the goal of highlighting and signal boosting teachers and researchers of color, those with disabilities, neurodivergent thinkers, and those offering a new way to think about design in the classroom. We hope sharing our failing as authors will encourage you to go easier on yourself if it takes you awhile to find the balance as you experiment with dancing in the rain, chasing the thunder, dangling on the clock tower, embracing the turbulence, and adopting a design-minded approach.

CHAPTER 1

But Seriously, What Does *Design Minded* Mean?
An Overview of Design-Minded Teaching

You keep using that word. I do not think it means
what you think it means.

—*Inigo Montoya in* The Princess Bride

Generally speaking, it's good practice for a book about a particular construct to include a section where the authors define the terms related to that construct. One option is for the authors to quote directly from the dictionary. Another is for the authors to list how other authors define the term or to provide the different meanings of related terms before offering their own definition (for example, "Other people define it like that; we define it like this") while others do delightful semantic dancing ("they say de-SIGN; we say DE-sign").

We're not going to do that.

And here's why: American teachers do not have a shared professional lexicon, and we're not lexicographers. While doctors and nurses across the United States can use the *Merriam-Webster Medical Dictionary* (Merriam-Webster, n.d.), psychologists in every state refer to the *Diagnostic and Statistical Manual of Mental Disorders: DSM-5-TR* (American Psychiatric Association, 2022), and lawyers reference the *United States Courts' Glossary of Legal Terms* (Administrative Office of the U.S. Courts, n.d.), teachers are left with only an online search engine.

A surgeon in California can say to a surgeon in Massachusetts, "I'm going to be doing a laparoscopic appendectomy today," and they will both understand the procedure without asking follow-up questions. Lawyers in Ohio can file an unlawful detainer action and a lawyer in Alaska will know what they mean. Meanwhile, if a fifth-grade mathematics teacher in one school district says to a fifth-grade mathematics teacher in another school district, even the next district over, "I'm starting a PBL unit today," the odds of them both picturing the same thing are slim to none. The odds are increased if they've read the same book, attended the same professional development, or worked together to design PBL units.

Even more confusing and frustrating, definitions in American education are so blurry that even the letters *P-B-L* require clarification. For many, that abbreviation means *project-based learning* (Lenz, Wells, & Kingston, 2015). To others, it's *problem-based learning* (Pete & Fogarty, 2018). Also, PBL is described differently than PBT, which refers to project- or problem-based *teaching* (Boss, 2018). Meanwhile, PBL is different from the *maker movement*, which is different from the *creativity movement* (Burvall & Ryder, 2017; Hatch, 2014), to say nothing of *inquiry-based teaching* or *learner-centered practices* or *engineering thinking* (Kaiser, 2020; Spencer & Juliani, 2017; Tollefson & Osborn, 2008). All of this is to say, when a teacher says they use design in their classroom, the nature of the design can look vastly different from the design another teacher uses.

The point of our highlighting the jargon confusion in education, especially as it relates to design, isn't to throw shade at others who meddle in the same space we do. We cited some of our favorite books in the previous paragraph, and each one offers something powerful to the field. Rather, we want to make it plain that if we were to put a stake in the ground and say, "This is what *design minded* means," we would be, in effect, saying our fellow meddlers are wrong. And they're not.

If once a week a teacher supports students through a five-step process to create a specific physical object, that teacher is doing design. Or, if a teacher coaches students through a seven-step project ending with students delivering food to housebound senior citizens around town, that teacher is doing design. If a teacher calls student rough drafts "prototypes" and has students iterate toward a solution when working on mathematics problems in a group, who are we to say they're not doing design?

We've made it pretty clear there are lots of overlap and disagreement, so it won't help to share how other people define design. (However, it is amusing how often the statement "design is hard to define" turns up in books about doing design in the classroom.) That said, it probably behooves us to clearly define what *we* mean when we say that word. We define *design* as . . . but wait—what does it mean to design when students have limited control over their days? We're going to resist the urge to create a graphic with arrows and color coding and instead offer an analogy. From this foundation, we'll explore critical aspects of our approach to design in the classroom: thinking about your thinking, your identity as a teacher, and your own thinking about design.

The Boat Analogy

If we think of the school year as akin to an oceanic journey, teachers are the ones responsible for getting students from one shore to the other. The classroom space functions like a boat. By the time students get to fifth grade, they've spent six years on nearly identical boats. The second-grade boat may have looked a little different from the third-grade boat, but the main idea was the same. Even if the first-grade captain ran things differently than the kindergarten captain, the six-year-olds learned the system quickly. Students likely knew how to impress the captain and where to find the oars and life jackets.

Using this analogy, we can think of one approach to design as *rocking the boat*. This approach is additive; teachers add design and design activities to their classrooms to change up the routine. This can range from helping students take part in traditional structures like invention or science fairs to making scheduling changes like adding a *genius hour* to students' day or week, in which they engage in a combination of inquiry-based and passion-based learning to learn about something they wonder about or are passionate about (Krebs & Zvi, 2016). They get to pick the topic and type of project for that hour. Other teachers rock the metaphorical boat by adding design to one or more subject or content areas. For example, a teacher can apply design concepts to a writing workshop or organize science units around creating or designing experiments (Stockman, 2016). It can also mean changing existing assessment structures by adopting a particular framework such as adapting a unit test using learner-centered practices and having students create multiple-choice items based on their understanding of the content.

In contrast to rocking the boat, *transforming the boat* means students hoist the anchor, trim the mainsail, and chart the path. The teacher sets out the standards (which we can think of as star maps), and students do the work of creating and adding. The teacher has, in effect, said, "First Officer, the helm is yours." If you're familiar with the work of democratic schools, that's transforming the boat at the schoolwide level; students write schoolwide policy, play a meaningful role in budgeting, and shape curriculum (Apple & Beane, 2007). As we mentioned earlier, we're advocating balance, so we're not proposing total schoolwide transformation in this book. This is the headspace Doug lives in and where we hope you'll visit. Perhaps even pull up a chair and stay.

There are more than three million teachers in America, which means more than three million different mental models about how to be a captain—er, teacher (CCD, 2020). However, the boat, the water, and the journey from shore to shore remain the same. Or, to put it in more concrete terms, the concept of the classroom as a fairly self-contained space, the existence of state or locally created standards as an immutable reality of teaching, and the reality that what comes after third grade is fourth grade remain the same. What changes is how teachers position themselves in relation to students. They're still watching the boat's railing to make sure no one falls overboard, but if the wind dies and the boat stops moving, or a waterspout suddenly appears on the horizon, the teachers don't tell students how to solve the problem. Instead, they turn the problem back to the group and develop a solution together. To be sure, the teacher stays in contact with the lighthouses on the other coast to ensure the boat arrives on the right continent, but the teacher is less worried about making sure the boat arrives at one specific port. Keeping enough focus and determination to steer the boat true and help students learn to solve problems on their own requires an intentional mindset. A design-minded classroom requires a teacher with a firm understanding of design-minded thinking.

Various contributors to this book are likewise learning and growing with their students and revising and updating their process. They learned from their mistakes and want to pass along those lessons. When we asked self-identified design-minded teachers, "What do you see as the attributes of a design-minded teacher? That is, in your opinion, what does it look like when a teacher embraces design in their classroom?" they said the following.

VOX MAGISTER (VOICE OF THE TEACHER)

"Design-minded teachers see themselves as the person who is most informed and capable in making the best instructional decisions for students. The teacher is the person who best knows the needs, interests, and other intangibles like relationships, culture, and so on. The design-minded teacher therefore doesn't rely on preconstructed curriculum and programs. Of course, they may be inspired by components of instructional materials other people have created, but the instructional design lies with them. Because design-minded teachers know they are capable of designing the best learning experience for their students, they also know their students are capable designers. They understand the students' role in codesigning their curriculum, meeting them in a place of ambiguity to invite the students to take an active role in shaping their own educational experience. As an expert in pedagogy, the teacher is mindful to ensure standards and outcomes are met, but students take the lead in designing experiences and making the best choices for themselves."

—Erin Quinn, teacher, personal communication, August 22, 2020

"I see a design-minded teacher as someone who is keenly aware of the various ways we produce, communicate, represent, value, and discover meaning and thoughtfully designed learning experiences for students. A teacher who embraces design in their classroom is one who is constantly reflective of the ways their choices impact student learning. These can range from the workflow of their class time and the aesthetic of their materials to the setup of their room. I feel like ingenuity is an important attribute of a design-minded

teacher. When one is aware of the endless number of choices they can make in the classroom, a certain element of creativity is needed to leverage them appropriately."

—Trevor Aleo, teacher, personal communication, November 9, 2020

"This is a teacher who is more of a facilitator of learning than the possessor of all knowledge. Students are not overly relying on the teacher as the one with all the answers. A design-minded teacher curates resources and makes them accessible to students so they can discover by themselves. Teachers create the conditions necessary for students to collaborate, challenge, and deepen each other's thinking."

—Sherien Sultan, teacher, personal communication, November 13, 2020

"Teachers who embrace the concepts and dispositions of design are willing to look closely at their practices, learn from others, receive feedback from students, and decenter their power as the owner of information."

—Krystle Merchant, teacher, personal communication, September 3, 2020

"The primary ambition of this book is answering the question, What makes a design-minded teacher? But, in twentyish words or fewer, a design-minded teacher is one who embraces the flexibility and mess of working with students who are actively involved in their own learning."

—Doug Robertson, teacher and author of this book, personal communication, December 15, 2020

Thinking About Your Thinking

At this point, we're going to turn the lens from our and other people's thinking about design to what's between *your* ears. When we wrote this book, we had in mind educators in all sorts of roles: classroom teachers, administrators, support staff, and professors in teacher preparation programs. Our goal was to reach anyone looking to better understand what it means to use design in the classroom. While, hopefully, anyone in education will find this section useful, it is primarily a space for you as a teacher to (1) think about your teacher identity and offer some affirmations, (2) articulate thinking you've likely not revisited since your student teaching days if you're a veteran teacher, or (3) focus on just one topic at a time if you're a student teacher. (Mental clutter never goes away, but it does get easier to handle.)

While we think spending time thinking about teacher identity is important for several reasons, the most relevant reason is what's coming up in part 1 of this book. In effect, Doug will be doing a *think-aloud*, a "metacognitive strategy in which a teacher verbalizes thoughts aloud . . . thus modeling the process of comprehension" (Harris & Hodges, 1995, p. 256). We want to add as much transparency as possible to the thought process a design-minded teacher goes through. In part 2, you'll think about three things as a form of diagnostic assessment before heading into specific pedagogy.

1. Your identity as a teacher
2. Your memories of design as a learner
3. Your memories of design as an educator

The following sections will help you explore both your identity as a teacher and your memories of design as a learner and educator.

What Is Your Teacher Identity?

The rush and push of teaching don't allow for a lot of time to think about identity. Having a clear sense of identity, however, makes curriculum design, lesson planning, assessment work, and teaching easier. As a result of considering his identity, Doug has a mental process ready when faced with a difficult standard or text to teach. His mental process starts with the question, "What about this is the biggest problem for planning?"

Once he has found an answer, he can move to asking, "How can I design my way around this problem?" For example, if he must teach the concept of summarizing through a story, but the story from the curriculum is disconnected from students' lives, Doug might just find a more culturally relevant or meaningful story. If he doesn't have time or resources at hand, he could decide students will summarize this story by way of a wordless comic strip. The words *comic strip* will catch most students' attention. And because students won't be able to just copy words straight from the story into the characters' mouths, they'll have to think deeper about what the story is saying to draw accurate pictures. Thus, a boring story becomes more engaging through a simple *redesign* of the lesson.

Because of his strong sense of identity, Doug has a ready answer when parents ask, "Why are you doing this?" or when worried parents raise concerns about their child falling behind. As a result of years of reflection and understanding how he approaches his curriculum, Doug can say to his parents:

> *"I'm a design-minded teacher, and the students are building trebuchets during mathematics because they are having to measure every single piece of this build, and then they'll have to measure how far their build throws this object. And those*

> *measurements include weight, which is like a bonus standard right now. Did you notice how excited your child is to show off their trebuchet? Would they have hopped to their mathematics book with the same enthusiasm? So, you're right; it doesn't look the same way you remember school. But did you like mathematics when you were in school?"*

Even if you get to the end of this book and decide design-minded thinking isn't the right headspace for you, hopefully you'll have a better sense of the kind of teacher you are or want to be, as well as a better understanding of the power of slowing down and thinking about your thinking. So, please consider this an invitation to start thinking about your identity. As a first step, use the reproducible "My Teacher Identity" (page 20) to articulate how you see yourself based on the words and phrases describing teachers as well as the other prompts provided. This reproducible is located at the end of this chapter.

If you attended a traditional four-year teacher preparation program, you may have developed a teaching manifesto or philosophy for at least one professor, and you may even remember some words you used for those tasks. You're welcome to use words you would use to describe who you are as a teacher or how you hope other people would describe you. Use as many or as few words as you like. You can even draw pictures if you prefer. In this exercise, though, try to avoid superlatives such as *good* or *effective*. Think about what useful feedback looks like for students. It is not useful to only say, "You did good." This exercise is not for cataloging your strengths (because you're reading this book, we're pretty sure you're awesome), but rather for thinking about how you orient yourself when you teach.

What Are Your Memories of Design?

You may have picked up this book for any number of reasons, and we won't presume to know why, but we know the idea of design must appeal to you. It could be a love-hate, or even hate-hate, situation. There is no judgment here either way. However, please spend a few moments thinking about your relationship with design. This book's introduction (page 1) offered a variety of ways to think about design in the classroom. Use those thinking strategies as a foundation to create your own definition in figure 1.1 (page 18). Again, you are free to use words, pictures, or even stream-of-consciousness thoughts to capture what the word and concept of *design* means to you.

Working with the definition you created in figure 1.1, reflect on your experiences as a student and the times an adult led you in a design experience. The Boat Analogy section (page 12) offered two ways to think about design: (1) rocking the boat (adding design) or (2) building a new boat (organizing the classroom around design). Please use the graphic organizer in figure 1.2 (page 18) to reflect on your experiences in grades K–12 and college. Consider describing what you did, what the teacher did, and what was involved in the project, activity, event, or class.

What is your mental model for your teacher identity?

_____

_____

_____

_____

_____

_____

_____

_____

_____

_____

FIGURE 1.1: Define your teacher identity.

Visit **go.SolutionTree.com/instruction** *for a free reproducible version of this figure.*

	Rock the Boat (Add design.)	**Build a New Boat** (Organize the classroom around design.)
Describe a time when a content-area teacher (English language arts, mathematics, and so on) or professor in your major used design in the way you defined it previously.		
Describe a time when a specialist teacher (art, music, physical education, and so on) or professor of an elective course used design in the way you defined previously.		
Describe a time when an adult who supported your education outside of school (a scout leader, a sports coach, a theater director, and so on) used design in the way you defined it previously.		

FIGURE 1.2: Your design experiences as a student.

Visit **go.SolutionTree.com/instruction** *for a free reproducible version of this figure.*

Use the definitions you created to reflect on your career as an educator and times you led students in a design experience. Use the framing of rocking the boat (adding design) or building a new boat (organizing the classroom around design) to guide your thinking. In figure 1.3, consider describing what you did, what the students did, and what was involved in the project, activity, event, or class.

	Rock the Boat (Add design.)	Build a New Boat (Organize the classroom around design.)
Describe a time when you used design in the way you defined it in a context related to a core content area (English language arts, mathematics, and so on).		
Describe a time when you used design in the way you defined it in a context related to a non-core content area (art, music, physical education, and so on).		
Describe a time as an adult when you used design in the way you defined it with students or young people outside of school (as a scout leader, a sports coach, a theater director, and so on).		

FIGURE 1.3: Times you led students in a design experience.

Visit go.SolutionTree.com/instruction for a free reproducible version of this figure.

Our goal when designing this activity was to create a space and structure for the reader to think about one aspect of identity as it relates to design. As we head into part 1, remember that a teacher's pedagogical identity is only one aspect of their teacher self. The next part is about considering a design-minded approach as just one of many headspaces teaching requires. We are offering not the only way or the right or best way but just a way that's worked for one particular teacher and his students.

My Teacher Identity

The following are words and phrases describing teachers. Mark those that you think most accurately describe your teacher identity. (Choose as many as you like, and even add your own on the blank lines provided.)

I am:

☐ A traditionalist   ☐ Culturally responsive

☐ A sage on the stage   ☐ Learner centered

☐ A progressive   ☐ Design minded

☐ A guide on the side   ☐ _____

☐ A conservative   ☐ _____

☐ An anti-racist   ☐ _____

☐ A meddler (or mediator) in the middle   ☐ _____

To further establish or develop your identity, write your answers to the following questions in the space provided.

- When I think about myself as a teacher, I want to be . . .

- The phrase I most connect with is . . .

- If someone summarized my teaching style in a single word, they'd use . . .

Based on your choices in the preceding sections, describe your mental model for your teacher identity. Use words shared here or other ones, such as those you would use to describe who you are as a teacher or how you hope other people would describe you. Use as many or as few words as you like. You can even draw pictures if you prefer. Try to avoid superlatives such as *good* or *effective*.

PART 1
Putting Design-Minded Teaching Into Practice

The following chapters are written from Doug's point of view. In part 1, Doug provides firsthand experiences anchored in research on performance-based assessment, project-based learning, teacher action research, and teacher mindset. We aim to make the design mindset accessible and understandable by exploring how Doug thinks about it. You'll learn how he uses his design process to think about nearly every action in his classroom. To revisit the analogy of the boat for a moment, Doug uses phases of a design process in the same way a boat captain calls out orders. If you've ever had occasion to be on a sailing boat or you know how to sail, you know what it means when the captain yells, "Step the mast," "Furl sail," or "Fend off." This habit isn't unique to captains. If you've been to a curling match or you curl yourself, you know the difference between a skip yelling, "Hurry," and a skip yelling, "Hurry hard." In both cases, and in the following chapters, this habit is a shorthand way to summarize or signify a needed change, a particular stage in a process, or what a listener should do. To restate it plainly, five design *steps*, *stages*, or *phases* (we changed our minds several times during the writing process) serve as Doug's organizing structure for thinking about his classroom. As a reminder, the five design phases are as follows. This is not a claim that five is the right amount or that having, say, seven phases is wrong.

1. Define.
2. Design.
3. Build.

4. Test and revise.

5. Reflect.

Unlike Mary Shelley, who used artistic license and vague terms while she invented the genre of science fiction to avoid walking readers through the mechanics of impossible science, Doug must use clear explanations when teaching students about the design process. He cannot simply say, "And once you have gathered the instruments of life and learning around you, while rain patters on the windows and the candle burns low, suddenly you will learn." As a design-minded teacher, Doug uses a set of terms including *problem*, *plan*, and *test* to describe both what students are doing and what he's thinking.

At the end of each chapter, we'll invite you to reflect on your teacher identity and the implications of the chapter's content for your classroom. You can then return to the "My Teacher Identity" reproducible (page 20) as a home base where you can reconnect with the teacher you see yourself as and the teacher you want to be. And you can use the reproducible as a base point from which to fill out the reflection sections you'll encounter going forward.

CHAPTER 2

Define
What's the Problem? What's the Goal?

If there was a problem, yo, I'll solve it.

—*Vanilla Ice, "Ice Ice Baby"*

The elementary classroom can present a problem, but in the best possible way. The problem? Twenty, twenty-five, thirty, thirty-five (been there, and more) individuals are expected to be part of a community for 180 days—working together, struggling together, and growing together. Class sizes are huge, and they seem to only ever get bigger, while the number of teachers in the classroom stays a steady *one*. Teachers have limited control over which variables are involved in this problem and must accept they are a variable too. In fact, these variables are so variable they respond differently depending on which variable they are next to. Perhaps a simpler way to think about this is to think of a classroom's seating arrangement as a chemical experiment. You must get all these chemicals into your beaker, but some will combust when mixed. Some will go completely inert. And, at the beginning of the year, you've never seen these chemicals this close before. You've seen them around the school, but this is the first time they have combined in your classroom.

A classroom is the best kind of problem because a teacher must take these disparate variables and turn them into a working whole. "You do not all have to be friends, but you do all need to be able to work together with respect," I say many times during the year. But teachers can't just tell students to work together respectfully; they've got to provide a model. I provide it through design.

On the very first day of school, students choose their own seats before they do anything else. I give no seating chart. "You are a smart fourth grader; I trust you. Find somewhere to sit. I'm here if you have questions or need help," I tell them. I don't make my students earn my trust. I assume it. When teachers invest the time to engage with students, the students will believe the teachers when they call it "our classroom."

The second thing that happens on the first day of school is part of a project I stole from someone at a training session, though they probably didn't intend it as a year opener. During this project, students build spaghetti and marshmallow towers. Arrange the classroom into random groups of four to six students, depending on class size. Each group has ten raw spaghetti noodles and ten tiny marshmallows. Once everyone has chosen a seat, say, "Working together, build the tallest freestanding tower. You can only use the spaghetti and marshmallows. You have fifteen minutes. Go."

This is a massive step toward solving a major problem in any classroom: building a community out of random students. I've found it immensely beneficial to immediately force them to work together on something nonacademic. I do it before students are being pulled for special education services and before students get a chance to fall back into old habits related to personalities and peer groups. I don't mention a prize to avoid embedding a sense of competition into the project. The sense of "this is unusual" hasn't yet failed to capture my students' attention. As an observer, I can see who leads, who steps back, who gets frustrated, who tries to step forward but gets run over, and who does the running over. I jot down observations and begin collecting data about students' approach. At the same time, the beautiful "problem" of the classroom starts to take shape.

Once time runs out, I celebrate both the freestanding towers and the collapsed piles of marshmallow mush and noodle debris. Look for positives from each group. Inevitably, the students are bonding over clever ideas, creative solutions, and safe failures. The beautiful problem of the classroom has begun to solve itself, though in truth, a classroom is never solved—only figured out over brief stretches of time before morphing into something new. That's how it is with students.

REDESIGNING FOR K–2

I do not expect that kindergartners should choose their own seats or build a tower on the first day of school. Waiting until after winter break, or perhaps spring break, may be a better choice. What could a student in kindergarten through second grade do independently on day one instead to give them a sense of ownership of the classroom? Help younger students feel like the classroom is theirs just as much as it is yours using bonding games, organizational projects, and group discussions.

The biggest lesson I've learned about problems is a simple one: it is impossible to solve a problem before the problem is clear.

In this chapter, we'll explore the best-use practices of the design process's define phase to identify problems, prioritize them, and set about creating a plan for solving the major problem a design will tackle. You'll learn how to re-envision curriculum goals as problems with design solutions and how to apply that innovative thinking across multiple content areas.

The Problem With Too Much Structure

School can be stifling in its rigidity. To solve that problem, I use *free builds*, in which students have a certain amount of time to themselves to construct something with cardboard, tape, and whatever other materials they can find in the classroom. I've found nearly all my students love free build time, and research supports the benefits of unstructured time for students. Work from Jane E. Barker, Andrei D. Semenov, Laura Michaelson, Lindsay S. Provan, Hannah R. Snyder, and Yuko Munakata (2014) finds short- and long-term benefits for students given time to engage in less-structured activities. There are times when students will sit and look at the building task with no idea what to do, and I tell them that a bit of boredom is good for them (Malkovsky, Merrifield, Goldberg, & Danckert, 2012; Mann & Cadman, 2014). I've seen students start to idly build something during free time, doodling but with cardboard, only for them to suddenly see something in their build and attack it with a sense of purpose. I've had a conversation that started with "Mr. Robertson, we were looking through the reading book and the next story is about weather, and we thought what if we, like, built the kinds of weather? Or, oh—I just thought of this—what if we used the iPad and made news reports? No! We put those together! Do news reports with weather!" Honestly, I was tapped for ideas going into that story, so we did what the students suggested, and it was great.

THINKING LIKE A DESIGNER

While teachers often suffer from a lack of student input in their class, the flip side of that coin is they are inundated with too many good student ideas and not enough time to implement them. I want to do everything they suggest, but I've got things to do too. I solve this particular problem by having students keep a list of ideas in their journals, and the last two weeks of school, when materials are getting packed away and everything is winding down, I say, "Many of you had ideas we never got to. Make one of those. Go."

The following section details how to use free builds to alleviate some of the rigidity in the classroom structure.

Free Builds

In chapter 1 (page 11), we talked about the complexities of teacher identity. Sometimes, educators have elements of those identities forced upon them through administrative policies; that includes ensuring our students attend to schoolwide behavior structures, such as Positive Behavioral Interventions and Supports (PBIS). The nature of such programs is the topic of another book, but to solve the problem presented by being a teacher in a PBIS school, I use free design in place of structured rewards. Some of my colleagues who've adopted a rock-the-boat mentality about design offer things like a goofy hair day, free time on the computer, or a build-your-own-sundae party in exchange for hitting PBIS goals. In my classroom, an unstructured opportunity to design is treated as a reward. When students hit a particular target, I give them free access to cardboard, scissors, tape, and other building materials in the room and forty-five minutes of challenge-free creation with no plan more explicit than to "go for it and make something." It's worth noting that in the beginning of the year, I teach students about different techniques for working with cardboard so they have options beyond cutting, taping, and stapling. Figure 2.1 illustrates a poster I keep up in my classroom about the cardboard building techniques students learn in this orientation.

Because I've seen students embrace free build time in ways they don't respond to other rewards, I don't limit my students to the supplies I provide them. Oftentimes, they want to carry forward earlier learning. For example, during a technology unit when I was teaching how to use slideshows to create stop-motion movies, students used the free build time to create their own slideshows and discover tricks they hadn't encountered in the more structured class time. I never showed students how to add textures to their slideshows, but someone did some independent research and discovered it on their own. The knowledge was quickly disseminated throughout the class, and soon, everyone's slides looked better. As a helpful byproduct, students are learning computer literacy, which furthers the technology education goals I have for them anyway. Sometimes, the problem is as simple as "How do I find something to fill these thirty minutes Mr. Robertson has given us?" Sometimes, students are inspired to follow an interest.

I informally document the types of learning that happen during these free builds and, if I need to, circle back or reinforce content goals during direct instruction time. Free-range creativity is valuable, but for a design-minded teacher, free builds are never the only choice. No principal will accept "Just go build!" as a pedagogical foundation. Structure always matters.

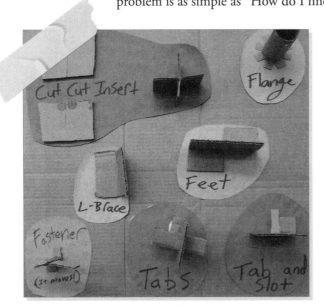

FIGURE 2.1: Cardboard techniques poster.

Structured Builds

Structure and constraints allow creativity to thrive because we can aim creativity in a purposeful direction (Drapeau, 2014; Rosso, 2014). One cannot push the envelope if there is no envelope to push. A creativity hero of mine, writer and director Guillermo del Toro (he of Best Picture winner *The Shape of Water* [2017], mecha-versus-monster masterpiece *Pacific Rim* [2013], and Gothic love story *Crimson Peak* [2015]), says that limitations are how he gets the most creativity from himself and from those he works with. Del Toro's philosophy is "You have to give everyone complete autonomy within a narrow bandwidth" (Savage, 2019, p. 212).

This same concept holds true in the classroom, where, just like on a movie set, too much freedom leads to chaos. Even the most self-directed elementary school students need direction. I once (or thrice) made the mistake of throwing my arms into the air and proclaiming, "Do whatever you want, *and learn from it*. Go, be free!" I gave students can openers and set them loose on a proverbial pyramid of cans of beans. Some students thrived. Some were petrified and frozen in place. Most struggled and suffered while wanting to grow. The sweet spot is structure but not too much. It is possible to offer students too many free builds. Students appreciate structure in their lives, and we know some structure and routines are good things (Burvall & Ryder, 2017; Hammond, 2015).

I have trouble finding the sweet spot between chaos and teacher-led control during the leveled-reading groups that are part of my school's culture. As a way to solve the problem, I tell students to make and write something that summarizes their reading. Then I go to specific groups and assign specific tasks based on their grouping needs. For example, I told one group, "You're working on your phonemic awareness, so I'd like you to turn what you've read into a dialogue you'll be reciting aloud." The students are reading their assigned text and working on phonemic awareness by reciting the vocabulary from the text aloud, and thus, I have solved the problem of design when my class is split into smaller groups based on academic needs.

Another problem the classroom presents is related to the nitty-gritty work of teaching and learning. As a design-minded teacher, I want to lead students beyond where knowledge is only information a teacher feeds them. Consider, for example, teaching about the Declaration of Independence in American history. A design-minded approach is to identify the problem to solve, and in this case, it's how to help elementary students understand the plight of the American colonies and the conditions people were rebelling against after immigrating to America. A fellow design-minded teacher in my building solved the problem by starting a class economy a few weeks before his unit on the American Revolution. During the previous unit, he paid students x for working quietly and y for turning something in. "But then come the taxes," he told his students. "Oh, those pesky taxes." He began to take a percentage of whatever unit of currency the classroom was using in place of money to imitate taxes. He even implemented the Pencil

Act of 2018 and taxed students differently based on where they were sitting in the room. When the time came to start the American Revolution unit, he had solved the problem (while creating a few new ones, as some students took the concept of revolution a bit too far). My view is that teachers don't lift students into the tree to grab the apple, but do offer students a boost. I will point to lower branches the students could probably jump to and catch the students if (and when) they slip.

Thinking Like a Designer

A teacher's job is to *define the problem*. A good problem will act as an energizing lightning rod to activate the design process for students.

The Importance of Listening and Questioning

The first obligation of a design-minded teacher is to teach students to clearly define the problem they are facing. A teacher who is rocking the boat might tell students, "During structured design, you're going to build a car, and here's how you're going to do it." Breaking down the problem into parts isn't a bad thing and can be a great place to start. But since the goal is to rebuild the boat, make it clear to students when teaching them about the design process what you are going to use and that the problem is more expansive (for example, "Work in a group to make a wind-powered car using only the materials given to you"). In terms of curriculum goals, I focus on only a few: writing a step-by-step process, explaining their thinking, and making exact measurements. But they don't need to know that—yet. I've done my part; now students need to do theirs and find the problem, or problems, within the challenge.

Once I've defined the challenge, students will likely ask, "But how do I do it?" A well-stated challenge can organically generate many questions, and questions define problems. The first few times a project or challenge is presented, the students won't ask, "What do I need to build, design, understand, and think about?" If you keep up a design-minded approach all year, the questions students ask in September will be vastly different from the questions they ask in June. Students will ask, "What does *wind powered* mean?" and "I've never done this before. How do I do this?"

"Good questions," I will reply. "Now we're finding problems," I tell them. "Write that down."

I've learned to perfect my poker face and develop a whole suite of redirection answers. When a student replies to a clearly defined challenge like, "Make a wind-powered car using the materials given to you," with a question like, "But what if instead of wind, we used a nuclear engine?" I might reply, "That is a very interesting thought, but it might defeat the purpose of the project: to make a *wind-powered* car. Plus, I don't have access to nuclear engines . . . that you know about. I'm going to ask Natalie if she'll come over and help us brainstorm." Never shut down an idea directly. Instead, acknowledge the student's creativity, restate the problem, and ask a student who has demonstrated they understand the problem's parameters to share their thinking.

There will likely be lots of awkward silence as you wait out students' responses to your questions. Spend time modeling good questioning (see table 2.1).

TABLE 2.1: Modeling Good Questioning

Question	What This Question Teaches Students
"What is the main goal I am trying to accomplish?"	This question helps students focus their energy in the proper direction, which is especially useful when dealing with story problems in mathematics. They will face more of these problems than they can count, and the first tripping point of all of them is figuring out just what the problem is actually asking students to solve.
"Am I looking at this problem from the best angle, or is there a better way to come at it?"	Students will find the longest, most complicated way if you let them. This question acknowledges, yes, there are multiple solutions to this problem, so it's OK to work on a few until one clearly becomes the best.
"What do I absolutely know before I start, and what do I need to know?"	Students, especially students early in becoming design minded, think everything is important. They might highlight an entire chapter of a book. Clearly defining a problem helps students look only for solutions.
"Have I seen a problem like this before? If so, what did I do then?"	Accessing prior knowledge gives students a huge store of information and honors who they are and where they've come from. It also starts them on the path to generalizing solutions from disparate locations.

All of this takes experience and guidance. A strength of the design process is it might be teacher guided, but students direct it and find their own learning through their own questions. This will only happen, of course, once they've gained enough experience to know what questions to ask and when.

THINKING LIKE A DESIGNER

How to define the problem for students will grow more detailed as the students also become more design minded. Designers *evolve* their thinking.

Avoid presenting problems in the form of a question. It's less effective to ask, "Can you make a wind-powered car?" because that opens the door for the student to respond, "No, I can't, thank you very much." It will become much harder to move forward after a student has already answered a question this definitively. So, take that option away. The framing of the problem as a statement assumes it is solvable: "Your project is to make a wind-powered car." In the form of a question, it becomes, "What's the best way to build a wind-powered car?" or "What's the best way to build the lightest possible wind-powered car?" depending on your curriculum goals.

Another aspect of the design-minded classroom that requires explicit instruction is working in groups. This includes teaching students how to ask each other questions in open, genuine ways as well as practicing active listening and being thoughtful about their words (Denton, 2013; Fisher & Frey, 2014). A key attribute of learning to work in groups is understanding and approaching other people as if everyone's input is valuable and everyone has something to contribute. The Common Core State Standards for Speaking and Listening (National Governors Association Center for Best Practices [NGA] & Council of Chief State School Officers [CCSSO], 2010) lay out the importance of communicating in the classroom, using expressive language, expressing your own thoughts and feelings, and using receptive language. Too often, students are left to figure out how to communicate well on their own. By connecting to the standards and drawing attention to what it looks like, educators can prevent a number of tensions related to group work.

The Hierarchy of Problems

Not all problems are created equal. Along with the main problems, students must think about and plan for secondary problems and unknown problems, examples of which appear in figure 2.2. Before we can design something that fulfills our educational purposes, we need a reason for designing it. That means understanding the type of problem we hope to solve.

The ability to define these types of problems, and to define what is a problem in the first place, matters because it will serve students well for the rest of their lives. I tell my students that people cannot grow or move forward unless they can name what is holding them back. Students practice naming their drawbacks in spaces the design process made safe to be vulnerable. By learning to define problems externally, students gain the language and tools to name and confront them internally. This theme also runs throughout the design process. Everything educators teach their students should apply in and out of the classroom. It's up to educators to help students see the complexity and holistic nature of the learning they are doing.

Main Problems

The main problem is the *big problem*. (What are we trying to find out?) This is the problem that would go in the bull's-eye. The main problem drives every decision and

Main Problem	Secondary Problems	Unknown Problems
Address the primary problem or goal.	Tell students there will be more problems to consider during the design phase when they will draw blueprints and make plans, and during the build phase when they will execute the blueprints and plans.	Expect students to show up! Be flexible when it comes time to design and build.
Build a moving car.	How do I make sure my car travels in a straight line and rolls easily?	Axles are hard to make and can be complicated, especially given the limited materials.
Build a freestanding tower of only spaghetti and marshmallows.	Once I break the raw noodle, I can't repair it. So, I have to be sure before I act.	Marshmallow is unforgiving as a glue and will remain tacky through only one connection.
Build a small room with an open top using tape and cardboard.	We only have some cardboard and tape, so supplies are limited.	Getting walls to stand and join is much harder than most students think until they learn about different kinds of joints.

FIGURE 2.2: Examples of discussing different types of problems during the define phase.

choice the teacher and the students will make. The first question students should ask themselves, and the first question the teacher will ask students who are doing something suspect, is "How is this addressing the main problem?"

Secondary Problems

Secondary problems are trickier. They're often things students don't know will be problems because they lack understanding regarding the stages of the design as a whole. Conversely, students will occasionally misname a secondary problem as a main problem either because the final goal was not made clear or because they misunderstood what the final goal is.

Secondary problems often do not become clear to students, especially early in the learning process, until the design or even build portion of my design process. When students are building something, a potential secondary problem would be, "How will we join these two pieces together?" It should not be a major part of the define phase, but students should have an awareness of it. Students won't be able to identify problems if they are unfamiliar with how to build something.

Unknown Problems

It's impossible to plan for unknown problems. Design-minded students and teachers can cope with unknown problems in only one way: by showing up and being flexible when it comes time to design and build. With experience, students' unknown problems become secondary problems and are replaced by smaller, more project-specific unknown problems. If an unknown problem becomes a main problem, then the real problem is with the teacher's design and explanation of the project.

Vox Magister (Voice of the Teacher)

"The biggest piece of advice I'd give teachers new to design is to embrace ambiguity. I know this feels really scary, especially to someone who is used to teaching in a stand-and-deliver kind of way. But if you resist the urge to succumb to your own anxieties, you will be astounded by what your students can do. To trust something amazing will come out of the process, even though we have no idea what it might be, is so exciting."

—Erin Quinn, teacher, personal communication, August 22, 2021

Design-Minded Thinking Across Content Areas

Students will encounter problems in all aspects of their learning. Problems connected with builds are just one of the most concrete examples. Teachers might need to help students flip their thinking so they see the word *problem* not as a negative but as an opportunity. Visualize the following examples.

- **Student:** *We have a problem? Oh no. We should ask the teacher how to solve it.*
- **Student in a design-minded classroom:** *We have a problem? Good. Here's a chance to learn.*

Every subject in school is made up of problems for students to solve. The following sections examine the kinds of problems teachers and students might encounter as part of specific content-area learning. Although only addressing English language arts and mathematics directly, I believe in taking a science, technology, engineering, art, and mathematics (STEAM) approach to subjects and de-siloing the content areas as much as possible. Thus, I have also included a STEAM section to nod to science, social studies, and the other content areas we all too often feel forced to cut from the daily schedule.

Redesigning for K–2

These sections will frequently refer to curriculum goals and content areas. Rather than be grade level specific, these will be general enough to apply to any grade level.

English Language Arts

Reading is full of problems where teachers can apply the design process. In fact, turning stories from the textbook into design opportunities is one way to make the lesson and story more interesting and engaging, especially if the textbook story is particularly boring to students. Take this prompt: *Write an essay about the main idea and details of the story using evidence from the story.* Now add the questions you want to ask and the questions students are going to ask anyway, such as the following. In the beginning, you would do this as a whole group, but the goal for this—as for most things in a design-minded classroom—is that at some point, students will be able to do this alone or in their small groups.

- ▸ "What's the problem here?"
- ▸ "What does *main idea* mean?"
- ▸ "Where can I find the main idea?"
- ▸ "Is this detail good for supporting the main idea?"
- ▸ "Does it address the main idea at all?"
- ▸ "How long does this essay have to be?"
- ▸ "Can I go to the bathroom?"
- ▸ "What does this word say?"
- ▸ "What did that word mean?"

So many other questions can come from defining the first problem. As students improve at defining problems and thinking like designers, some of those more vestigial questions will drop off and the process will streamline and simplify.

Mathematics

Teachers ask elementary students to solve mathematics problems every day. "I have five tanks of water. Inside each tank of water are three man-eating sharks. How many man-eating sharks do I have?" appears to be a straightforward problem. We can use the design process to solve it despite its simplicity. Students must first understand the problem's story. Even this short, simple problem includes many extra details, and students must learn to break it down to find three times five. Three times five what? Sharks. So, the answer of not fifteen but fifteen *sharks* is the one that shows total understanding of the problem.

Mathematical thinking is like design thinking because students cannot answer a mathematics problem without first knowing what they're trying to answer.

STEAM

The scientific process begins with defining a problem. We cannot create an experiment until we have a question we need to answer. Scientists think like designers because they are designers. Educators want students to think of themselves as scientists, and when teachers use the same language in science they've used in other places, it will create a bridge for students to cross. If *designer = scientist* and *student = designer*, then *student = scientist*.

History is the unraveling of problems from years past: What problems did those being colonized face? What set of problems led to this war? Why did these things happen? What problems persist today because of those original problems? How do all these problems interconnect? It's easy to get lost in the problem-to-solution cause and effect of just about any historical event. By defining a problem we need to solve, we are making the process of learning about history a more active and investigative one, which can help generate student interest in it. A pair of excellent questions to always ask are these: "How long ago was this?" and "What else was happening around the world at the same time?" For example, by asking these questions, students will realize that Ruby Bridges, who is an American civil rights activist and the first African American child to desegregate an all-white school in Louisiana during the New Orleans school desegregation crisis in 1960, is still alive and younger than they might think. Or Neil Armstrong, the first person to walk on the moon, was born nine years before the first successful helicopter was invented. Or perhaps you, their teacher, were born before most families had a computer in their home. Make history personal.

The Joy of Defining Problems

I can't claim that the design-minded classroom produces more thoughtful, more reflective adults than other types of classrooms. I can say, though, as I've transitioned to keeping a design-minded classroom over the years, I've noticed more instances when students stopped to describe a problem they were facing. For example, during one design project, a student recognized that a house was inaccessible to people who use wheelchairs. The student named the problem, leading to a class discussion about the inaccessibility of buildings, including our school.

After defining the problem comes the next step of the design process: designing solutions.

Define Reflection Template:
What's the Problem? What's the Goal?

This chapter was about articulating and defining problems. Use the space provided to articulate the problem of your classroom, a problem in your curriculum, and a problem you'd like your students to solve. You're welcome to use as many or as few words as you like. You can even draw pictures if you prefer.

What is the problem of your classroom?

What is a problem with your curriculum?

What is a problem you'd like your students to solve?

CHAPTER 3

Design
How Can We Solve the Problem?

There is beauty and humility in imperfection.

—Guillermo del Toro

In chapter 1 (page 11), we offered a ship as a mental model for thinking about how a teacher approaches design in the classroom. A *mental model* is a model "constructed and simulated within a conscious mind" (Merritt, n.d.). In effect, think of the classroom as a ship and the teacher as a captain with the goal of getting students from one shore to another. This helps the teacher (and the students and their families, if the teacher shares the mental model) think about the roles, responsibilities, structure, skills, knowledge, and dispositions the teacher needs to ensure students have in order to get there. Visualization is a key ability in this mental model (and part of navigation). Those visualization skills become explicit and implicit parts of a design-minded teacher's classroom.

The design step is where designers develop their strategic plan. We can think of it as imagination or visualization, but regardless of what we call it, design involves building in your head. When students learn to think as designers, they often learn to hold something in their minds; turn it around; look beneath it, above it, and inside it; and grok the thing. Some practiced designers can make an object or idea malleable in their minds and can therefore manipulate it.

Some are unable to do it at all because of the myriad mysterious ways the mind works, and that is certainly OK too. This is what paper, small models, and computer programs are for (if you have access to such things). To help students understand that not everyone can visualize or that not everyone visualizes the same way, tell them about "tongue turning"—the ability some people have to turn their tongue upside down without touching it. I tell them that bodies and brains are weird and different, and that's wonderful and OK. We don't give up on students learning to read just because they can't do it after one year, so let's apply the same grace and flexibility to other processes. In this phase, teachers may exert the most influence over a project. I try to be as hands-off as possible when students are actively in my design process, but of all the phases, the design phase is where I'm likely to step in (or, more accurately, where I need to step in to avoid catastrophe). That doesn't mean teachers *should* step in, but now is usually the time. In this chapter, we will review how flexibility and detail both contribute to a great design visualization and how design-minded thinking applies across various content areas.

Designs Must Be Flexible

Designs (and designers) must be flexible. Expect to read that statement multiple times in this book. Design thinking requires a willingness and ability to change plans and tactics as soon as a problem seems to be insurmountable or a better idea is formed. Give students a visualization exercise early in the school year to help them understand this. The following passage is an example of a visualization exercise I've given to students.

> *"Close your eyes. Imagine you are running through a forest, sprinting as hard as you can—head down, and deeply focused. You are trying to get through the forest as fast as possible. Then,* bam! *You run headfirst into a tree. The impact knocks you backward, but you know you're supposed to get through the forest as fast as you can, so you pick yourself up and start sprinting again. Then,* bam! *You smack right into the same tree again. What's the problem?"*

Students will eventually realize they can't see the tree if they're looking down. They're going to run headfirst into it. They often respond, "We should look up and go around the tree!"

This can become shorthand in the class for getting around problems students get stuck on. "Did you look up and step around the tree?" I'll ask.

Teaching students to *think around the tree* lets them know it's OK to not know something. What's important is accepting the not knowing, pressing forward as best you can, and being ready to modify what you know as more information comes to light. We can think of this a bit like the state of flow we encourage in our students (Csikszentmihalyi, 2014). Mihaly Csikszentmihalyi's (2014) *flow* is a state of complete immersion in an activity. Focus on staying present with students and moving forward. Even when they make mistakes or experience failure, they're growing and progressing rather than stagnating. That's learning. That's thinking as designers. And there will be points during the design phase where we don't know things and we run into seemingly insurmountable trees. We can choose either to let the design grind to a halt or to step around the problem as best we can for now. The only time this approach does not work is on some computerized or standardized tests because those are built to not let students progress until they've answered the question on the page. But students can usually flag the questions they're unsure about and come back to them later, which still allows some measure of looking up, stepping around, and moving forward.

REDESIGNING FOR K–2

Younger students may run into more or different trees because of their experience (or lack thereof). They can still learn that it's OK not to know, but they may require more guidance through the mysteries (or a flashlight in the forest, if you will).

Some design questions we can't answer until the build phase of the design process, but we should still ask them during the design phase. This is why design thinking demands flexibility. "I don't know" is a legitimate answer if *because* or *but* follows it. Table 3.1 features acceptable responses from students when they can't solve a design problem during this phase.

TABLE 3.1: Examples of "I Don't Know" Answers With Explanations

Sample Problem	Acceptable "I Don't Know" Answer With Explanation (Secondary Questions)	Question Developed by Students to Guide Their Plan Going Forward
Students need to give the measurements of all three sides of a right triangle in their blueprint when they know only height and length.	"I don't know *because* I haven't been taught to figure out triangle sides yet."	"What research might help me decide the length of right-triangle sides? Can I check the mathematics book or the internet?"
Students' trebuchet needs to be strong and stable enough to not fall over or come apart.	"I don't know, *but* I do know it can't fall over because it needs to be reusable."	"How can I make sure my trebuchet doesn't tip over or fall apart after each throw without taping it down (because Mr. Robertson said I can't tape it down)?"
Students don't know if the cardboard arcade game they are building is much too complicated and won't be fun to play.	"I don't know *because* I've never built a cardboard arcade game. I think it will be cool."	"The game makes sense in my head. It won't become clear until I have to try to explain it to another student, and then I'll have to make adjustments based on playtesting."
Students haven't learned wheels can't just be round things on sticks. Just because something is a circle doesn't mean it'll go around.	"I don't know, *but* I do know what a wheel looks like, and it can't just go directly on the side of the car's body. So that's something."	"How do I make sure the wheels spin freely without falling off? How do I make sure the wheels are round and not roundish?"

As this table illustrates, saying, "I don't know," is OK if designers can show their thinking and explain why they don't know. This might not be acceptable on a construction site, but it's perfectly appropriate in an elementary classroom.

Students are naming those unknown questions and turning them into secondary questions. "I don't know *because . . .*" and "I don't know *but . . .*" are ways of looking up, seeing the tree, and stepping around it while remembering it's there. If students answer, "I don't know," don't answer the question, even if you know the answer. Explaining the problem for students here undercuts the entire process. Students need to recognize they don't know and *why* they don't know so they can invent a question to guide their plan going forward.

Nothing we build in class is finished until it's submitted, and things can be changed even then. See the forest and the tree, take them into account, and do your best. Build the skills of visualization through explicit modeling and language. Remind students they are trying to see two things at once: (1) the trees *and* (2) the forest. The forest is the whole path, all the way through. The trees are the details. Tell students the entire project is always doable. Assure students you would never assign something impossible. When they do run into a problem, it's a tree and not the entire forest. The flexibility they show when they adapt to problems they face comes down to details.

Designs Must Be Detailed (Not Final)

Designing with details slows students down and makes them think about what they are going to do before they start doing it. These details could include how long each side or piece is, where students will join the pieces, how they will join them, and in what order they should join them. Designing with details comes with experience, but that does not mean students can't think about these things right from the start. As the tongue twister goes, "Proper planning prevents poor performance." Students new to being design minded likely want to build and build *now* because, to them, the entire point of the project is to build. It's fine to explicitly tell them that isn't the point. If they skip the details, their build *might* work. Or the wings of their build will come off because no one remembered to add, "Glue them here and here," to the plan. At first, the details will frustrate students. Pilots want to get in the air too. Flying is the fun part. Soon, students will realize that while flying is the fun part, landing (or creating a build that *solves the problem*) is the important part.

The details, what we'll call *blueprints*, to expect from students' designs vary depending on the project and grade level. I often say and will repeat as often as needed that all students—even kindergartners—can create blueprints, given the chance and support. Let's now detail those details . . . in detail.

Thinking Like a Designer

Expectations for student designs should be high. Students find it hard to spend quality time in the design and not rush forward, but it's important to help them see the benefits of thoughtful, deliberative planning (Drapeau, 2014). Letting students rush through the design piece to get to the building does no one any good. Rushing results in lots of unused cardboard scraps and group arguments because the students were not all on the same page before beginning to cut and tape.

Teaching high-quality design means teaching blueprints. Students will be bad at blueprints at first. I was bad at them at first. Getting better at blueprints helped me get better at unit design and long-term planning, as blueprints serve as a vehicle for making thinking transparent. I was building the muscle of taking an idea and putting it down on paper. One year, I shared with students while we were setting goals that I wanted to get better at creating blueprints. Another year, as we talked through the year's curriculum plan, I helped students see our curriculum goals as my blueprints for their learning. I had created a detailed plan, laid out clearly and carefully to achieve a goal. I try at every available opportunity to identify blueprints or ways in which someone has made thinking visible. For example, when students are drawing the standard algorithm process for a mathematics problem, they are creating a blueprint.

It's typically nearly impossible to build something if you can't articulate what it's going to be. However, failure and growth are baked into design thinking. Blueprints can be hard to draw because they're confusing to look at until you're used to their layout. What I've found, though, is the practice of creating blueprints has led to more students being able to notice and comment on connections between content areas or topics without me asking. Blueprints are also vital for the construction of anything. They're the literal embodiment of "show your work."

Redesigning for K–2

Start with blueprints of simple shapes like cubes. Students could make a blueprint of an existing shape they can see, hold, and measure rather than an object they thought of for practice.

Figure 3.1 is an example of an unfinished, imperfect blueprint a fifth-grade student created while working with a group of peers. In this particular case, students were solving a problem related to game design. I tasked them with creating a Skee-Ball game as I had instructional goals related to estimation, prediction, measurement, and area. (More information on this particular cardboard arcade project appears in chapter 8, page 119.) Always structure design time in groups because every class has students who are better able to visualize (and those who are better able to put a visualization down on paper) and those who struggle to make what's on the page match what is in their mind. The teacher must make sure those students who best visualize and whom their peers have deemed the best artists aren't always the blueprint artists no matter what the group or the project is.

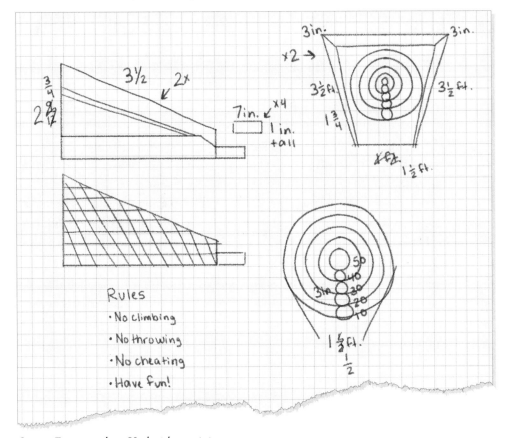

Source: Former student. Used with permission.

FIGURE 3.1: Example fifth-grade student blueprint.

Share this expectation with students: "Make sure you're not always the blueprint artist. Everyone needs to be able to do this." And then support them to organize themselves (Berger, Rugen, & Woodfin, 2014). In a design-minded teacher's class, students choose and take responsibility for their learning, and this student leadership must be *everywhere*. Blueprint visualization is one of those places. It's not beautiful, but it's real.

Vox Magister (Voice of the Teacher)

"I see intentional teaching and backward-design lesson planning as key markers for design-minded teachers. My experience is mostly with project-based learning, so I think of it as another way to assess what students have learned in the classroom, as well as making it a fun way to wrap up a unit and perhaps begin a new one."

—M. David López, teacher, personal communication, January 14, 2021

Students should also have the mindset that blueprints may not always look beautiful but they represent potential and a visual of their thinking. And that's a beautiful thing. That mindset will help them see the importance of blueprints. A complete blueprint for a design project will consist of the following three parts.

1. At least three specific views: front, side, cross section, top (optional), or opposite sides (needed only if the design is asymmetrical)
2. Specific measurements
3. Specific materials

The following sections will detail these parts and their respective values.

Designs Need Specific Views

The views students draw for their blueprints will not be perfect. Perfect is not the goal. The goal is for students to understand that what they are about to build will exist in the real world and, as such, will have width, depth, and height. All grades, from kindergarten upward, can do this. I will keep mentioning this because I have experience with K–3 teachers especially being unsure whether their students can do these things. Yes, emphatically and passionately—yes, they can, if the teacher releases control and allows for learning through repeated failure. Start small; don't go straight to a giant build. We don't jump right into algebra and novels. Why would design thinking be any different? The idea is that students build what is to them, at their level, a clear blueprint. They must know what the blueprint will look like from all angles before they start cutting pieces for it.

Inevitably, some students will complain they cannot draw. This is a perfect chance for them to practice perseverance. If they want to build, they'll figure out how to draw the blueprint. Tell students this is not an art project; we just need to know what they're looking at without asking them, "What is this?" so we know whether to intervene before they start building. Show students real blueprints, but offer the warning professionals created them. I don't have a magical source for blueprints beyond searching online for "blueprint samples." I have asked students whether any of their grown-ups work in a construction setting and would be open to sharing a blueprint. You can also keep student work samples as exemplars for the following years or share clips from home improvements shows, 90 percent of which include at least one scene where builders and designers stand around a blueprint and look thoughtful. Have students look at them for inspiration without feeling pressured to replicate them. Each blueprint reveals something different, but generally speaking, make clear connections to the curriculum when introducing these blueprints. For example, point out the use of scale and measurement and its role in estimation. Explain how blueprints work as a primary source to help us understand someone's thinking at a particular moment and how they are a form of modeling, which we do in science. The following are a few kinds of blueprints you might want to show your students.

- **Front-view blueprint:** This blueprint shows exactly what it sounds like. If you are standing in front of the object and looking at it directly, what do you see? How wide is the front? How tall is the object? What details are important? Where are the sections connected?

- **Side-view blueprint:** This blueprint turns the front view ninety degrees in one direction or the other. Are the walls a different height from the side than the front, or do they angle in a way the front view hides? How does the object stand (if it's supposed to stand)? The side view allows you to see supports that might not be clear from the front. It also allows you to see how long the object is.

- **Cross-section blueprint:** For this blueprint, students must imagine the side view but cut the object in half to see inside. How are the internal pieces attached and supported? What size are they? For example, in the Skee-Ball design, the students needed a cross-section portion of the blueprint because inside the game, there was the base piece of cardboard, and there was also a ramp halfway between the top piece and the base. The ramp is so a ball that goes through a hole returns to the player. A normal side view would not show this, hence the need for a cross section.

- **Top-view blueprint:** I don't always require or show this type of blueprint, as it involves a whole lot of drawing, and the side and front views are usually enough to communicate. A top-view blueprint provides a bird's-eye view of the design. How is the top of the build supported? What internal structures can you see from the top view? If the design has an open top, students will be able to see what their build should look like from above. In some designs, the actual top may only be a covering, so students may need to cross-section the top off as well to know what is happening in their design from this angle and ensure that all edges meet where they should, all angles are correct, any holes that should exist do, and any holes that shouldn't exist don't.

► **Opposite-sides blueprint:** Another optional view, this blueprint matters only if the object students are making looks different on both sides. Some designs may need left-side and right-side views if, for example, someone who is building a house wants two windows on one side of the house but a window and side door on the other. If that's the case, the blueprint should represent it.

When teaching students about blueprints, I also connect them to the concept of useful and relevant information, which connects to writing instruction (elementary-grade students love to add all sorts of irrelevant details). I want my students to show relevant details, like axles and how they connect to the body of a car, and leave off irrelevant ones, such as numbers of the speedometer on the dash. We revisit the idea of useful versus irrelevant details when we talk about communication in the classroom and when we do online research.

Blueprints are foundational to any design project that happens in the classroom because they set a goal and they set expectations. They can be seen as a teacher writing learning goals on the board before a lesson, but much more personal and functional because students make the blueprints themselves and must use them to be successful. A student with a blueprint is a student with a plan, and a student with a plan can get to work and be independent at whatever level is developmentally appropriate. Another beautiful thing about these blueprints is they are unique to each student. Our ideal classrooms include learning goals and assignments focused on individual students, down to their individual needs and strengths. That is impossible for some class sizes, but what *is* possible is a roomful of unique blueprints, diverse learning plans guided by the teacher but created by the students. Blueprints will result in different endings, each reflecting a student's or group's learning, even if that learning comes from the blueprint's initial failure (it's important to encourage students to think of failure as a good learning opportunity). Then the student, guided by the teacher, takes that learning and applies it to the next thing.

REDESIGNING FOR K–2

Detailed blueprints might be too much for younger students. However, including a drawing activity, where you draw a picture of something *on* a table or something *inside* a basket, on the morning calendar can get to the same type of thinking. The goal is to help students understand how the image reflects thinking.

Designs Need Specific Measurements

Specific measurements must be part of the blueprints as well. This allows educators to start checking off geometry standards much earlier in the school year than most mathematics curricula would have them do. In my experience, every elementary grade level has some sort of geometry standard in mathematics or measurement in science, even if it's measuring with nonstandard objects or estimating an object's size.

The practical reason for specific measurements is until students have a lot of experience with building and measuring things, they struggle to understand concepts of size. We know that students have a hard time understanding space and measurement, and the more practice they can get, the better (Carpenter, Fennema, Franke, Levi, & Empson, 2015). Blueprints are helpful in this area. Getting good at space and measurement means not only understanding what an object is but also learning how that object relates to other objects in space. As an example, I've had students label the height of a build as three yards. Three yards and other large measurements are often student shorthand for *this part is going to be really big*. So, we must teach them that specificity matters.

As a way to do that, I ask a student to bring me the blueprint with *three yards* written on it and a yardstick. I will admit, it's fun to watch a student walking back to my desk holding a yardstick (wielding it like a sword, probably) and realizing a yard is bigger than they imagined. A lot of students don't even make it all the way back; they just call to the rest of their group, grab the blueprint, and make edits. Good! They might not realize I just taught something, but they just learned something. Remember, all of this usually happens before anyone is allowed to touch cardboard, scissors, or tape.

REDESIGNING FOR K–2

Our younger students, on the other hand, are still developing the abstract reasoning skills to make the connection between three yards and the yardstick, so they may not make the connection as readily. So, guide them to it or explain to them, "We don't have that much cardboard, and it'll be bigger than you." And yes, I'll talk about scissors and such in the next chapter (page 53).

Sometimes, students will need to build a scale model or a proof of concept to be sure their idea and plan are sound. Students should build a scale model when something integral to their build is unclear in the design. For example, students were building traps to catch tree kangaroos in a project I assigned (more details in chapter 7, page 103). One group brought me a plan that included a pulley system. While the group had drawn what looked like a pulley system, I wasn't sure they'd actually be able to make it work with the materials at hand and in the time allowed. So, I quickly resketched part of their design with much smaller measurements and told them to try to build it as quickly as they could. It turned out they did know what they were doing, the scale pulley system worked great, and they built it full size with little problem.

My favorite design phase story encompasses everything I love about building in class and my design process in general. Every year, as I said, a group of students will want to build a Skee-Ball game during our winter cardboard arcade. And every year, I let one group do it, but I demand specific measurements before they start to build. Side-view blueprints come to me, and the base length is good, the height is cool, but the build's wall is effectively a right triangle. The hypotenuse of the wall is always a guess. It's always, in fact, either the exact length of the base or slightly longer by an estimated amount. Students aren't sure how long that side should be. Why should they be sure? They've not yet learned how to find the hypotenuse. They don't even know it's called a *hypotenuse* most of the time. The full geometry unit is late in the school year, and this is happening at winter break.

But they need to know the word and how to find the hypotenuse's length, so I, Mr. Robertson, will let them build. As a result, they ask. To be clear, students ask me how to solve a mathematics problem they created for themselves. They're asking me not *to* solve it but *how to* solve it. This is a true can-opener moment. I write, "Hypotenuse, Pythagorean theorem," on a sticky note and send the students away to grab a laptop and search the web for those terms. My parting words to them are usually, "When you find them, write down what you find. If you're still confused, and you probably will be, which is cool, come back and I'll help."

A few minutes later, students come back, completely confused by the exponents and equation and the "Pythag-whatever" word. Together, we work out what it all means. This group of students sits with me to solve the Pythagorean theorem, and I coach them through it. Soon, they have a good measurement for all three sides of their wall. But they also have a basic understanding of an advanced geometry concept they asked to learn. Measurement in design causes organic learning opportunities and constant student-driven problem solving. And later, during the official geometry unit, these students are all too eager to share their expertise.

It was an accident the first time it happened. I had no idea a learning opportunity for that kind of mathematics would happen when I started the arcade project. The project's design made those moments possible. I'd designed with flexibility and accidents in mind. I can only take credit for seeing a teachable moment and grabbing it.

Designs Need Specific Materials

Specific measurements make material needs clearer. Sometimes, it's a *good* thing teachers have limited resources. Students should become used to working with less than they think they need and planning using what they know they have. (Does our classroom have enough cardboard? Are these chopsticks long enough, or will something have to happen to make them longer?)

Secondary problems constantly appear and must be solved in material planning and in the measurement process. The materials in my classroom include a lot of recyclables, leftovers, old bottles and bottle caps, giant packs of chopsticks, cereal boxes (cardboard but thinner, which works better for younger students), millions of rubber bands, all the cardboard in the world (because I have a problem), and a random assortment of other things I pilfered from my house, from other teachers, from science kits, from LEGO kits, from Goodwill stores, or from anywhere, really.

Some teachers might look at the previous paragraph and want to be more purposeful and organized about what supplies they make available to their students. I've tried being purposeful and organized. I give students straws and chopsticks, thinking they'll use the straws as car axles and the chopsticks as masts for sails, and inevitably, students will use the materials in completely different ways. Not wrong ways, just different. I do, though, work diligently to keep structures and routines in my classroom for storing, using, and borrowing resources. Model what Jeff C. Marshall (2016) describes in his book *The Highly Effective Teacher* as *conscientiousness and curiosity*, if not cleanliness. Make sure to meet deadlines and prepare to explain what's happening in the classroom and where administrators or parents can find things whenever they ask. Being purposeful and organized can mean anything depending on the individual. Rest assured, a safe and functional design-minded classroom doesn't require a Pinterest-perfect classroom.

Buying things gets expensive. Scrounging is easier. We can't promise it will work for everyone, but rumor has it, grocery stores are a great resource for cardboard boxes of various sizes and thicknesses. Be aware of the brands advertised on any wild boxes you acquire, and keep in mind that some of them shouldn't show up in a classroom. It also doesn't hurt to become friends with managers of local big-box stores who have to deal with removing packaging material following shipments. Some design-minded teachers have had luck building relationships with staff at local secondhand stores. Some, not all, places allow staff discretion to set aside objects for teachers. If you do make a connection leading to a steady supply of cardboard and resources, send the individual (or store) a picture of how your class used the materials and a class thank-you letter. And if you bring in boxes from your home, take the address labels off first.

Materials are scarce in a classroom, so students should know what they're working with and where it came from. My goal is that they feel collective ownership over our resources. They should also have reasons for using what they want to use and consider the impact of using limited resources on the other designers in the room. Nothing in a design should happen because of the reason, "I guess, uh, yeah." Every measurement, every detail of the views, and every piece of material has a purpose. As a reminder, I have students articulate that reason during the design phase as they are creating their blueprints. This doesn't mean they can't change their design or approach, but I want them thinking about the connection between the problem, the solution they visualized, and the solution they create.

THINKING LIKE A DESIGNER

The educator modeling design thinking must take on the responsibility of asking, "Why?" at every available opportunity. Let your inner toddler free. If "why?" stumps a student, consider asking "I notice you used _____ in your design. What lead you to make that choice?" This is an important question. Here's an example: "You are using chopsticks here. Why?" Designers can justify their thinking. Sometimes, especially early in the process, a student might answer, "I'm not exactly sure, but I think they will work the best because _____." This is perfectly acceptable.

Design-Minded Thinking Across Content Areas

To be design minded as a teacher is to embrace the design phase of the design process. Why the repetition? Because it's important. The design phase is all in the design, the intent, and the plan. Embrace all aspects of this phase. Appreciate the solidity of having measurements, materials, and blueprints in place but also the *wibbly wobbliness* (flexibility) of knowing the plan can change at any moment according to the problem's needs. That's what teachers do. Teachers respond in the moment to student needs, to curriculum needs, to bells and fire drills, and suddenly, all the tape is gone. How did this project use all the tape? The teacher has a plan to restore the tape, though, even if the plan is "I was expecting to be surprised, so while I *am* staggered, I'm not knocked off my feet by the lack of tape, and progress may continue."

Students who are not used to design don't usually think about the planning portion of learning that much. Learning is receptive in a traditional classroom; students sit and read and listen and then write down what they learned. You don't have to prepare much for that as a student. But to be design minded means to be purposeful in all things, and that includes being responsible for what happens next. Students might not be designing the big plan (curriculum)—that's on the teacher—but they must prepare their part. Being design minded makes *learn* the verb it wants so badly to be.

English Language Arts

Outlines or bubble maps are the blueprints for writing assignments. If students can think about planning a cardboard arcade game with depth and detail, they can think about a writing assignment the same way. Part of the joy and struggle of using the design process in the classroom comes from translating it to the other subjects. It usually doesn't take long for students to see the relationship between a blueprint and an outline for a story or an essay. They can see how a story web has characters, story beats, settings, a beginning, a middle, an end, a driving problem, and a solution. It's also flexible and open to change, because sometimes, characters have minds of their own and refuse to do what the essay's writer expected. An essay's outline has research points to hit, a hypothesis, citations, and evidence, and can change based on what the research says versus what the writer thought it would say. In case this point hasn't come through yet, what happens in my classroom is usually very different from what students are used to. The novelty of it all means students willingly and excitedly create a blueprint for builds. When students reframe a story web or a brainstorming graphic organizer as a blueprint, the familiar becomes unfamiliar, which might be the bit of new and different that students need to use a tool they may have previously avoided or misunderstood.

Try to make connections between the design work students are doing in class, which reflects what people regularly do outside of school, and the work of school. Chapter 6 (page 87) will cover this in much greater detail, but during and after a build, have students write down their process and reflections and complete more familiar school-type works. For example, if students are doing a build to accompany a whole-class book, they will still do reading and writing activities related to that story.

Mathematics

What is creating an equation based on a story problem if not design? This is often smaller and quicker than creating a whole blueprint, but the concept is there. A multistep mathematics problem can be an intimidating beast for a student, so breaking it down into its parts and details is valuable. It's also valuable to write the problem out in a sensible way by considering multiple views. Remember, design means allowing designers to hold a possible solution or pathway in their mind before they can hold it in their hands.

Thinking like designers allows students to see the mathematics as a plan. This helps students get over mathematics anxiety because they can see it as something they are already confident about. If they can design a cardboard arcade game, which includes mathematics work, they can design their way through a story problem. A good design phase makes the build phase easier. It addresses potential problems and allows for steps to make the thing in the designer's head become a thing in the designer's hands.

STEAM

A great experiment to do with students once they feel confident in their blueprinting abilities is to have them draw a blueprint for an object, trade their blueprint with another group, and have them build from the plans they just received. This immediately shows the strengths and weaknesses in their blueprinting abilities. It's fun too. This works with essay outlines, mathematics equations, and presentation slideshows. Keep anonymity to protect students from embarrassment if needed. Call this experiment *mystery blueprints* or *mystery outlines*, for example.

On an episode of the television series *The Flash*, Captain Cold says, "Make the plan, execute the plan, expect the plan to go off the rails, throw away the plan" (Allowitz, 2017), and I'm prone to repeating that saying to my students (in April, never before the winter break). They need to understand the importance of planning ahead as well as the importance of having flexibility. The goal is to encourage them to grab hold of their learning, and activities like mystery blueprints can serve to acclimate them to that idea of adaptability and independent problem solving.

The Joy of Designing

So much of what happens in an elementary student's life is out of their control. To be a child is to be told, "You go here now; you do this now." So, while a design may (read: should) have boundaries and rules, it can still be a place where students freely flex their imaginations and explore. Remember, they do not have to build a design. The wonderful Treehouse children's book series written by Andy Griffiths, which begins with *The 13-Story Treehouse* (Griffiths, 2013), demonstrates this concept in a lovely way with friends Andy and Terry creating a treehouse that could not possibly exist. A design is a plan, a direction in which to go with purpose. A design mindset will let students set goals for themselves inside and outside of school. In my class, on the very first day of school, my students write a letter I call *Dear Future Me*. In that letter, they write to themselves on the very last day of school, talking about how they hope the year goes, what they hope to have accomplished, and how they expect their behavior to be. They make a design for their future. I take those letters, put them in a TARDIS-blue folder, and send them into the future (in other words, put the folder somewhere in my desk where I won't lose it). We talk about the planning for the year they just did and how that might help direct them going forward. The folder reappears on the last day of school, and students can see how their plans went. Most have forgotten the letters existed, which is fun. Be prepared for a lot of "Oh man, I can't even read this! No way did I write this bad." But in the end, they have a clear blueprint to look back on and reflect.

Design Reflection Template:
How Can We Solve the Problem?

Blueprints are a key part of the design phase of the design process, which is really a way to capture students' thinking.

In your classroom, how are you currently asking students to document their thinking?

When you think about using blueprints in your classroom, what's your initial reaction?

CHAPTER 4

Build
How Do We Create a Solution?

Close enough for theater work.

—Jack Spratt, the University of the Pacific theater department's head of set building,
while eyeballing a set of stairs leading to nowhere

This is the part students have been waiting for and most teachers (including me, even now) have been secretly worried about: the build phase. The ship is at sea. The sails are billowing, the oars churning. Prepare the trash cans and warn the custodians because the learning is about to get messy in here. This chapter details how to run the build phase of the design process while also doing the work of school, including formative assessment. Saying students will build is easy, but actually having students build in a productive manner is not, and we will address that in this chapter. Take from this what works for you, and change it to meet your needs. Build from what I've built. This is the essence of being a design-minded teacher.

Let Go of Control

The build phase of the design process is the scariest part, especially for teachers who are not used to stepping well back from their students while they work. I've spoken to many teachers about implementing design in their classrooms, and I've seen jaws tighten, pupils dilate, and hands shoot up with a full slate of clarifying questions ready to go. Their concerns and nerves are understandable because when I do it in my class, as I have done for years, I still get nervous about how it's going to go. Build-based projects in the classroom are an exercise of trust in your students and require a lot of not knowing what will happen; the latter may be unusual for teachers who organize their lessons down to the minute. Build-based projects can work for you too.

Teachers get lots and lots of messages about the need to control the classroom, from handing out papers to getting everyone's attention to walking through the hallways in certain ways (Marzano & Marzano, 2015; Wong & Wong, 2018). However, aiming for a controlled classroom when eight groups of students are spread about the room, each building something different, is simply too difficult. This is a time you don't want to simply rock the boat; instead, let the students rebuild the boat as they build their projects.

In other words, allow students to use trial and error to figure out what works for them individually and for the whole class. Nearly every single year, I've had a student work up the courage to say during a class meeting, "It's too loud when we work in groups. Can we brainstorm a way to keep the room quieter?" And every single year, students will talk through and figure out how to find balance between unproductive noise and productive rumblings. At the same time, try to avoid dictating one correct way of working in groups. I have found if I don't insist on flattening out individual quirks, I can see the way students work and learn what I never would have noticed. A student who appears to be doodling because she's bored might actually be processing and drawing to understand her thinking. Another student talks to himself (I don't even think he knows he's doing it), but when he's talking in class, he's probably more engaged than we assume. Observing these habits and individualities will serve you well later.

REDESIGNING FOR K–2

Gradual release of control is slower in the lower grades. I advocate for giving students the freedom to explore and fail while not sinking your own ship in the process. Independent group work will look different too. Students can gather around one group and the teacher, or the teacher could preview the steps that will be taken and choose volunteers to complete each step for the class. The end result may be less-complete builds but more teacher sanity and student understanding.

Students use the blueprints they created in the design phase to guide them through the build phase. Blueprints should be 80 to 85 percent solid when students move on to the build phase, and the final product should reflect about the same percentage of the blueprint. This takes time for students to learn. It will not happen until blueprints are good and design thinking has taken hold in their minds.

Depending on where you are in your journey, your enjoyment may vary. Your students, however, are going to love the build phase. You also must expect and accept the chaos of a classroom as construction zone. The build phase is a messy one. It's the least controllable environment.

Teachers who are used to having complete control of their classrooms may struggle here because the control is almost completely in the students' hands. As a reminder, the design phase is crucial, as it's your chance to influence the build as much as you feel you must, which should be as little as possible, or just enough to avoid disaster. Avoid pointing out flaws in student designs before you approve them, but do make an anecdotal record of the possible flaw so you can respond if the flaw impacts the design. You might even say something along the lines of "I noticed that you did *x*, *y*, and *z*. I think you're going to run into some trouble when you start to build. I'm going to approve this and see what happens." Be sure to have those notes handy during the build phase. The conversation in my classroom about students themselves finding flaws in their plans will usually go as follows.

> *"Mr. Robertson, how long does this have to be?"*
> *"As long as it needs to be to be well done."*
> *"Yeah, but like . . . is it good?"*
> *"That is an excellent question. Is it good?"*

Students will have internalized becoming designers when that conversation doesn't happen anymore. Teachers who have always pointed out how students can improve their work should try taking a step back. Let students look at and collect examples from the world around them to decide what *good* is and what *done* looks like. Leading these conversations with students, collecting models and discussing them with students, and annotating student work and annotations are part of what Silvia Rosenthal Tolisano calls *documenting learning* (Tolisano & Hale, 2018). Show students it's their classroom. (More on this in chapter 9, page 153.) Model what it means to be learner centered by soliciting feedback on what's working and what's not (Ahmed, 2018; Martin-Kniep, 2000; Tollefson & Osborn, 2008). Fifth-grade students and I created the following rubric (figure 4.1, page 56) as we worked together to develop a classroom community. We built it over the course of the first marking period, revising the language to make sure everyone understood what it means to be a member of a classroom community. Students used the rubric to reflect on how the day went at the end of a free build session, class discussion, or other activity that required interacting with other students.

Thinking Like a Designer

The best thing an educator can do for students during the build phase is move around the room, nudge students toward solutions, help solve interpersonal problems, and keep opinions private for the time being. Trust students and the process.

The build phase can feel the least like teaching in part because teachers are the least active during it. Sometimes, teaching looks like sitting on your hands, pacing the classroom without looking like you're pacing the classroom, and waiting for students to look up and step around the tree all on their own. Teaching is a verb in the most *gather around, children, and listen while I impart wisdom upon you* sense of the word. I call this, with all the respect in the world, *capital-T teaching*. If you set things up right, your

	Disrupter	Visitor	Member	Leader and Role Model
Focusing on the task at hand in a community means that I make sure I pay attention to what needs to be done.	I focus more on tasks of my own making. If someone asked me what I'm learning at that moment, I would have a hard time answering.	My focus switches back and forth between a task of my own making and the task at hand. If someone asked me what I'm learning at that moment, I would tell them the last thing I remember learning or something unrelated.	I do what I need to do to keep myself focused on the task at hand. If someone asked me what I'm learning at that moment, I could explain to them what I'm doing.	I do what I need to do to keep myself focused on the task at hand and make sure that I'm not interfering with other members of the community. If someone asked me what I'm learning at that moment, I could show and explain to them what I'm doing.
Asking for help and helping others are important when I'm part of a small group.	When learning in a small group, I get stuck when I need help. My questions may cause confusion for myself and others in my community. When others offer help, the words I use are unkind or harmful to others.	When learning in a small group, I help others when I have the same question or problem. I ask others for help, but the words I use make it hard for a classmate to know where I need help. I may ignore the suggestions others give me.	When learning in a small group, I help my classmates when they ask or when an adult asks me to help out. I ask others for help with general questions. I can explain why I'm stuck and am open to suggestions.	When learning in a small group, I look for opportunities and take the initiative to help my classmates. I ask others for help using specific questions and ask for feedback on the work I've done so far.
I'm an active participant in discussions (connection to Common Core standards).	I ask questions unrelated to what we're talking about. When asked a question, I avoid answering. I make comments that seem unrelated to what we're talking about. Other participants in the discussion aren't sure how to respond to my comments.	I ask questions to be part of the conversation and understand what is happening. When asked a question, I answer it in a way that others may not see how it connects to what we're talking about. I make comments that are related to what we're talking about. My questions and comments add to the conversation in a way that only makes sense to me.	I ask specific questions to make sense of what others are saying or to follow up on what others are saying. When asked a question, I make comments that contribute to the discussion and link to the remarks of others. I make comments that reflect what we are talking about.	I ask specific questions to make sense of what others are saying, to follow up on others' comments, or to encourage a comment from someone else. When asked a question, I make comments that elaborate on others' responses and provide further information or explanation. I make comments that contribute to others' understanding of the topic, text, design, or issue under discussion.

FIGURE 4.1: Habits and behaviors of members of a learning community.

Visit go.SolutionTree.com/instruction for a free reproducible version of this figure.

students will start the building and learning processes themselves, and you will be there to fill in the gaps and provide the proper support.

Focus on Engagement

Work by educators like Phillip C. Schlechty (2002) and Heather Lyon (2020) help explain not all engagement is the same. Just because students look busy or engaged in an activity, it doesn't mean they're learning. In this phase, you're doing important teaching work. You're constantly collecting formative assessments to ascertain the space between where students are and where you want them to be, learning-wise (Wiliam, 2011, 2018). I'm a big fan of clipboards with checklists—nothing complicated. Student names go in the first column, boxes for standards go across the top, and there's space to write notes. I recommend jotting down things like whether students' measurements are correct, whether students are attending to the *main problem*, whether they are reading the correct sections of the story to find the proper information, and the nature of what they tell you when you ask what they're learning or working on. These one-on-one conversations are essential to discerning if students are engaged in productive work. Stepping on, but not over, that line between monitoring and hovering takes some practice, and it takes a while to learn what each students' productive struggling looks like (Blackburn, 2018). For many students, this means teaching through letting learning take its course. For others, it means direct instruction in particular content or skills. My classroom routines and structures include helping students understand that when I sit down next to them, it doesn't mean they're in trouble. Rather, I'm helping. Everyone needs help sometimes.

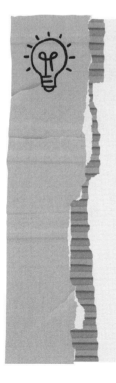

Thinking Like a Designer

Iterate. Iterate. Iterate. Constant iteration is a good habit to develop as a design-minded teacher in a cardboard classroom. This makes instruction more accessible for students who may have trouble with focus, memory, or hearing. Educational institutions should, and increasingly do, make it a universal goal to incorporate more practices from Universal Design for Learning (UDL) to ensure all students, especially those with sensory issues, feel comfortable in the classroom (Posey & Novak, 2020). A feature of UDL that speaks to me is the idea of *designing to the edges*— that is, ensuring everything in the classroom is accessible from the get-go rather than modifying or adapting to meet students' needs. Consider adopting the same goal to make it so no student with a disability, or their parent, needs to ask for an adapted assignment because everything will already be accessible.

Establish (Some) Rules and Expectations

We are about to embark on a journey that can involve a lot of mess, confusion, and disagreement. Before starting off, you must have a candid conversation with your class. Talk about mess. Talk about supplies, structures, and routines. Talk about all the things you need to make your class run smoothly or to find your way back to smooth when things go awry. The chaos must function, and function safely.

During the build phase, you can and should control the following ten things. All of these come from experience, and the list is always changing because students are infinitely creative, but the basic guidelines that follow should prove helpful for your classroom. Lay these out as rules and expectations for students.

1. **Put safety first.** You must be mindful that the materials and the tools you give students to use are age and skill appropriate for them. Consider the following.

   - Demonstrate how to move around a classroom holding scissors. Don't assume. Students forget. Demonstrate it. Demonstrate it again. Walk with blade down, gripped in your hand, point not sticking out.

   - Cut slowly. Say to students, "Cut away from your body. Do not cut down toward where your leg is." (Yes, you have to say that.) Explain and model for students how to cut up materials on a stable desk and *not* to use their laps.

   - Have students cut cardboard with scissors first, and then introduce cardboard knives. Cardboard knives are small cutting tools with lightly serrated blades you can find at any craft store or on your favorite online megacorporation's website. Schools don't like the word *knife*, and some administrators will get nervous if you use it, so call them *cardboard-cutting implements* or *single-blade scissors*. But really, they're knives. They cut cardboard better than even the best pair of scissors. Do not buy these if your school regulations forbid them. (In chapter 9, page 153, we get into relationships with administrators. It sounds small and silly, but talking about scissors is an essential part of those relationships.) Students can get cut with cardboard knives, and even if the resulting cut is no worse than a paper cut, answering for that falls on the teacher. I am very deliberate with my students when I demonstrate the proper ways to use these tools. The word *tool* is also key; they are not toys but tools.

   - Let students work with scissors first so they know the struggle. Then introduce cardboard knives so students know how good life can be. Afterward, remind them that misuse of the cardboard knives sends them back to scissor time for *x* long. No one wants to go back to scissor time. Scissor time hurts your hands.

2. **Be cool.**
   - This is the prime directive (right after "be safe"): be cool. Communicate to students, "Before you make a choice, before you say a thing, decide if you're being cool (as in calm, collected, and kind) or not. It's the easiest rule in the world to remember. Be cool to your partners even when you disagree. Be cool to those around you. Be like Fonzie. Be cool."
   - When working in groups, everyone does not need to be best friends, but they need to get along. Everyone needs to be cool with one another. Listen with an open mind and an open heart. Communicate like you know the people listening are also smart humans who want what is best for the project. (It's also worth revisiting that teachers, like all people, contain multitudes and don't slot perfectly into a single teacher identity. If you're interested in setting up an equity-minded classroom, *Equity-Centered Trauma-Informed Education* by Alex Shevrin Venet [2021] is a great resource.)
   - Students should be cool to the other groups. The build phase is never a contest. It's never a race. It's a community. We share ideas. No one is "copying" anyone else, but sometimes, ideas find their way into other builds. That happens. It's better if the groups ask and communicate, but overall, students are cool with each other and proud their idea inspired someone else. (Yes, you do have to specify the difference between this and plagiarism later. But in their final reflections, students can still give credit: "We added this kind of sail because we saw that group do it and it looked like a good idea.")

3. **Measure twice, cut once.**
   - Students will use all the cardboard in a room in a day and a half if the teacher lets them. Rulers are their friend. Blueprints have measurements for a reason. Students should measure, draw a straight line with the ruler, measure the line, and cut on the line. Thou shalt not eyeball it. Thou shalt use a straight edge.

4. **Respect the space and materials.**
   - The classroom is a shared space, and the materials are shared materials. Treat everything like you will need it next time. Treat it all with respect. No one can use broken scissors, and we don't have enough scissors as it is. Cranking on scissors to get them through thick cardboard will break them. If a pair does break, use it as a teachable moment for the whole class to show how it can happen to anyone if they're not careful.
   - Be careful as you move through the room. Groups will be working on the floor, so be careful of someone else's project. Do not assume a pile of stuff is garbage and throw it away without first asking around to be sure you're not throwing away small pieces of a larger build.

- Clean up. The room must look nice at the end of every session because other kinds of learning must also take place in the classroom. ("Look nice" is a relative measure. My nice is messier than that of many teachers I know. The students should know what *nice* means to you.) The students can clean. Budget more time than you think you'll need for this at first. Remind the students the custodian can shut down a build project even faster than the principal can.

5. **Follow. Your. Plans.**

- Remind students to look at their plans. You do not need to make them follow every step, but you can ask questions and nudge them. Point at something on the build, and then point at the blueprint and ask where it is on the plans. I like to ask *why. Why is this there? Why did you cut this like this? Why are you googling pictures of kittens when you asked me if you could search for trebuchets?*

6. **Consider timing.**

- A project is like a gas; it will expand to fill the space it is given. If you give students a week to finish, they'll be done in a week, and some will be rushing to finish on Friday. If you give students three days to finish, they'll be done in three days, and more students will be rushing to finish on the third day. It takes time to figure out how long is right for each build.

- Projects finish when they finish, just like anything else. I wish I could tell you every student will build at a certain pace. But alas, I cannot. What's important is to communicate clearly with students and be present with them while they work. Shulman (2004) gets into this idea in his writing about the thinking that teachers do. In effect, his foundational work on teacher mindset offers that actively listening, thoughtfully honoring students' thinking and work, and setting aside preconceived notions about what's supposed to happen are key classroom teacher skills.

- All things must end. Teachers experience an internal struggle between wanting to give students enough time to do great and not wanting the project to drag on forever. Are students really using all the think time to think, or are they spacing out? Doing well and dragging out a project look different with every group. If students have naturally moved on to the test phase, they're done. If they're cutting out pictures of sloths and gluing them to their build (true story), they're probably done. If they're tinkering and don't want you to stop them, they're also probably done, even if they don't think they are. If they're fighting, they should be done, at least for a while. If they're panicked, use your teacher judgment. Will ten more minutes really make much of a difference?

- In the beginning, students will come ask you, "Is this done?" You can respond, "Is it? It's not my project." Eventually, they learn designers decide the end point.

7. **Build quality.**

- You cannot control the final quality of a build, especially not if the build is truly student centered and student driven—not if the student is the one thinking like a designer. The designer decides when something is done. The designer decides when something is the best it can be. This is a struggle. We teachers influence this not in the moment but later, during the reflection process. As students build, all we can do is nudge, encourage, and provide explicit instruction when students' formative assessment data call for it.

- Make sure builds are "close enough for theater work." In college, I had a job working in the theater department building sets. I quoted the man who ran the department, Jack Spratt, at the start of this chapter (page 53). He kept things in perspective. He knew we were building for theater, which meant the sets needed to look good, work, and then come apart. When a detail wasn't perfect, he'd always say, "Eh, close enough for theater work." I say that in class too (and yes, I have to tell the whole story for it to make sense). The takeaway here is we're not looking for perfection. Perfect wastes time. We're looking for *close enough for fourth grade*—high expectations for fourth grade, granted, but still only fourth grade.

8. **Keep in mind group dynamics.**

- Decide how you'll determine groups in your classroom. I believe specific jobs don't keep everyone busy, and they don't instill a sense students are all in this together. Many teachers develop group jobs: artist, planner, timekeeper, scribe, whatever. If assigning jobs works for you, great. Elizabeth G. Cohen and Rachel A. Lotan's (2014) book *Designing Groupwork: Strategies for the Heterogeneous Classroom* is a useful resource for elementary teachers thinking about how to manage large and small groups. Personally, I prefer groups to be more dynamic and flexible because students will often divide and conquer jobs on their own: "You build that, and I'll build this."

- Students' saying, "That's not my part," is unacceptable. "It's all your part," I tell them. Projects are not judged in pieces. Projects are judged as a whole. Students cannot step away from something as if it wasn't their responsibility because, at the end of the day, there is no group leader, and there are no specific jobs; there are only the goal, the problem, and hopefully, the solution. You can explain this to the students, but it's up to them to find their way through it. There must be differentiation within this, as teachers each know their class and their students. In a class with strong relationships, the students understand they are all different, but the overriding expectation, "We're all in this together to do the best," remains.

- It will occasionally become clear one student is not pulling their weight. Judge the project as a whole, but also give students an opportunity during the reflect phase to explain their individual additions to the whole. If a student is holding their group back on purpose through lack of effort or even sabotage somehow, have a conversation in the hall. Ask the student why. Try to come from a place of understanding. Talk to the student; then give them a choice: "The project must be done, and we must solve the problem. Return to your group, and contribute or work alone. If you work alone, you can make your own project, with no extra time, or you can answer the problem a different way while still showing the same amount of work and following my design process." Most students will return to their groups. Issues arise when too many students try to take control and communication breaks down, and we forget everyone is doing their best.

9. **Modify and iterate as necessary.**

- As students are building something, they're discovering things about their blueprints, their problems, and their solutions. This is the best learning of the build phase. Things are changing. Students can find improvements and modifications as they build. Blueprints are guidelines, not directives. As Captain Barbossa says in *Pirates of the Caribbean*, "The code is more what you'd call *guidelines* than actual rules" (Verbinski, 2003). Students *should* change and modify their blueprints. That's learning. Occasionally, students will have to throw out and completely rewrite their blueprints. That's also learning. Whether it works is completely up to how much time students have.

10. **Don't forget to teach.**

- To take our extended analogy from the water to the air for a second, consider that every new pilot learns this simple rule: "Don't forget to fly the plane." Pilots are usually told to remember this when they're troubleshooting a problem, but it's a helpful point for the build phase. It acts as a good reminder to keep an eye on what's happening, to document what students are doing, and to step in when needed with direct teaching. Think of it as "just in time" teaching or coaching.

- Be aware of the distance between students and the curriculum learning targets (more on this in chapter 9, page 153). If the learning gap starts to widen or shows no sign of closing, it might be time for a minilesson or content refresher.

Figure 4.2 offers a student-facing version of the rules to keep in the classroom.

Class Rules

1. Put safety first.
- Be careful with the materials and tools you are using.
- Hold scissors the correct and safe way.
- Cut slowly. Cut away from your body.
- Respect the implement, or work without it.

2. Be cool.
- Before you make a choice, decide if you're being calm, collected, and kind.
- Be cool to those around you.
- You don't have to be best friends with everyone. You do have to listen, collaborate, and get along.
- Be cool to the other groups.

3. Measure twice, cut once.
- Rulers are your friend.
- Blueprints have measurements for a reason.
- Thou shalt not eyeball it.
- Thou shalt use a straight edge.

4. Respect the space and materials.
- The classroom is a shared space, and the materials are shared materials.
- Be careful as you move through the room.
- Clean up as you go and after you're done.

5. Follow. Your. Plans.
- Look at your plans frequently.
- Check them before any major cuts or decisions.

6. Consider timing.
- A project is like a gas; it will expand to fill the space it is given. Use your time wisely.
- All things must end. Be mindful that you'll eventually be out of time for a project. Plan.
- Only you decide when the project is finished.

7. Build quality.
- The teacher cannot control the quality of the build. You must do that.

8. Keep in mind group dynamics.
- All parts of the project are your part. You are all equally responsible for making sure the project gets done.
- Pull your weight.

9. Modify and iterate as necessary.
- Don't be afraid to change your blueprint if you find something that works better.

10. Don't forget to learn.
- All your projects tie in with subjects you are learning. This isn't just fun build time! Take care to learn the lesson here.

FIGURE 4.2: Build phase class rules.

*Visit **go.SolutionTree.com/instruction** for a free reproducible version of this figure.*

REDESIGNING FOR K–2

A few of the preceding points deserve clarification for K–2 educators. Please see the following.

- **Concerning safety:** Cardboard cutters are sharp and dangerous. But paper is thin and hard to build with. As a compromise, I suggest using your standard classroom scissors and cereal boxes. Cereal box cardboard is sturdy enough to build with but won't break little scissors when cut. I did not come up with this idea; a second-grade teacher I work with did. Use the experience and help of those around you when you don't know.

- **Concerning project timing:** I maintain that our smaller students can also judge this, but the teacher should directly teach this to them by modeling the questions students should ask themselves and creating (read: having students create) a question anchor chart featuring questions like, "Can I show the teacher how this works? What was my goal, and does this do that? Will this work multiple times? Do I know why every part exists?"

Encourage Growth Through Failure

Things change during the build phase. Design thinkers embrace this. Students learning design thinking worry about this and follow their designs either too closely or not at all. Early in the school year, when your students are still learning to think like designers, they might see blueprints more as hoops to jump through than as tools integral to the final product. They'll think this way no matter what you say as you introduce blueprints and go over them. Students will draw blueprints because you say they have to so they can get to the fun parts: cutting and gluing and measuring (if they remember). That's OK.

Yes, it's OK that students will see their blueprints as hoops to jump through at first. It's OK that the first time they build something, most—if not all—of them will completely forget about their blueprints about five minutes into the excitement and adrenaline of the building process, and freestyling will ensue. It's OK because those builds will be, almost without exception, bad. Early student builds are nearly always bad. They fall down. They are fragile. They look terrible. They are laminated in packing tape. They're uneven, and they just barely solve the problem stated at the start of the process.

This illustrates what we in the ed biz call *natural consequences*. Teachers who teach design thinkers never say, "I told you so." Instead, we say, "How closely did you follow your blueprint?" or "Can you talk me through the steps of your design process?" When students are still learning to be designers, they are usually able to explain the thinking behind a part of their build they are excited about but completely unable to articulate any clear thinking behind another part. So, ask direct questions like, "It seems to me the problem in your build is stability. When did you notice it tends to fall over, and where in your process did you address the problem?" If the class is feeling fragile, which happens because failure is hard, craft feedback such as the following to guide the students closer to their goal while respecting their autonomy.

> *"I see you've put a lot of thought into the overall look of your build. It looks great, and it's clear what you're trying to make. When it's placed under certain kinds of stress, like when the table is bumped or when you try to make this part move, it all kind of goes sideways. Have you thought about other internal structures or shapes—[cough] triangles [cough]—that might make it stronger without ruining the nice outside design you've got going on? You've got the time. I know you can figure this out. Feel free to take a walk around the room and check out other builds if you need some inspiration."*

Guidance such as this clarifies the idea that *failure is good* so students can understand it easily. I don't teach formal lessons on grit, which is Angela Duckworth's (2016) term for the perseverance and dedication to long-term goals. I also don't directly teach students about growth mindset or use its concepts to organize my classroom, but I do try to keep them in mind (Dweck, 2016). People with a growth mindset believe they earn skills through good habits, regular practice, and constructive criticism from others, while people with a fixed mindset have a kind of "you get what you've got" mentality about skills, meaning they are born with innate abilities and should learn to live with their limits (Dweck, 2016). While teachers don't commonly walk students through the concepts of growth mindset and grit, these concepts can help teachers recognize when students are bummed because they failed at something they were excited to do. By applying a growth mindset in themselves *and* encouraging it in students, teachers will know when students need assurance that they can be successful, and teachers will learn how to recognize the confidence that comes in the beat after failure.

Students who are good at "playing school" know the rules and the tricks and have never really struggled with school. They come at building projects like they do every other school assignment: with a confidence born of good grades and lots of praise. Then the wall of their build won't stay up, or the wheels fall off for the seventeenth time. They get frustrated. They get worried they're not going to pass, even though no one has mentioned grades. You don't want students thinking about grades. You want them thinking about whether their build solves the problem. That's all. The grade—hold on, come closer as I whisper this: "The grade does not matter." When it comes time to show off their build, some students will be embarrassed because they think they failed. That's when you get to help them see all the value in what they did. That's when you get to do more teaching.

Redesigning for K–2

Here, K–2 teachers may have a leg up on grades 3–5 teachers. Their students have less to unlearn about what school "should" be, which may make their transition to being design minded easier. This will help the students who might have otherwise adopted an "I'm good at school" mindset.

A bad build is a failure students can see, but it doesn't hurt. A bad build is so much easier for students to understand than a bad essay or a missed mathematics problem or a boring presentation. It's right there in front of them, falling apart and looking sad.

But it's not the last build they'll do. It might not even be the last time they'll do this specific build. The very first build project in my class is a quick build I call *wind-powered cars*. (See chapter 8, page 119, for details.) The short guide to this build is to "make a wind-powered car." Many of these cars fail. But sometime after winter break, as a fun interjection between all the big tests at the end (of the semester, unit, or lesson, whatever cumulative test students are anticipating), we revisit this build, and students get a second crack at those wind-powered cars. The second crack turns out so much better. Cars roll. They roll straight. They roll far. There's cheering. There's evidence of learning and growth clearer than any big test at the end can offer.

Thinking Like a Designer

In the build phase, reinforce the lesson you've been communicating throughout the year: it's OK to be bad at first. Encourage students to make the second build better using what they learned from the bad build.

Students have successfully internalized design thinking when they no longer need teacher approval of an idea before they try it. They should still ask for help with small things or general advice, but if they have an idea and it's not completely outlandish, they should be confident enough in their thinking as a designer to try it. A designer does not need constant head pats. A designer moves forward with a well-thought-out plan, and when problems appear, a designer evolves the design to adjust to those problems. A designer still asks for help and works collaboratively. If anything, a designer might need a subtle nod and smile from the teacher at the start.

Once you feel your students have embraced being design minded, you can start throwing curveballs at them in the middle of their build to see just how flexible they can be. If they have been building cardboard arcade games and you've noticed all the games seem fairly static (nothing on the games moves), add a new requirement like this: "All games must have some moving component." Say nothing more and let them discover; unless you're giving them robotics kits or something (which would be really cool), this means cutting slits in the cardboard and having someone hide behind or beneath the game to move a piece back and forth. These curveballs, or challenges, ensure students are always thinking flexibly and actively and, thus, learning.

Thinking Like a Designer

It is our job to point out what the students have done and use it later in other subjects. Iteration and revision are essential parts of the learning process (Berger et al., 2014; Schlechty, 2002).

Design-Minded Thinking Across Content Areas

There is academic value in the mess. The build phase is about as far away from large-group direct instruction as you can get. Some of your teacher colleagues will not get what is happening in the room. I have had conversations with teachers where I sat down and explained all the thinking behind every step of what happens in my room (basically the nickel version of this book). One teacher replied, "Oh! I thought you all were just, you know, building stuff because it's fun in there." I worked next door to that teacher for years prior to this conversation. After the conversation, she was much more open to trying new stuff.

Some people will not see the academic value in the mess. It is up to each person to decide how much the mess bothers them. The principal is the only person who needs to get the purpose as a whole and understand teachers are in control of their room, even when they're *not* in control; principals can make or break the project time. The guardians around students need to understand what's happening, so spend time during parent conferences having students show off what they are building. Most parents love nothing more than seeing their child excited to show off something they've done at school.

If this process is truly student driven, teachers do not interfere even if they want to. I specifically mean teachers don't interfere with designs and plans, but also, remember rule 10: don't forget to teach (page 62). The goal is to find a sweet spot between chaos and control, between play and productive learning. The following sections detail how the build phase in the design process translates across content areas.

English Language Arts

The first official five-paragraph essay students write is unclear, disorganized, and in dire need of an editor and a citation check. I teach fourth grade as I write this, and by fourth grade, some students already think they can't write. They can't see writing as creation. Your job is to help students see they are creating something when they write. They are building with words (Stockman, 2016). Once students can connect a blueprint to a build, they have the pathways to connect an outline to a finished essay. They have done the process, and they have a better understanding of the work it takes to go from one to the other.

Mathematics

There is confusion the first time students divide fractions. As with making measurements, the mental models needed for dividing fractions can be difficult to develop (Carpenter et al., 2015). During this time, there is hair pulling and tear shedding, gnashing of teeth and rending of workbook pages, not to mention how the *students* react to it. In the build phase, my students learn they can both literally and abstractly construct mathematics problems; they can take the problem-solving design they came up with and give it form. Mathematics stops being this abstract thing and becomes something students can see on paper or create with manipulatives. Anyone who has taught adding or subtracting fractions (let us leave multiplying or dividing aside, because who has the time?) knows we all start by drawing fraction bars. That is building the problem. Even if you say, "No, it's not, because I did fraction bars before reading this brilliant, wonderful book," that just means the soul of a design-minded teacher is within you. It means the best way to teach something is already by using design thinking, and the design in this case is drawing a fraction bar to represent one whole, then drawing lines (or cutting out pieces) to represent fractions. Your students are making something. Not all design thinking involves big projects, remember. Design mindedness describes where your head is at.

STEAM

The first science experiment students will try in my class is a baking soda volcano, which teaches them exactly nothing about science, experiments, or volcanoes. But the build phase helps my students see what a science experiment could be and gives them the confidence to make something worth testing. My students have tested regular fourth-grade things like how a plant grows with x, y, and z (variables such as type of soil, amount of sun, or kind of seed), and they made the planter themselves. They felt control over the parameters of the experiment because they learned to control a build.

Social studies lessons take on a new dimension when students build a city themselves—not in a "here are some sugar cubes and paint; build Mecca" kind of way. (I remember doing this specific example as a child and snacking on sugar cubes as I did.) Rather than use an example from my own class for this, I will reference the teacher across the hall from me, who is the kind of teacher who makes *you* better because he is so good. He uses an architectural building simulator on the computer and has students create operable cities. He puts in constraints forcing students to work like historical figures might have. And once they have their own city, they can do whatever they want within it. They own this place; they're invested. Then, the teacher talks about revolution, civil rights, and taxes. Students then have a proportionate understanding of those concepts' scale of impact because they have their own city to think about when they consider the concepts.

The Joy of Building

Building like a designer is methodical. It's planned. It's thoughtful. It's also a lot of fun. There is noise in the classroom. There are students everywhere. There's a mess to clean up. I would never suggest all learning should always look like this, just as I would never suggest no learning is happening when students sit quietly in rows looking at journals. But there is a unique joy to the build phase of design. More than any other step, building helps bring students back to the room and get them excited to learn. No matter their reading level, mathematics level, language level, or public speaking confidence, there's something fun about getting on your knees with three other students and making something you drew on paper become a reality. It only gets deeper in the next phase, test and revise, where designers learn to evaluate their builds and consider what it means to be successful.

Build Reflection Template:
How Do We Create a Solution?

The idea of control comes up a lot in the build phase of the design process. Take a moment to consider what control means to you and how it manifests in your classroom.

How do you currently manage your classroom? How do you plan out routines and class structures?

How does the idea of a messy design-minded classroom make you feel? Why?

CHAPTER 5

Test and Revise
What Happens When We Try Out the Solution and Respond to Data?

> How fast will it go until it breaks?
>
> —*Doug's children, with any new toy*

Students generally love building. As we learned in the previous chapter, building is when you get your hands on the materials to cut, glue, tape, and make a thing. It doesn't feel like schoolwork to students; it feels like play, or like they're getting away with something. Testing, though, is an entirely different phase.

Testing has taken on a bad name in education, especially for teachers who lean toward progressive pedagogies. *Test* is often said at best with a sneer and at worst with a rude gesture. So many in education say *test* as if they need to have their mouths washed out with soap after saying it. (I ought to back up this claim with statistics because this is a research-based book, but I can hear you nodding your head from here. You know it to be true.)

But what if students and teachers didn't associate testing with negative emotions and wasted time? What if students were excited to test? What if they knew testing was an important part of the learning process, and because they were taught to think like designers, they *valued* the data collection process testing provides them? This chapter explores the ways design-minded thinking can communicate to students that testing is a learning opportunity rather than just a way to evaluate their skills by applying it to the design process after they have built something.

The design process helps students become more engaged with measurement, research, and preparation and enables them to focus on something they might not have initially cared about. But what if it also showed them tests have value? What if it showed them the data collected from the tests and the actions resulting from data collection have value? What if they felt they could use what they find out from tests to make amazing things? These are things about testing students can latch onto. What if designing got students excited about conducting multiple tests, and they ended up asking to be tested, and they cared about the results not because they want to know their grade but because they want to know what actions can happen next?

Thinking Like a Designer

As a design-minded teacher, be very clear with the language you use about tests and why you use it (Denton, 2013). Proudly use the word *test* in your classroom. It will help reduce some students' anxiety around large-scale testing mandates (Greene & Melton, 2007). You can explain how mandated tests come from the people in the state capital trying to understand whether the experiment of school is working. This can help students feel less stressed about the test day because they know they are doing their part by providing information about their learning to those who will read their tests.

I've trained my brain so that when I think about testing, I go to testing designs and builds first to learn how well they address the defined problem. Because I've been in a design process mindset for so long, I have to switch gears to think about traditional tests like spelling tests and the big tests at the end (I call them all *the big test at the end* because I've found that a little hyperbolic teasing goes a long way to relieve student anxiety about the tests). Such is the goal for my students as well. When I say *test*, I want them thinking about what they get to do to help themselves. This, of course, does not mean I don't test. We all have to do the *other* administrative or subject-based tests. By becoming design thinkers, my students are better able to sit for the other tests because they understand the mechanics behind them (most of the time). I'd never claim students actually like those tests, especially the big tests at the end because they hate that they can't use the data they'd gather from these tests right away.

I do avoid more traditional "everyone do this worksheet"–type tests as often as I can because they're not as flexible as I need them to be. As long as what students are doing shows proficiency in the standard, they can do it. What I'm tempted to put here is this: embrace project-based learning, avoid standardized tests as much as possible, and know these are harder to grade but more rewarding to read, watch, or see. But I won't, because I know the difference between the ideal school in my head and actual schools in the world.

From here, we move to testing what students created and seeing if it does, as your students will surely have assured you, solve the problem you've presented them and follow the design. In this chapter, we will consider the word *test* itself and make connections between the test phase of a build process and large-scale, state-mandated tests.

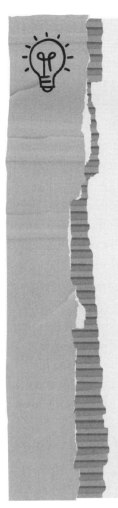

Thinking Like a Designer

A brief digression of clarification: the design process is not a way to trick students into doing school better. Design thinking is not a trick. Magic is a trick because it's not real. It fools your senses against your better judgment. Teller, of the magic duo Penn and Teller, says, "Magic is *unwilling* suspension of disbelief" (Stromberg, 2012). That's a trick.

Design thinking is not unwilling. Design thinking is all about belief—specifically, students' belief they are capable of something. We are not in the tricking-students business—not here in this book, not here in this thought process. If we were, I'd trick you into buying a copy of this book for everyone at your school; then I'd fill it with trapdoors and mirrors instead of something real. Becoming design thinkers means we work along with the students, not against them. We can best introduce design thinking through engaging projects. That's the initial motivation. Expecting students to be initially motivated by or interested in something "because it's school," in my opinion, deflects the burden of responsibility away from the teacher and onto the student. We, the teachers, must find ways to engage the students. But the design-thinking process is never a trick. It's real.

Model Testing and Test the Model

Modeling testing is important because students will almost never, in my experience, push their projects as hard as you'd like them to. Not at first. I, as the teacher, need to demonstrate what I mean when I say, "Test your build." I can use a student product, or I can use something I've built myself, but students need to see exactly what I expect from them.

When students are in the design and build phases of the design process, they should have a clearly articulated understanding of the problem in front of them—the problem statement ("Build a wind-powered car") or question ("What's the most efficient design for a wind-powered car?"). In my experience, when students are first learning this process, they lose track of the goal in their enthusiasm. Some will forget they even have a design or a problem to solve. Some will follow their design without thinking about whether it does what it's supposed to do. And some will get caught up in making the build pretty rather than functional. Having learning targets or goals in a place where students can see them makes it easier for them to self-assess their progress (Moss & Brookhart, 2012).

In the test phase, put the main goal front and center in everyone's mind again. Even though you've left the project's purpose on the board this whole time, now you can call everyone's attention back to it and repeat it while underlining it and circling it over and over and over. Use this theory of comedy I gleaned from George Carlin's work: once is cute, twice is clever, three times is funny, six times is annoying, and at twenty-three times, it's funny again. Ask students to tell you the main goal. Hopefully, at this point, every group is done with its first build.

Modeling what testing a product looks like is important here because students will experience a push and pull familiar to anyone who has ever created anything: the desire to get it right versus the urge to protect the ego versus the need to just be done. Knowing when to push and when to hold back is again shaped by Angela Duckworth's (2016) grit and Carol S. Dweck's (2016) growth mindset. During the test phase, you as the teacher face the challenge to help students overcome their ego and impatience in favor of honest evaluation. It's better to be right than to be fast. You cannot be subtle about testing with students. Explain you know it's hard to look at something you've made and see its flaws.

THINKING LIKE A DESIGNER

Keep in mind that, like your students, you're a designer. You're solving the problem of getting students from one shore to the other, of teaching learning standards, and preparing them for the next grade. When your students are working independently, you're testing if you've successfully taught them how to work in groups. The data you're collecting about their learning are data about your teaching. They will serve as the evidence you'll use to reflect on your teaching.

My students know I've written books, so on my computer, I keep a list of all the corrections I made on a book right before it went to press. I pull it up and tell them, "Dig this. I read this book two dozen times. A bunch of friends read it. And I still found all these missed things. This is hard to see. But if I hadn't looked one more time, if I had wanted to just be done, if I had been scared it would make me feel bad to find mistakes and problems, my book would have been worse. Please go slow, be honest, get it right." (I will show my students all the different iterations of this published book and all the ways other people helped shape the final design and look of it.)

To model this, you must learn to quell your ego and fight the urge to just be done and move on already. Do this with creating a lesson and with growing as a teacher. Pinpoint a challenging hobby and fail at it. I write. I also picked up learning to play the bass. Re-experience what it means to be a learner. It's good for us teachers to embrace creative pursuits in our personal lives, as it helps us be more creative in the classroom (Henriksen & Mishra, 2015). It can also help us get better at design thinking and problem solving (Henriksen, Richardson, & Mehta, 2017). Sew, knit, build things, make models, draw, or make music. Do something that risks a blow to your ego but is also rewarding. Make something fun. How can you teach students to put themselves in this mindset if you don't?

You, dear reader, have embarked on a journey by reading this book. You've opened yourself up to a viewpoint, teaching style, and mindset possibly very different from your own. You're willing to learn new ways of teaching to help your students, even if you don't use them. This is hard because our egos are closely tied to our teaching. By writing this book, I am holding some of my deeply held beliefs up against research and seeing where they fall apart. I'll change what I do in response to what I find. We are always modeling the test phase because we're always modeling our ability to be wrong in public. Students will want their thing to work and look good because they won't want to look bad. Students will want to test their thing honestly so they can make something good looking and functional.

Thinking Like a Designer

Design mindedness is a flexible method. Designs are living documents, built to change. The goal may be set in stone, but the path is not. Flexibility and autonomy can help protect the student ego and stave off impatience because at the end of the day, they determine the path. Students control their learning.

Use the Cyclical Nature of Testing to Teach

In the test phase, stress this idea to students: testing is not the end of the process.

Write it on the board where students can see it. The first time students hear this, they might blink and cock their heads in confusion. Tests have been the end of the line in their experience—take a spelling test, then move on to the next spelling list, pass or fail. We must help students see the test might have been the end of formally learning those words, but it didn't end learning spelling. Testing is not the end of the process.

That's why testing is combined with revising in this design process, rather than having two separate stages. While all steps in the design process are interconnected, none are as intrinsically linked as test and revise.

Students who think of testing as designers do should not see their tests as pass or fail. That takes some retraining after years of school-enforced thinking. The retraining comes through these projects and the process. Tests are also situational, which you'll have to explain to students.

Sometimes, students test to collect data on a build's ability to confront a specific problem, which they can use for immediate revision. Sometimes, they take a test connected to grades and scores because *school* demands it or because the teacher needs a snapshot of what students have learned at this moment in order to make the next instructional move (Wilson, 2017). I'll mention again my student review system of clipboards, notes, and sticky notes. I also ask students to regularly share their best thinking or do a *brain dump*, during which they just write down (or draw or recite into their tablet using a text-to-speech app) everything they remember learning from the build period that morning or the previous day (Agarwal & Bain, 2019). Collecting and reviewing these things is incredibly useful, especially when a student has a blank page or not a single student mentions the content they've spent all morning learning. But even that doesn't mean the learning has ended. Students are smart, and they can hold two (or even more!) thoughts in their heads at the same time. If they internalize thinking about tests as data collection to improve performance, this might change their outlook on testing as a whole, and they'll be able to connect to the idea that grades are data used to track and guide revisions. I try not to talk about grades at all in my classroom, but when I do, I always tie them back to the test-and-revise phase.

Though the testing portion is straightforward in that we're checking to ensure the build phase went well, the revision phase has an important sequential nature to it. Figure 5.1 illustrates the flow of the cyclical test-and-revise phase. The more you test and revise, the more chances you have to improve your design; this holds true even when you apply the cycle to schoolwork other than a build project.

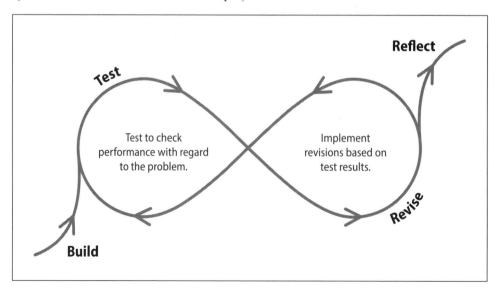

FIGURE 5.1: The test and revise cycle.

*Visit **go.SolutionTree.com/instruction** for a free reproducible version of this figure.*

When I assess my students' learning at times when we haven't been doing a direct project or build, I still try to use alternative tests. I will sometimes have students write one test question and answer for each big idea in a unit. I'll look through these questions, choose the best ten, and create a test. So it is a test, but the students have their hands in it. I'll also have students make something called *paper slideshows*, where students use construction paper, instead of a computer, to create a "slideshow" that expresses a concept. This gives students a chance to be creative and do what they'd call *art* while doing what I'd call *testing*.

REDESIGNING FOR K–2

This may be too abstract for our younger students to grasp as a concept, but a teacher concretely drawing a line between design-minded testing and pencil-and-paper or curriculum testing will help students understand the relationship.

Test the Build

Students can test their builds in whatever way makes them and their teacher the most comfortable, provided the focus is on seeing how the builds conform to the problem's parameters. If your build is a puppet show to demonstrate the main idea of a story, you better rehearse that puppet show for someone and make sure they can identify the main idea. In my classroom, students test in their own groups first, pushing and pulling on their design to see what makes it fall over while safely away from everyone else. My students and I sometimes call this *throwing rocks*. That's because it's also how I describe the rising action of a story. First, a writer gets the main character stuck in a tree. That's the problem driving the story. Then the writer throws rocks at the character. That's the rising action. Then the writer gets the character out of the tree. That's the resolution.

As students throw rocks (metaphorically speaking, unless they're building something *really* specific) at their designs, they should make notes and discuss what they're seeing with their partners (see figure 5.2, page 78). They should be honest with themselves and each other. I suggest the first phase of testing happen in the same small groups that built the thing. Students find it easier to be honest with the people they've been working with the whole time. However, be aware some students will magically change their goals or designs in response to how their build reacts to the tests, rather than changing their build. "No, no, we *meant* for it to fall over like that. It's a feature, not a bug," they'll say. It is up to the teacher to know how to deal with this on a situational basis. Decide whether the group members are protecting their egos, are trying to just be done, or have actually found a working solution. Sometimes, they come up with a legitimate change. Ask students to reflect before telling them what to do.

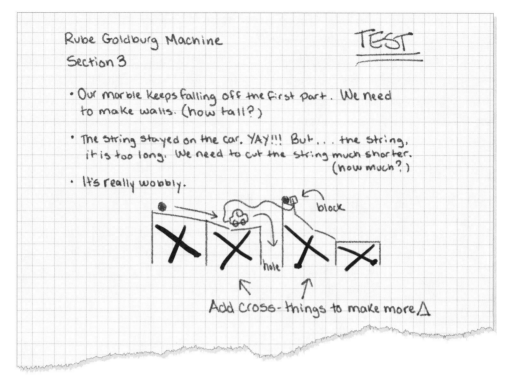

FIGURE 5.2: Student test notes for a Rube Goldberg machine.

For example, in one of my classroom's more challenging builds, my students create a trebuchet, which is like a catapult but with more moving pieces. It's hard to make these strong enough to stand up to the repeated stress of multiple tests without breaking down and coming apart. As a result, some groups will try to minimize their testing so the trebuchet survives to the final presentation, rather than figuring out how to make the trebuchet stronger and more reliable. Asking questions often reveals flaws in the student testing process (especially ones like, "Is this change to make the build better or easier?"). At first, I was surprised by how many groups would honestly say, "To make it easier." A face always gives it away too. Student innovation doesn't surprise me any longer because through becoming more design minded, I have learned to trust my students more.

REDESIGNING FOR K-2

Pictures count as test notes if writing is too difficult for our younger students. Pictures still show thinking if the students can clearly explain what is happening in the pictures. This round could also be done as a whole class for both modeling and control purposes.

The guiding thought through testing needs to be this: "Does this design solve the problem? If yes, how can it solve the problem better? If no, why and how can we change it?"

Complete the First Revision

After the first round of internal testing is complete, then comes the first revision phase. Rarely does this mean going all the way back to the drawing board. Occasionally, a group will find nothing works and they need to restart. This decision is up to the teacher to make based on time and materials. Sometimes, students need to do the best they can with a bad build, not to embarrass them and never to shame them, but to deal with the consequences of a bad build, and we teachers are here to learn these consequences and how to avoid them.

What's most helpful to model revision is to illustrate a group build's need for revision with the group's permission. In the beginning, I tried to fake mistakes in builds; the students always got wise to me and knew I had made mistakes just so I could fix them. *Always* get permission from the group first. Say something like, "Can I please use this to show everyone how we're going to revise? We're not going to make fun, and we're going to make this better together. You can say no." If the group says yes, have the class gather around and talk through what they see. The class will ask the group members questions about how their tests went while taking clear notes about what needs to change. Together, they'll draw simpler, revised blueprints or mark up the existing blueprint. I created the quick-revised wind-powered car blueprint in figure 5.3 based on experience. At this stage, make sure students are always referring to the main problem or question, which should be driving every choice.

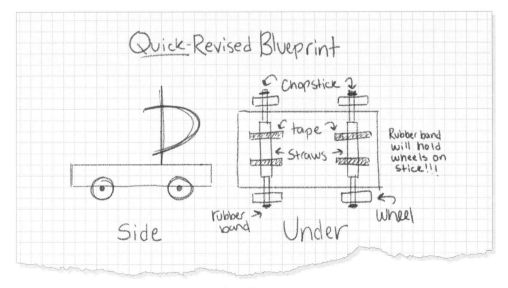

FIGURE 5.3: Quick-revised wind-powered car blueprint.

In my class, students make wind-powered cars at the start of the year. This means they build a body and attach wheels and a sail so the body rolls when air blows on the sail. Students commonly make the mistake of not securing the sail well enough, and with enough air pressure, the sail will spin around the mast and the car will either turn or stop moving completely. Students can normally see the sail is the issue when this happens, but they're not sure how to solve the problem. So, we brainstorm: "What did you see happen?" I ask. "Let's watch it again and see if the same thing happens. OK, you're saying you notice the sail is turning. How can you stop that from happening? Draw up an idea or two, and then try them out."

What's really cool about this process is it does not give groups the answer, so builds can range from slightly to wildly different. We're not correcting a mathematics test as a class. Groups are seeing what they could do based on what other groups are doing, but they still have to translate this new knowledge to their own builds. We're creating guidelines, not answers, together.

Early in the year, my students run their planned revisions by me before they get to work. This is because they are new to the process and emotions can run high. Some students will be despairing at their lot in life and swearing that they need to scrap everything. Interject, talk them down, and focus together on what works and how to make those parts stronger.

REDESIGNING FOR K–2

The previous passage about emotional regulation may resonate for teachers of K–2 students even more than it does for teachers of older students because younger students tend to have more heightened emotional responses. Remember to focus on the positives and reframe problems from *not working* to *not working yet*.

I have seen students who have a hard time with a build not working correctly and need a minute to collect themselves. But more often, students are eager to take the results of the first test and fix what needs fixing because they want it to be right. And those revisions just require a quick look, in which you'll likely say something like, "What are you gonna do? Why? OK, cool, go do it."

Your job during the revise phase is not to fix problems or solve problems. It's to lend an ear and give a nudge. Student projects can still fail after they are revised, and that's still OK. But hopefully, they fail less, and students learn through both the revision and the failure. There will also be groups that think they don't need to fix anything and their project is perfect as it is. A first build is never perfect. Find a way to make it better. Revise to get closer to the goal. "Impress me," you might challenge them with a smile at this stage. "I dare you."

Repeat for the Second Round of Testing and Revisions

The second round of testing and revisions, if you have the time, takes place in small group gatherings. Put two or three groups together and have them demonstrate their builds for each other. This is the second phase of testing. Then everyone gives feedback—quality feedback. Getting to that level of feedback requires teaching students *how* to give quality feedback to each other in the same way educators had to teach them how to work in community. This means going beyond "Good job!" to specific, useful feedback. Get students to "Have you thought about . . . ?" from where they usually are: "I think you should . . . ."

You *must* model feedback and constructive conversation here (Berger et al., 2014; Denton, 2013; Sprenger, 2020). Teach students words to use, and give them sentence starters for peer-to-peer feedback such as the following.

- ▸ "You can also address _____ with that."
- ▸ "This could also be combined with _____."
- ▸ "This might allow your peers to understand _____."
- ▸ "If you included _____, you could also _____."

Designers can talk about designs without making it personal and without getting their feelings hurt. We're back to the ego-versus-quality problem again, only now it's a peer who seems to be attacking the ego but isn't.

Stop here and have a class meeting–type conversation about giving and receiving feedback. My class and I frequently talk about kindness and how no one here is out to hurt or tear down anyone else. We're all in this together. Design thinking works best in a strong class community. Everyone needs to trust everyone else. We talk about framing feedback as suggestions and questions and not orders and absolutes.

Talk about how feedback could hurt someone's feelings but hurting feelings is never intentional. Talk about the best ways to give friendly feedback to sound helpful instead of critical. As teachers, we want students not saying, "I didn't like this" or "This was bad," but instead asking questions like, "Can you explain what this means?" or grouping a criticism with a compliment like, "I think what you did here is great, and it would be cool to see it here too." Sometimes, I will tell students, "These are friends trying to make your project better. You are not your project. A problem with your project does not mean there's a problem with you." We must break students out of the impulse to wrestle between *protect the ego* and *get it right*. There may still be students who try to be mean here. If you notice such behavior, ask the student what they hoped the person hearing their words would feel. Talk with them and the class about intention versus impact and the difference between feedback on work versus feedback on the work's creator.

Once this round of testing and feedback is over, students return to their groups to revise. Hopefully by this point, everyone is polishing rather than rebuilding. I know books like this one are not supposed to say, "Hopefully, this is happening," but let's be honest: a classroom is a fluid thing, and sometimes, things don't go to plan. When in doubt, remind your students that flexibility is a must-have for a designer. Mr. Murphy of Murphy's Law (an old adage that claims anything that can go wrong will go wrong) fame lurks around every classroom, waiting to foul things up. So yes, hopefully, everyone is polishing rather than rebuilding. However, it's inevitable that someone's project will get stepped on or someone will damage something in a short burst of frustration, and the group will have to enact a mini–design process as quickly as possible to stay on track.

THINKING LIKE A DESIGNER

During the revise phase, always point out the working parts of a build to try to get students out of a negative headspace. "What's working?" is a great question to ask, as students will often exaggerate the problem. Remind them of their guiding question: "We're trying to make it do _____. Show me what parts should be doing that." Breaking the problem into bite-size pieces reduces the stress and helps students see any specific problems.

Do the Final Test or Demonstration

The final test happens in front of the whole class, and it's the first time you, as the teacher, *officially* pay attention to whether the builds fulfill the goal set before students. (Remember, you are *always* observing and gathering data about what your students are doing.) Your job switches to part feedback giver and part evaluator. In my opinion, the teacher never wants to go full evaluator here. Even though students are smart and can understand you're there to help them, you also have to assess and score, so jumping back and forth over that line without confusing them and yourself is difficult. No build is ever finished; it's just stopped.

When it comes time for the final test, my students and I gather around, and everyone shows what they've done and talks about it. I still call this a test, but it's a test *and* a demonstration. Calling it a test means failure is still safe, assuming the idea of growth from failure has taken root. In my class, every group goes, even the groups that did not complete their build or satisfy the goal. The purpose is not and will never be to embarrass these students. Reiterate to students often that the test phase is about learning from mistakes rather than laughing at them. Every group will have done something worth celebrating and something everyone can learn from. Failures hold the seeds of better ideas. We can watch the car not roll anywhere and still talk about its design. We can hear the group discuss things they think went well. There is rarely another revision process after the whole-class tests and demonstrations because we will have run out of time.

VOX MAGISTER (VOICE OF THE TEACHER)

"Trust students. Let them do the heavy lifting."

—Scott Cody, teacher, personal communication, January 14, 2021

Design-Minded Thinking Across Content Areas

The test-and-revise cycle is a living, flexible thing that a teacher can adjust at will. Because of this, you can find a multitude of ways to use it in your classroom beyond what I suggest here. We teachers are often given assessments as part of the curriculum our schools have bought, and that is fine. Some of those assessments aren't always great, and that is also fine. Being design minded means never throwing away something just because it's bad in its current form. If your school gives you the flexibility—and not every school does this, and few educators might have the time to do this for every unit—take what you're given and break it into usable pieces. Redesign the test based on what you already have so it's more student friendly and more design minded.

English Language Arts

The teacher and students look at the goal of the writing assignment as a class. This is when rubrics become essential. Does the student's writing fully explain the life cycle of the North American rattlesnake? Does the story contain dialogue and have a strong setting and theme? Have students checked their spelling, grammar, and capitalization yet (because this is where grammar learning happens)? Have students read what they wrote out loud? Yes, out loud. If they don't want to read it themselves, they can recruit a classmate or use the "read aloud" feature in Word or Screen Reader tool in Google Docs.

Students will check the performance of the test-and-revise phase with their writing by reading a paper to someone who has no idea what the paper's directive is. Make friends with the other teachers on your grade level and experiment with joint editing time.

Maybe you can even share documents along with a short feedback form digitally between classes. The form includes the question, "What is the main idea of this writing?" This is *throwing rocks* at the writing, which means testing the strength of it. If another student from a different class has no idea what your student is writing about, that's a problem. (OK, maybe the other student hasn't read closely, so have students share two or three times just to be sure, time allowing.)

In reading, you are probably testing and revising understanding of the text, specifically whatever reading goal the book has decided the students should be working toward. Most reading goals strive for comprehension or summarization. When students work together to check their understanding through partner or small-group conversations, they are looking for consensus or clear reasoning. They throw rocks (politely, respectfully, and *only* metaphorically) at each other's thinking. Educators teach a similar review process most of the time anyway, so this is a way to reframe the process to make it design minded.

Mathematics

In mathematics, the test phase is solving the problem, running the equation the students built, and then checking the work. It's fairly straightforward, but it's not just solving the problem. That's not a test. Students test the result by checking the work in another way. We're supposed to be teaching mathematics using testing and revising anyway, so it makes sense to group those two steps together. Revision happens if the two solutions don't match. Most teachers already teach concepts like *addition is the inverse of subtraction* or *multiplication is the inverse of division*. This is the test-and-revise process for those kinds of problems. Every time my students do a multiplication problem, they (are supposed to) check it with the division problem.

STEAM

Because the design process has similarities to the scientific process, this is where students run the experiments they designed. Revision isn't really part of an experiment. If you change the parameters of an experiment, you start invalidating data. Here, revision is more about running the experiment multiple times to get the best data possible. So, if my students were testing to see which mineral in the school-supplied science kit is hardest, they would check the rocks against the surface given. Then, students would check them again in a blind order and see if they got the same result. So many people love the show *MythBusters*, but most of the time, the show was looking to get a result, not repeatable data.

Students have most likely only experienced testing as a one-and-done event. They take a test at the end of a unit, and how they did is how they did. Period, put it in the gradebook, we have to move on. But here, students are using those results immediately and concretely. There is less stress around the test because students have a chance to fix things and make them better. It is my hope that teachers will take this idea to heart and apply it across their whole classroom. Would you rather students feel that they're stuck or that they always have a chance to improve? Yes, there's not always time, and eventually, they can't go back and retake the unit 1 test because you're on unit 3 now, but at least the option was given. The value is in the student learning the material, not the student learning the material *right now*.

The Joy of Testing and Revision

The test phase of any subject is where people check their work. Does the thing do the thing it's supposed to do? Can they make it better? With the removal of ego, is it good? Is it valid? Students do this while keeping in mind the test is not the end. The test is a valuable part of the process because it's not scary. Students eventually learn to look forward to the test because they want to see if their thing does "the thing." They have put a lot of work into it. Time to light the candle, as it were, and see if it flies.

Once the teacher decides the class has done test-and-revise cycles (I do two rounds in my class, but I wish I could do more), they move on to the last phase of the design process: reflection.

Test and Revise Reflection Template: What Happens When We Try Out the Solution and Respond to Data?

Considering how words are used with students is a valuable part of the test and revise phase of my design process, answer the following questions.

What are the benefits of connecting testing out a design to formal testing (such as exams)?

How do you talk about failure with your students in your classroom?

CHAPTER 6

Reflect
What Did We Learn?

I'm starting with the man in the mirror,
I'm asking him to change his ways.

—*Michael Jackson, "Man in the Mirror"*

Reflection is the final phase of the design process, but reflection doesn't happen only at the end of the process. It happens during *every* stage of the design process. Being design minded requires an awareness of several phases at the same time and how they interact with each other. All through the process, students should be thinking about what they are doing and why. This awareness of their own thought processes, or *metacognition*, will aid them in understanding both the pieces of their learning and what their learning looks like as a whole. When educators teach the design process to students, they teach it in phases so it's clear. It's done in phases in practice too. With repetition and understanding comes the ability to synthesize the phases and see all the connective tissues and how to apply them to different contexts. The better students can do this with build projects, the better they will transfer the skills to other content areas. Design-minded students and teachers can see the matrix behind the process. As such, when students are thinking and acting like designers, they are in a constant state of reflection. You, dear reader, will hopefully take the information you've encountered thus far, reflect on it, and interpret it in your way. Your distinct teacher (or administrator, or well-read guardian) voice will make the information yours.

If you've been completing the reflections at the end of each chapter, then you already know what I'm talking about. (If you haven't been, why not?) Hopefully, you have done them not just because I told you to but because you know the power of reflection. If you're thinking perhaps you don't need to go back and reflect because you're the teacher, consider that Willingham (2009) has an entire chapter in his book *Why Don't Students Like School?* about the power that thinking about teaching has for teachers. He reminds us teaching is a cognitive skill. As with all cognitive skills, we need purposeful time to think about our practices. Use the reflection spaces to combine information from your immediate environment, past experiences stored in your long-term memory, and working memories you have just made by reading chapters from this book (Willingham, 2009). Just as students need time to process new content and learning, and to sit with what they've learned, so do we. In this chapter, you'll learn about the active, equitable, and informative nature of reflection. Then, you'll consider how to identify what students are learning and why.

Thinking Like a Designer

Stay aware of not only what students are *doing* but also what you are *teaching*. Remind students, "Remember, I need you to know not only what you're doing but what you're *learning* while you do it. Otherwise, all we're doing is playing with cardboard, and even the coolest principal in the world won't let us keep it up."

Reflection Is Active

Personal preference and group dynamics play a large role in how each group communicates and cooperates. Yes, there will be one or two groups, or just a few students within one or two groups, wearing scowls while trying so very hard to remember what their teacher has been trying to teach them about mature disagreements and problem solving. They know they *should* listen with respect and with the assumption everyone is working for the common good. Even when things get tense and interpersonal issues rear their heads (mostly in the form of students being unable to clearly communicate their thinking or hear someone else's thinking until talks break down into frustration), most students will enjoy themselves. Making things is fun. For the most part, there's music playing, laughter, and lots of overlapping conversation. This is what solving problems and reflecting in a group can sound like. Not everyone works this way, of course. But sometimes focus sounds like a dozen non sequiturs strung together because the group members have developed their own shorthand and inside jokes over the course of the project. Just because I hear someone shout, "Sloth!" followed by raucous laughter, it doesn't mean I won't also hear reflections such as, "This wall could be joined in a better way. Have you tried tabs? What does the blueprint say?"

When you're reflecting at the end of every chapter, think about what your classroom sounds like when everyone is working with focus, and consider the possibility your idea of focused noise and the students' idea of focused noise might not match. How do you reach an equilibrium if those two ideas don't match?

Reflection Is Equitable

I know what my students are doing when they're being loud because I'm a loud teacher (ask anyone who has ever taught across the hall from me); therefore, I have experience with loud classes. I am confident in a design-minded approach because I have spent time with and had lots of exposure to design. I also work to be very thoughtful about the nature of conversations when students are working (Johnston, 2012). I've made a conscious choice to step in when I hear students of any gender say that a particular task is something only one gender can do, or the inverse—that something is, for example, "not for girls." These statements often happen when a project involves traditionally gendered things like sewing, knitting, or exerting strength of some kind.

I've also made the choice to be strategic with my English learners. I step in to help model being a good listener when I overhear a student getting frustrated with another student's English, or I pull aside students who are having trouble expressing themselves to try to prevent frustration. I have zero tolerance for racist or stereotypical comments about other students, and as much as my students know I sit next to them to discuss rather than punish, I'm clear about what will and will not be tolerated in our classroom. I've only reached that kind of clarity because I reflected on what happened when I didn't step in fast enough or I didn't respond clearly enough when a student said something hurtful. One time, I didn't react quickly enough when I heard a student complain about not being able to understand another student because of how they spoke. In truth, I didn't hear the comment. I just saw the way the student who was targeted pulled back and stopped participating in discussions. Eventually, I found out what happened, thanks to other students in the group who trusted me enough to tell me. Moments like these happen quickly, but it's important to sit down with the person who made the inappropriate comment and help them understand how they have caused harm.

REDESIGNING FOR K–2

All students at all ages can and should be having these kinds of conversations. Period. You can begin by asking younger students what they meant when they said what they said and if they'd heard that kind of language used somewhere else in their lives. Then, ease them into the larger words like *racism* and *sexism* by defining them simplistically. We cannot implement an age limit to knowing about these subjects, especially if there is a chance this kind of intolerance will impact the student in question directly. Some students lack the luxury to not know about intolerance from a young age, as they may be subject to it.

Figure 6.1 features explicit examples of intolerant beliefs infiltrating the classroom. The right column includes examples of what you can say if something discriminatory is said during class time, but prevention of this kind of interaction starts on day one by building respect, understanding, and empathy among students and making it clear everyone will be seen and treated as valuable humans. There's not a project for building respect; just tell students what the subject is, and talk openly about it. You can't build necessary conversations out of cardboard. But you can strengthen and deepen respect by building in groups with cardboard, where communication must be clear and respectful. The best-case scenario is my students and I have time for such discussions, and I build them into our weekly meetings where students and I routinely discuss classroom current events and routines.

When a Student Says . . .	You Could Say . . .
"[Girls or boys] aren't as good at _____."	"We do not judge someone based on their gender in this class. Gender doesn't determine what we're good or bad at. Everyone is equally capable, and I don't expect anyone is treated any differently based on their gender. Be cool."
"Ugh, we can't understand what you're saying." (Toward a student who is an emerging English learner or emerging bilingual speaker)	"I am going to need you to be a more empathetic human right now. You know they are doing their best. Do you think this is making it easier for them or harder? What have you tried to help communication go smoother?"
Any kind of slur	"Let's pop into the hallway, please." At this point, a much longer conversation about respect and the meaning of words takes place. I don't get angry, but I do get firm and serious. I will ask students if they understand what they said and, if they do, ask them to explain what it means. If they don't, I will explain how it is a hateful thing to say. I don't avoid the hard subject, because students must know, clearly and without doubt, that a slur is hate speech and that it is not tolerated.

FIGURE 6.1: "When a student says . . ., you could say . . ." examples.

In chapter 1 (page 11), we explored the role of teacher identity and acknowledged that teachers bring all sorts of different ways of thinking about teaching into the classroom. I want to revisit that for a moment and extend you an invitation to consider making *active bystander* part of your teacher identity as well. Although it has a variety of connotations, the word *bystander* describes someone who witnesses interpersonal conflict but is neither the target nor the aggressor (Katz, Heisterkamp, & Fleming, 2011). In effect, when one student says something racist, sexist, or unkind to another student, you and the other students who hear it are bystanders. An active bystander is a bystander who takes action upon hearing or seeing an act of violence.

This action does not need to be a grand pronouncement or a dramatic intervention (I recognize the limits of my own expertise and strongly recommend the Right to Be website [https://righttobe.org] for more resources and specific information on how to be an active bystander). Such interventions, though, are more likely to be successful when a classroom has a culture of shared responsibility and accountability. To that end,

I recommend resources like Liz Kleinrock's (2021) *Start Here, Start Now: A Guide to Antibias and Antiracist Work in Your School Community* and Sarah M. Stitzlein's (2008) *Breaking Bad Habits of Race and Gender: Transforming Identity in Schools.* Design sessions can get intense. Creating an environment where young people are held accountable for words they say in the heat of the moment (and where they can learn better ways to express their frustration) is critical to a successful design-minded classroom.

Reflection Is Informative

I have an idea of what my students are learning (and this phase makes that idea become a reality) because I take anecdotal notes (see figure 6.2) and continue to document what I see. This way, I make sure I accurately understand where they are in terms of learning goals (Tolisano & Hale, 2018). The students know what they are building, and they know how that building connects to their learning. This means I've heard a wide range of reflective conversations. To bring back a previous example, during the cardboard arcade project, some students are talking about finding the hypotenuse of a triangle. Meanwhile, a group on the other side of the room is discussing whether the game rules are written clearly enough for both a kindergarten student and a fifth-grade student to quickly understand them (a skill seen in Common Core Writing standard W.4.2d: "Use precise language and domain-specific vocabulary to inform about or explain the topic" (NGA & CCSSO, 2010). Students are aware of the range of their learning.

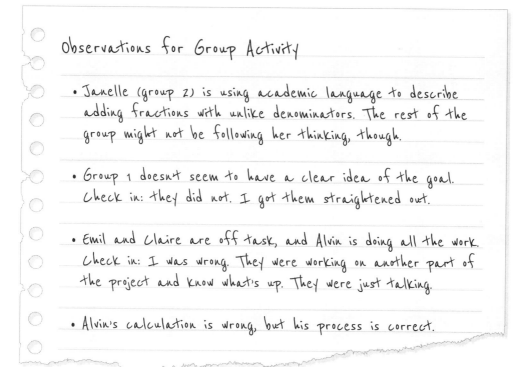

Observations for Group Activity

- Janelle (group 2) is using academic language to describe adding fractions with unlike denominators. The rest of the group might not be following her thinking, though.

- Group 1 doesn't seem to have a clear idea of the goal. Check in: they did not. I got them straightened out.

- Emil and Claire are off task, and Alvin is doing all the work. Check in: I was wrong. They were working on another part of the project and know what's up. They were just talking.

- Alvin's calculation is wrong, but his process is correct.

FIGURE 6.2: Example of anecdotal notes (names are pseudonyms).

continued →

- Group 3 is referencing specific pages in the book before they make a decision.

- Olivia looks checked out. Did the group leave her out? Check in: she felt her group had moved on without her, so I helped get communication back on track. Everyone understands project goals.

- I just heard group 5 help group 4 with a problem using design language. They even shared blueprints. I will need to make note of this as good practice during whole-class discussion.

- Group 6 thinks they're done. They aren't. Check in: I gave them a reminder about deeper goals and had them talk me through their work so they could find holes themselves.

- Erik asked for clarification on a specific expectation, and he was able to explain his thinking. He's on track and adding good details.

Reflection Always Asks Why?

Students' knowing *what* they are building is not good enough. As builds are happening, students must think about *why* they are choosing to build a certain way. As they plan builds, they need to think about why they are making certain choices. As they make changes to accommodate the results of tests, they need to know why they make specific changes.

Why is a driving word. It's a power word. As a teacher, you can ask why to get to the heart of any design choice (and you can try to use it to get to the heart of any behavior choice, though you'll likely get much fewer "I don't know" answers when asking why about a design choice). The following are good why questions for a teacher to ask during any phase of the design process.

▶ "Why are you putting this piece here?"

▶ "Why is this part not going to be taped down?"

> ▸ "Why is the section this size and shape?"

> ▸ "Why are we making this?"

You want students to think about their why. You want them to be asking why all the time. Learning to interrogate their own work helps students naturally become more self-reflective, which benefits the design process and makes them more independent learners.

Vox Magister (Voice of the Teacher)

"I am one of the authors of this book, but I am not a design-minded thinker. It's simply not an identity I connect with, likely because I haven't had my own K–5 classroom in quite some time. Rather, if pushed to identify my pedagogical identity, in addition to my personal and political ones, I'd likely go with *systems thinker*, as in one who uses systems thinking. Much like Doug uses design thinking to problem solve with his students, I'm a fan of using the work of systems thinkers like Daniel Kim, Linda Booth Sweeney, and Peter Senge. It was in Senge's 2002 book, *Schools That Learn: A Fifth Discipline Fieldbook for Educators, Parents, and Everyone Who Cares About Education*, where I first learned of the *five whys*. Although it's been used in different contexts, my introduction to the strategy was at a systems-thinking conference where a group of us were working through a particular problem. The first few times, I thought it was silly. But each time we did it, each time I got better at clarifying, I realized the power in the simple question.

"While we were working on this book, there were multiple instances where Doug would explain something he did in his classroom and I'd ask, 'Why?' So, he'd explain some more, and again, I'd ask, 'Why?' and so forth, until we got to the clarity we wanted to convey in this book. While Doug doesn't count his or his students' whys, they are a critical part of the classroom and of class vocabulary."

—Jennifer Borgioli Binis, editor and researcher, personal communication, January 10, 2022

Reflection is active. It's purposeful. People can build something without thinking about it. They could even build something aimed at a specific goal without thinking about it much. Just get it done. Every teacher in the world has watched those presentations and read those essays. Words were said. Things were done. And yet, nothing happened—*nothing* here being *no learning*. No learning happened. There was sound, there might have been fury, yet it signified nothing.

Without reflection, nothing of consequence happens in a classroom. Anything of consequence happening in a classroom must involve learning. Taking in information, making a project, writing an essay, and doing research are all equivalent to just dishing up the food and putting it in one's mouth. Reflection is the rest of the digestive process. During reflection, students extract the nutrients from the meal and convert them into usable energy applicable elsewhere.

THINKING LIKE A DESIGNER

Being design minded isn't just about the act of design. It requires embedding reflection into the process and routines because people get better at design by reflecting on it. Reflection is part of design thinking and the design process, so it's built into everything students are doing. It's how they are learning from the steps they are taking, and in the end, it's how they generalize their learning to something broader than whatever they just did.

Reflection Defines What We Are Learning and Why

Design-minded students should be able to say what they are learning and why in a generalizable way. They have to do more than tell you about the project; they need to tell you about the ideas they're using to complete the project successfully. This has a huge sliding scale too, because students each come to understand what generalizing their learning means in their own time. So, figure 6.3 says "early in the year" and "late in the year," but the timing will be different for everyone, including you, because you'll get better at communicating what generalizing their learning means.

In a student's explanation, there could be mathematics, science, reading, and whatever term your school uses to describe "having a positive learning mindset when frustrated." My school mascot is the Panthers, so keeping a positive mindset during challenging learning moments is one of the "Panther life skills." These pieces de-silo education and are at the heart of science, technology, engineering, art, and mathematics (STEAM) as a concept. What mathematics are students learning? Where is reading coming in, and how is this making students better at it? Where is the science in this, and what is it? I say to students, "You tell me; I don't tell you." Prompting students to take charge of answer seeking creates independent learners (Parrish, 2022).

Example Student Reflection Early in the Year	Example Student Reflection Late in the Year	What the Students Are Doing Differently
"We learned to make the car go by checking the internet about cars. It had wheels, but they didn't spin great. We learned to fix wheels not spinning well."	"We learned to research and experiment to find the best way to get the wheels to move. In the book, it said friction slows wheels down, so we are trying to figure out how to make the friction less. We also didn't think our wheels got cut round enough, so we measured the diameter in a few places to check, and they weren't, so we fixed it."	By talking about the diameter, the students are bringing in learning from a mathematics lesson. And they used prior knowledge gained from research.
"We learned a trebuchet throws objects through the air, and if it's heavier on the one side, then the other side will throw farther because of weight and gravity."	"We used angles to figure out that, when the trebuchet arm goes past ninety degrees, the payload gets thrown into the ground, so we had to stop the arm at about eighty-five or eighty degrees. We borrowed a protractor to measure. We also figured out it throws better if the weight is two times or more heavier than the payload. We had to figure out the scales for the counterweight."	Students are using tools to make their build more precise. These are tools they will need to use later in the year.
"The main character is nice, and the villain is mean, so we wrote the script just using the words from the book. We learned to read the book better so we could see the characters' feelings."	"We had to compare and contrast the main character and the villain to write our script because we wanted it to be funny how different they were. So, we also looked at the problem the villain caused and the solution the main character found, and we noticed it relates back to their personalities, which was neat."	These students are reading deeply by choice to make their script more creative and fun for their audience. In doing so, they stumbled across the bonus lesson that authors will often link character motivations to plot problems and solutions. Compare and contrast was the main lesson, so extra learning is great discovery learning, or *incidental learning*.
"I had to measure five of the things, but they didn't line up easy on my ruler, so I looked where one ended. Then I held my finger down at the ruler and moved the next thing in, and it took me to a whole number. And then I added that number three times."	"Because we had to measure five things that were the same, I measured one of them. It came out to 4 ¾ inches. So, I multiplied four by five to get 20 and ¾ by five to get 3 ¾. Then I added 20 and 3 ¾ to get 23 ¾. I didn't stack all five things because they were longer than the ruler together, and I didn't think I'd get a good answer using the method."	This student is generalizing by using a skill they learned in mathematics to solve a measurement problem. They realized stacking the items was easier but less effective in the long run.

FIGURE 6.3: Student reflections early in the year and late in the year.

Once your class arrives at independence, you can simply guide. You can course correct. You nudge or directly instruct as the case may require. But you won't have a line of students around your desk asking, "Why are we doing this?" They'll be too busy trusting there is a reason they're doing it, and they need to figure out what it could be.

It has happened before. When my students can answer, "What are we learning and why?" in a generalizable way, previously closed doors in learning open because you no longer need to invent a special way to engage students. They've already bought in. The lessons still must be good. Buy-in is a delicate thing and easily spoiled. But when students learn to reflect and learn how reflection answers the *why* question every student has, things begin to slide along much smoother.

Reflection Happens Across Content Areas

Reflection happens as students design their builds because they must think about what they built last time, how it worked, and how to do it better or differently. Reflection happens as students actively build based on the same factors, plus more immediate reflections like these: "I saw our neighbor group try this, and it didn't work, but I think if we change it a little, it will." "I remember what we were doing in mathematics with fractions, and I think we're not dividing this section up right. Hold on." "Wait, this is based on the research we did, but our conclusion doesn't line up with our research. How do we change our conclusion?"

At the end of the process, my class makes their reflections concrete. My students know we formally reflect last. Every time a project is finished, the last presentation has been presented, and the last cardboard flap has been secured, every single student in the room waits for me to say, "But wait, there's more!" And, if they're feeling saucy, they say the next line with me: "Time to reflect!"

REDESIGNING FOR K–2

This is done independently in the upper grades, but it should be a whole-class activity in K–2 classrooms to aid in modeling thinking and writing.

This reflection—the *big reflection at the end*, you could say—forms inside students' heads and is born when they write it down. They will reflect in their groups later, but the process starts alone. I supply seven general guiding questions applicable to just about any project with little modification. Figure 6.4 lists these general guiding questions.

The most important questions here are five and six, but students must follow the breadcrumbs of questions one through four to get there. I have found jumping straight

Questions for the Big Reflection at the End

1. What worked?
2. What could have worked better?
3. If I could change one thing about the final product right now, what would I change?
4. If I could change one thing about the process we used, what would I change?
5. What did I use in the process that I learned in this classroom?
6. Is something I learned from this process applicable elsewhere in school?
7. Any other thoughts?

FIGURE 6.4: General guiding questions for after a test.

*Visit **go.SolutionTree.com/instruction** for a free reproducible version of this figure.*

to five and six does not give students the chance to warm to the reflection process. They need to work their way through the project itself first. No project goes perfectly, and failure is always an option, so those first four questions help the students think through it and get out any grumbles or frustrations. Plus, things always come up as they watch the other groups present. "Oh, we should have done that!" is a great thing to hear because it means students are paying attention to each other. "We should have secured our sail in the corners! That's way better." They get excited thinking about the whole arc of the project and sometimes need to think for a little bit or talk to their groups depending on how long the project took. This is a practical reason in-class projects in my room ideally happen within a week. Students need to remember all the way back to Monday, and teachers know the challenge of student recall. The following list breaks down each of the final three questions for the big reflection at the end.

▶ **Question five ("What did I use in the process that I learned in this classroom?"):** This question connects the learning from the project directly to class. It helps the students see what they're doing in class *does* have something to do with other things they're doing in class. It's the de-siloing of STEAM in reflective form. It makes them again aware they're expected to use what they're learning from their projects in other ways. This provides a form of motivation when they're doing work not as inherently interesting as building a car, like regular schoolwork out of a book or on a computer program. They know they could apply the learning to building a car later, which is a goal I have as a teacher: that my students think about applying the skills they learn now toward the future.

▶ **Question six ("Is something I learned from this process applicable elsewhere in school?"):** This question gives the student even more ownership over the work because it assumes new learning happened and the student can spot a learning opportunity and can generalize it. Generalization is a tenet of learning. Often, mathematics concepts fly around here because those, in my experience, are the hardest to make real-world sticky for students. For example, when students don't have access to the yardstick they had yesterday, but they do have a ruler handy, they quickly figure out how to convert measurements.

▸ **Question seven ("Any other thoughts?"):** This question lets students note anything else they want to say. Sometimes, they note something about working in groups, which they didn't feel fit into any of the other questions. Sometimes, they note they got frustrated halfway through but then persevered and are glad they did. Sometimes, they note how someone in their life knows about what they were doing, so that person shared some ideas with them at home, and that really helped. Students must have a voice, even at this point in the process.

REDESIGNING FOR K-2

Keeping a daily chart of whatever process the students will be reflecting on will help students with recall. You can use butcher or kraft paper to make this chart.

After students work out all these questions in their head and in a journal, they share with each other in their original small groups to strengthen a welcoming and learner-centered classroom community, model different reflection strategies, and support students' academic mindsets (Berger et al., 2014; Hammond, 2015; Tollefson & Osborn, 2008). Students can revise and add to what they have already written down based on these conversations. This helps the students who are stuck writing, "I don't know," on a bunch of questions as well, because even though this whole process does promote and aid in student-directed learning, it doesn't help everyone all the time. Nothing does.

Once small-group sharing is done, I have my students share as a whole class. I go around the room once and make it clear everyone must contribute something; everyone's voice is valued. I will let students pass but only on the second time through. Accountability and equality matter, and by now, everyone should have something to say, even if it's repeating what someone else said. That's passing without passing, and I either have to be OK with it or make a student very uncomfortable, and I won't do the latter. Sometimes, students turn in the reflections as evidence; sometimes, they keep them as evidence. The reflections are not thrown away. Consider using protocols like Two Cents to help formalize turn-taking and equitable contributions (MrWilliamsD8, 2016).

Here's What You Do With All Those Projects

Speaking of throwing things away as a metaphor, the reflection phase has one final metaphor lying in wait, and it's the answer to the question some of you have been asking yourselves: What do you do with all those projects? That is the final piece of the reflection process.

What do you do with all these cardboard builds? They are projects your students worked hard on for a week. Students are not taking them home. The bus driver doesn't want them on the bus; the parents don't want them at home. How do you split a Skee-Ball game four ways without a fight? So, what's the solution?

You take them apart.

Students will *hate* this the first time they hear it. They get so mad. I explain my reasons, as listed here, plus one more: as much as I buy from a certain massive online store, I do not have infinite boxes. So, my students and I are going to carefully break down these projects, and all the reusable cardboard will go back in the cardboard box for the next project. Anything not laminated in tape, impossibly broken in some way, or just put together in a manner where getting it back into usable pieces would require safety goggles, a blowtorch, and possibly dynamite, the class recycles. You will get good at knowing what can be kept and what can't be, and the students will also figure it out with time. Did you catch the metaphor? Just as we just deconstructed our projects into learning, which we can then use to create better projects during our reflection, so do we deconstruct our materials into pieces we can later use to create new, better projects. The materials are our learning.

Thinking Like a Designer

As a design-minded teacher, remind students, "Just as we just deconstructed our projects into learning, which we can then use to create better projects during our reflection, so do we deconstruct our materials into pieces we can later use to create new, better projects."

Nothing described in this section happens the first time, the second time, or the third time. As with everything else in school, students must learn to reflect. They must learn the mindset needed to do this and train themselves to be reflective designers. The first reflections of the year, much like the first projects of the year, are bad. They're sparse, and you have to do frequent reflection modeling to make the students' submissions acceptable. That's OK. Expect this in your classroom. Students should be bad at reflection at first. But set the expectation for where you want it, not where the students are, and then meet the students where they are. The teacher cannot give up on the reflection process when it gets hard. Designers reflect, but first, designers must *learn* how to reflect.

VOX MAGISTER (VOICE OF THE TEACHER)

"Far too few teachers who are interested in principles of design pedagogies are also well versed in equity principles, and thus teachers end up reinforcing, replicating, and building on inequitable practices in their use of design in the classroom. Many think, as they do or did with gamification and other ideas, they are immune to considerations of equity and injustice in their work because 'everyone can design.' My favorite disaster and success happened at once: I worked really hard to find an object for a 'take apart' protocol with sixth graders, gathered tools, introduced the topic, and let them get to work. As they moved through the steps, I slowly realized the object I selected would not fully come apart in eleven-year-old hands in the forty-five minutes. Whoops! However, since we were doing . . . a metaphor for a system of inequality, a few students started to realize their inability to take the item apart or even access all of its pieces was not dissimilar to how the system of homelessness worked in our city. My cold sweat was for naught!"

—**Krystle Merchant, teacher, personal communication, September 3, 2021**

The Joy of Reflecting

Designers reflect on their reflection process and improve by doing so. Reflection is not only part of the design process but also part of being design minded. It makes the learning thorough and valuable by reinforcing what students have already learned and reminding them of things they may have forgotten; or, if they reflect with peers, it gives them the chance to hear how others learned from the same lesson they did. It provides me with a chance to consider what to change for the next project, which groups to adjust, and what supplies to restock. Now that you've learned about how the reflection phase fits into the overall design process, it's time to look holistically at how the phases fit together over the course of a single project lesson. The following chapter will combine all that you've learned thus far and implement it through real build strategies in the classroom.

Reflect Reflection Template:
What Did We Learn?

What does your classroom sound like when everyone is focused and working? Consider the possibility your idea of focused noise and the students' idea of focused noise might not match.

How do you reach an equilibrium if those two ideas don't match?

CHAPTER 7

Put It Into Practice

I'm lookin' for a mind at work.

—*"The Schuyler Sisters," from the musical* Hamilton

Now you know all the phases of the design process, but what do they look like in practice? In this chapter, I (Doug) will take you through a project from beginning to end, from coming up with the project to carrying out the final reflection right before tearing it to pieces. It's important to see these things not as separate steps but as a whole.

The reason I'm going to do this is based on the work of Lee S. Shulman (2004), who coined the phrase *pedagogical reasoning* to describe the processes and practices teachers go through as they make teaching-related decisions. He professionalized an essential part of what generations of teachers did: absent transparency around thinking, they fell back on replicating what their own teachers did because they did not openly review their pedagogical reasoning. As we shared in the introduction (page 1), way back in 1975, Lortie was describing the fact students spend up to twenty years in the "apprenticeship of observation" and young teachers arrive to their classroom with more experience *watching* other people teach than *doing* the job they're tasked to do. As a relatively new concept built on recent research, being a design-minded teacher wasn't an identity available to teachers in previous generations. This chapter makes plain what the mindset entails. Using a build example called *a trap for a tree kangaroo*, I'll methodically go through every phase of the design process so you can see what it actually looks like when a class completes a design project, and I'll review issues and variations as they arise.

When to Expect Inspiration

It's impossible to guess when an idea for a project will hit. Hopefully, it hits while planning a unit because that's the best time for it to happen. When I'm alone in my room playing music while staring at textbooks and standards and mulling over the team meeting I just left, the seed sprouts slowly. In this moment, I have the time to watch it grow. Curated moments to just sit and think about your classroom and your goals may be the place you can expect inspiration. It is important to carve out times in your day where you can let your brain talk to you.

Sometimes, an idea hits right before the actual teaching starts, as I'm pouring my first dark, rich cup of coffee and the bell rings. The aroma hits me, it goes straight through the nasal canal and into my brain, and *zap*—it's idea time! Better scribble it down somewhere quick before it vanishes like a spare charging cable at an edtech conference. Or, more likely still, the idea for a project arrives midsentence.

In any of these scenarios, what is important is to give yourself permission to catch the idea and record it somehow, not to edit it or deconstruct it in the moment; there's no time for that yet. You just have to write it down. Sometimes, I'm organized enough to put it in my plan book or capture a full thought in a notebook. I recommend you take that route more than I do. Sticky notes or index cards work just as well, though, even if you just add the idea to the growing collection on your desk. One time, however, a student found a sticky note in my handwriting that just said, "Milwaukee? Elephants?" and I still don't know what I was trying to catch there. Either way, make a space for yourself to brainstorm project ideas. Keep a notebook, a computer document, or even a voice recorder nearby, and value those little moments where half an idea comes to you in the middle of something. If you write down those ideas (yes, even the incomplete ones) and revisit them later, you might be able to make sense of what your brain was trying to say. After reading this chapter, in which you and I walk in slow motion through a full build project, step by step, you'll have a skeleton you can apply to any of your own project ideas that relate to your curriculum standards.

How to Build: A Trap for a Tree Kangaroo

Being a design-minded teacher means freeing yourself to stop, experience a minor brainstorm, and then grab what is good and put it into action. Sometimes right away. Sometimes as a sticky note on your laptop. Occasionally, I free myself to brainstorm by instructing a student, "Remind me about *x* in twenty minutes, please." Some students make good reminder alarms. You know the one in your class.

The inopportune brainstorm in question occurred during language arts. My class and I were reading a story in our language arts textbook called *Quest for the Tree Kangaroo* by Sy Montgomery (2006). The tree kangaroo is an animal living in Papua New Guinea. It is a shy, arboreal marsupial and, as one might guess from the title of the story, scientists go on a quest to find and study tree kangaroos because they hide in the trees. To paraphrase the story, a native of Papua New Guinea locates the tree kangaroo hiding in their tree, climbs a nearby tree, and scares the animal enough to jump out of the tree. Then, the scientists on the ground catch it in a net and take it back to camp to tag it and do noninvasive science on it.

When my students read about how the tree kangaroo was captured for study, their empathy kicked in, and hard. "Aww," they said in chorus.

"Aww?" I asked.

"Aww, that's so mean, scaring it out of the tree! There has to be a better way to catch them than that."

Stop. That's it! That's *the moment*—the moment and opening a design-minded teacher needs. I didn't force or plan it; a student created it. This is a much stronger, more valuable type of opening. In my mind, I told myself, *All I have to do is step through it and bring students with me. What is on the other side of the opening? It's right there, if only I can find a way to* . . .

> *With a click, it all falls into place.*
>
> *"Who knows what the word* humane *means?" I ask. Some do; some don't. Perfect, an organic vocabulary lesson. We define it as an adjective meaning "having or showing compassion or benevolence."*
>
> *I continue, "So, what's the problem with how they catch the tree kangaroos in this story? Remind me, why the* aww*?"*
>
> *"It doesn't seem very humane!" one student calls out.*
>
> *"Good use of the word! Is that a problem?" I ask.*
>
> *"You're so mean! Yes, of course it is!" comes the reply.*
>
> *"So, let's fix it."*

There you have it. The students identified a problem. It was a natural progression from an organic in-class conversation, wherein the students recognized something they wanted to fix. And thus, the design process begins with our first phase: define.

Define

Per chapter 2 (page 23) of this book and step 1 of the design phase, we must define the problem with the way the tree kangaroo is caught so that our course of action is clear.

> *"Here is your challenge," I say. I begin writing on the board now to describe the problem and goal. "You must design and build a humane tree kangaroo trap. You think the scientists' way is bad? Then do better. Today is Tuesday. I want to see traps by Friday. Make small groups—no, you three can't work together, you already know; sit down. Make small groups of no more than three and no less than two. Remind me, are you going to go grab cardboard and materials right away?"*
>
> *"No!"*
>
> *"What comes first?"*
>
> *"Defining the problem."*
>
> *"Good." I write* define *down on the board. "Then can you build stuff?"*
>
> *"No."*
>
> *"Good. What's next?"*
>
> *"Designing our build," they shout.*

This is all said with boundless enthusiasm, like in some teacher instructional video with six of the best-behaved students you've ever seen.

"Good." I write design *on the board under* define. *"Then what?"*

One student says, "Then we can start building!"

Another student pipes in, "After you approve the design!"

Back to me: "What part of your design needs to be approved before you can start building then?"

"Measurements!" yells one student.

"Three blueprint views: front, side, and cross section!" adds another.

Someone calls out, "Details!"

Then another student suggests, "Materials!"

"OK!" I write down measurements, blueprints, *and* materials *to the side of* design. *"Then what?"*

"Then we can build our trap!"

"Awesome! We'll review the other steps later. Find your groups, run them by me, then get to work. Go."

At this point in the year, my students know the steps. They know I expect detailed blueprints. And they know they're never going to touch scissors, cardboard, or tape until I approve a design, checking all the boxes I've laid out for them. We review the steps anyway because, as the cliché says, *reteaching is part of teaching.*

The define part is easy. Ask the students the following questions.

▸ "How do we catch a tree kangaroo in a humane way? What do we know?" Possible answers: It lives in trees. It can jump high. It's about *this* big.

▸ "Where does the information come from?" Possible answer: the story (the kind of dry, not-terribly-interesting story losing their interest a few minutes ago, which they are now poring over, motivated to wring every little fact and detail out of it).

▸ "What was the reading focus for this story?" Possible answer: main idea and details.

The define part will check those *students will* learning standards while engaging students more than a story like that normally would. Students will understand main idea and details and be able to cite sources from the text to support their ideas. *Check.* Students will read and understand grade-level nonfiction. *Check.* Students will love being in school and have active academic conversations with their peers without the prodding of their teacher. (That's not a standard, but it should be.) *Check.*

Students have to know this stuff before they can begin to design a trap. I do walk around and ask what the problem is so I can hear them say it out loud and so those in their groups who don't know can hear it said out loud too.

Design

It doesn't take too long for define to give way to design. In this case, it took less than one work session. Design does take some time because students know a plan like, "It's a box. It . . . uh . . . falls down and traps the tree kangaroo," isn't going to cut it. Students' designs need to show their thinking from their work during the define phase. The designs need to be complex enough to satisfy all the requirements while still being simple enough to pull off both in the classroom and in the middle of the jungles of Papua New Guinea.

Blueprints are hard, and none are perfect. It's an abstract thing to have to visualize an object from multiple angles well enough to draw it and then to cut the object in half and draw what it looks like on the inside. So, while I'm hard on the measurements and basic dimensions, I'm less strict on the drawings themselves (an example of which appears in figure 7.1). If the students can tell you what something is and why it is there when you point to it on the blueprint, that means they're completing the requirements of design.

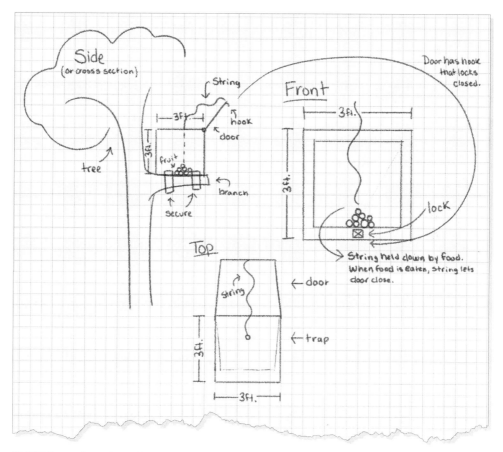

FIGURE 7.1: Sample student tree kangaroo trap blueprint.

I'd like to emphasize this: as long as I can point to something on the blueprint, and *any* student in the group can tell me what it is and why it's there, then I'm OK with it. No one gets to hide behind "I'm the artist; I'm doing the coloring." If everyone doesn't know what's happening, then nothing is happening yet. Still, the drawings don't have to be perfect or to an exact scale. Blueprints get better as the year goes on. The point is blueprints serve as a guide. Without them, students will run to the cardboard with no plan and, after three days, will have nothing to show and will have completely abandoned the learning.

As designs come in, I approve them or offer suggestions. It's rare a design is good enough at first draft. Measurements are tricky, and students often need one or two cracks at them to make a design workable. There will be some small structural issues they won't see. You probably *will* see those structural issues but not correct them because problem solving is part of the process, and the design process allows students to discover and overcome those hurdles on their own. Teachers are not building a trap. Students are. Teachers are facilitating by getting out of the way and biting their lip.

Build

The build phase takes the longest time, often two or three work sessions, which in my class means no more than an hour or however long I have for my English language arts block. This changes from school to school as well depending on how willing the principal is to let teachers move times around while still fulfilling the learning objectives. Getting things lined up and put together is never as easy as the students think it will be. My students and I have learned techniques to join cardboard and other materials together while avoiding the strategy "laminate with tape until immobile," which is their first choice. I, and most school administrations, simply do not have the money to keep classrooms supplied with enough tape to fulfill the plans of a student's imagination. (Buying this book helps me buy tape for my students, by the way. So, thanks for that. Tell your friends.)

Problems, both interpersonal and build related, come up constantly. Sometimes, a group's vision splinters and it slows them down because now they're building interpersonal skills and a tree kangaroo trap at the same time. Good. That's part of the overall plan. In these situations, tell students things like, "How do you compromise and work together? You don't expect Mr. Robertson to immediately solve your build issues, so why do you expect him to solve your friendship ones? Both solutions are the same: talk to each other, listen to each other, and most importantly, respect each other." (Use your own name instead of mine here, of course.) If a problem is really bad, step in. As much as you should stay hands-off, it's also important to stay vigilant to situations where only the teacher should be mediating.

Every time a multiday project is underway, I feel panic and doubt at some point. Here is where I think, *This is not going to work.* It happens about halfway through. I stand in the middle of the room, look around, and worry I'm wasting time, nothing will get done, and nothing is being learned. I must trust it will work, and these half towers and collapsed boxes do represent growth and learning and will be something real in a few hours' time. I encourage you to do the same. It's usually in the moments when you feel the most nervous that you need to do the most trusting.

Test and Revise

Once I see it is time for the next step, which usually means I've already had the following conversation with a few groups one on one, I stop everyone.

> *"OK, your builds are coming along nicely, which means what comes next?"*
>
> *One student responds, "Test and revise!"*
>
> *"Right! Make sure your build does what you told me it would do—not it does something, but it does what you intended. If it doesn't, figure out why and fix it. If it does, but it's only OK, improve it. If it does what it's supposed to do well, how can you further improve it? Could you make it more realistic or efficient?"*

This portion can take a long time for some groups. Failure is always a possibility. Some groups will not build successful tree kangaroo traps. That's OK. An unsuccessful trap does not prevent them from revising the trap or from reflecting on the design and learning from it. This part will also go super fast for those students who have not yet internalized the idea of continuous improvement and growth and who think their design is just good enough. They need a push. Even if their trap is good, could it be better? Revise, test, be sure. With these groups, I do give specific suggestions if I have to because I want them thinking harder about the problem so they can be more successful.

Both testing and revision happen in stages. In the first stage, groups test and talk on their own. They make changes they see, and we move on to the second stage. The second stage allows for greater testing and revision because I will put two or three groups together and have them present to each other. Groups must go through everything— their thinking, their design, their build, what they improved—and do all of it just as if they were in front of the whole class. Then they demonstrate the trap. Then they give feedback to one another.

We will have talked at length about giving constructive feedback and being open and egoless to what classmates are saying. It's hard. It takes maturity on the part of both the feedback giver and the feedback receiver, but they can do it, and it helps them see each other as intelligent individuals with valuable things to say. Every student in every age group can do this. Feedback focuses on the product and not on the person who created the product and often can be couched in reflective questions. Instead of saying, "I don't like this," students can ask, "Can you explain your thinking in this part?" Simply by asking the other group to explain their thinking, students create a feedback loop whereby the act of answering causes reflection, which leads to a deeper understanding of the work. Students can also say, "This is unclear here. Can you tell me how this works?" This is better and more specific than many students' first instinct, which is "I don't get it."

Feedback should never be judgmental. Teach students to avoid statements like, "I don't like *x*" or "I like *x*," and "*Y* is really good" or "*Y* is kind of bad." These are closed ended, and the only possible response is either "Thank you" or something much ruder, as the case may be. Questions during feedback time should allow the other person to explain and justify. It's a conversation or a loop, not a one-way street.

Vox Magister (Voice of the Teacher)

"The powerful thing about design is it's all about intention. If you are aware of the systemic and structural issues affecting students' education, a design mindset can help you make choices to mitigate them to the best of your ability. I'm not naive enough to think design is some panacea for white supremacy, surveillance capitalism, and the patriarchy, but it can at least begin affording some tools to help dismantle and rebuild one classroom at a time."

—Trevor Aleo, teacher, personal communication, November 9, 2020

Another minor revision time follows for last-minute changes based on the small-group sharing. Students compare their notes and discuss what they absolutely must change for their build to best meet the main question and their design.

Then students share in front of the whole class. This is the first time they will have run through everything with an instructor present. You will have been around the whole time, watching, poking, offering small bits of advice and questions, but not in control. This is their build, and you do not want students coming to you to ask how to do something. You don't know how to do it either. They will still try to ask for teacher help. This is how the conversation goes until students get the picture and stop initiating it.

> "Mr. Robertson, I've never made one of these before!"
> "Me neither! It's going to be cool! Can't wait to see what you figure out. I know you can."

I'm not being deliberately unhelpful here, but guiding rather than directing.

I'm always surprised and delighted by student builds. Even the bad ones. They get so creative. That's something important to remember and something I couldn't articulate about the design process for a long time: it is delightful how your students will surprise you. This isn't a negative kind of surprise, like, "Huh, I didn't think you would pass this math test." Instead, it's surprise in a wonderful way, like, "How did you think of that? That's so cool!"

The best example of a student design surprising everyone is a trap a pair of students designed that attached a box to a branch midway up the side of what was supposed to be a tree trunk in front of the class. They had extra time, so they designed the tree trunk to be covered in brown cloth and the box in brown and green. A green cloth covered the top of the box. The following conversation ensued at the time.

"Here is our trap. It's camouflaged so the tree kangaroo can't see it. It's x by y by z big, so the animal will fit inside comfortably."

It has to be asked, "Wait, so the tree kangaroo is supposed to just randomly jump in there?" I usually try not to interrupt presentations, but I do here anyway. I need clarity.

"No, of course not, Mr. Robertson. On top of the box, we have placed an arrangement of leaves that will look like a solid branch, but actually hides the box's opening. And, before you ask, we placed food on the center of the leaves, so that's why the tree kangaroo would jump onto it."

I'm still trying to poke holes. "OK, but it's obviously an open-topped box, then. Did you forget about how strong of jumpers they are? That thing is going right back out the top."

"Of course we didn't forget," the presenters reply. "Have you ever seen a lobster trap?"

I am taken aback. You get asked the strangest things in a design-minded classroom. "Uh, yes. Have you?"

"Uh-huh. My uncle catches lobsters. You know how lobster traps open inwards so when the lobster crawls in, it goes in easy, but then the doors won't push back open because of the angle they are at? So, it's easy to get into but impossible to get out of?" He shows with his hands.

Much like the lobster, I take the bait. "I do . . ."

The students whip the covering off the box, revealing a vertical lobster trap door. "So that's what we did! It can't get out!"

They're so proud. I'm so impressed. The design is clever, and an excellent use of prior knowledge. At this point, push just a little bit more to see if they have covered all the bases. "Aha! Now you have a panicked, frightened animal capable of jumping incredibly high trapped in this box! It's going to hurt itself!"

"No, it won't!"

"Prove it! That tree kangaroo is going to bang its head on the opening! Your trap is inhumane!" I shout, now standing and pointing because I can't resist a bit of drama and they're playing along. I'm expecting them to have used what the previous group did and reveal padded walls. But no . . .

"It won't be jumping all over because"—pause for effect—"we drugged the food!"

The class and I exploded into applause. I also detected pencils scratching as everyone else magically remembered they, too, had drugged their bait. Awesome. Collaborative learning.

Reflect

The process continues even after students each present their projects, and they know it. Students must reflect. Always write the seven reflection questions on the board or in another location visible to the whole class.

1. What worked?
2. What could have worked better?
3. If I could change one thing about the final product right now, what would I change?
4. If I could change one thing about the process we used, what would I change?
5. What did I use in the process that I learned in this classroom?
6. Is something I learned from this process applicable elsewhere in school?
7. Any other thoughts?

Again, the penultimate question is the real kicker. The others are important to get the gears moving, but everything leads to that one. Every time the class makes something, a teacher and their students must have this conversation: "There's nothing in the standards saying, 'Students will learn to make *x*.' So why did we do this? What does it have to do with school?" This process takes awhile for the students to figure out.

Students work in their groups or alone (their choice) to write their reflections. Then students go once around the room and share out loud with the class. Everyone has to say something. The process happens once more, allowing students to skip if they want this time.

Generalizing is hard. Specific generalizing is harder. Yes, students learned about tree kangaroos. Good. They learned about making traps. Good (especially if you have a younger sibling or cousin). *But what does a tree kangaroo trap have to do with anything else in school?*

Eventually, the class works all the way back to understanding the following main ideas and details.

- ▸ Students learned to read a text carefully and look for valuable information.
- ▸ Students learned to use the information they found in new and unique ways.
- ▸ Students learned to express and justify their thinking and use evidence to support it.
- ▸ Students could, if asked, write a multiple-paragraph essay about the story because now they know it front to back.
- ▸ The class actively discussed the finer points of the story all week.

This project closed with us keeping the traps around for a while and putting them up in the hallway display case for the rest of the school to see. It tickles me to know there were just a bunch of intricate traps on display in the hall, even though we provided context and textual evidence in the description next to them.

I've included a quick build to get you started on your own design-based project, should you like to use it to adapt your own idea. Figure 7.2 features the full quick build guide for the trap for a tree kangaroo project. This quick guide will take you through every step of the process.

Guide to Build: A Trap for a Tree Kangaroo

Here are the supplies required for this build.

- *Quest for the Tree Kangaroo: An Expedition to the Cloud Forest of New Guinea* by Sy Montgomery (2006)
- Blueprint
- Building supplies (paper, pencils, cardboard, tape, scissors, and so on)

Design Process

1. Define:
   - *What's the problem?* Scaring tree kangaroos out of a tree isn't nice or humane.
   - *What's the goal?* Design and build a humane trap for a tree kangaroo.
2. Design:
   - *How can we solve the problem?* Students submit blueprints for approval.
3. Build:
   - *How do we create a solution?* Students work together to build a trap.
4. Test and revise: Try out the solution and respond to data.
5. Reflect: *What did we learn?* Reflect individually or in groups using the key questions.
   - What worked?
   - What could have worked better?
   - If I could change one thing about the final product right now, what would I change?
   - If I could change one thing about the process we used, what would I change?
   - What did I use in the process that I learned in this classroom?
   - Is something I learned from this process applicable elsewhere in school?
   - Any other thoughts?

FIGURE 7.2: Guide to build a trap for a tree kangaroo.

*Visit **go.SolutionTree.com/instruction** for a free reproducible version of this figure.*

What was the final result of this design-thinking exercise? The students could not wait to get to the next story in the book. "What are we going to read next?" they'd ask. Can you ask for anything more as a teacher than a roomful of students who are pumped to do more nonfiction reading and can't wait to come back to school after the weekend?

The Joy of Putting It All Together

A large-scale, multiday build doesn't happen every week. It's not every single lesson. But if I didn't follow the design process, and if I didn't trust design thinking, this wouldn't happen in my classroom as often as it does. All this experimental learning, all these adaptable projects, and all these impromptu experiences are thanks to being open to inspiration. They're thanks to thinking like a designer and letting experimentation and change happen, then following the threads those changes make visible. These kinds of projects are worth a few duds every year. And the duds get fewer and further between the better I get at thinking like a designer, and the better my students get at thinking like designers. Students can make a bad idea good and an OK idea great. Teachers just have to let them. In part 2 and the next chapter, we (Doug and Jennifer) will contend with ways that you, as the teacher, administrator, or other school-related person, can think about becoming design minded. We'll explore initial steps, potential setbacks, curricular connections, and negotiations with administration to ease you into the process.

Put It Into Practice Reflection Template

Here we are, at the end of part 1, and the tour of the design-minded classroom is complete. Consider using the space provided to write out what happens in your head while you're teaching or how you might tell the story of how your teaching unfolds. You might use analogies, metaphors, or even drawings to capture the process.

Post Assessment

Having read all of part 1, revisit your definition for *design* from figure 1.1 (page XX). Using what you now know that you didn't know before, write a new definition of what design means to you in the space provided. You might use words, pictures, or even stream-of-consciousness thoughts to capture what the word means to you now. If you prefer, you may instead update your definition by crossing it out of figure 1.1 and adding new text as needed.

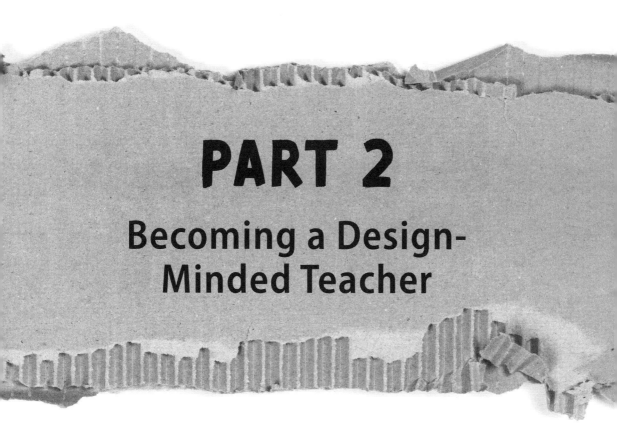

PART 2

Becoming a Design-Minded Teacher

There is a particular kind of silence, unlike any other, that occurs during professional development. It usually falls after the presentation of an idea and before a question or a clarification as participants do the mental calculations to figure out how much new work the idea will entail. You can almost hear teachers weighing the pros and cons of adopting the new idea and negotiating whether it will benefit themselves and their students in the long run.

In part 2, we aim to answer those questions before you ask them regarding design-minded teaching. We explain the reasons why specific designs are worth the effort and the benefits to jump-starting creativity. Our goal in this part is to provide starting points regarding design and lots of options for specific design-focused activities.

CHAPTER 8
Specific Designs

Zhu Li, do the thing!

—*Varrick in* The Legend of Korra

This chapter covers seven specific projects I (Doug) do in my class. The projects will bring life and excitement to the classroom as well as meet a multitude of curriculum standards, like drawing on information from multiple sources, providing logically ordered reasons supported by facts and details, solving real-world problems involving multiplication of fractions and mixed numbers, and converting different types of measurements. Project reviews will include everything from the nitty-gritty details of the project to the project's genesis, the project's learning goals, and the reasons why the project belongs in the classroom. Along the way, the chapter will clearly list potential issues to look out for as you have students complete these projects or projects like them.

I generally don't use worksheets or reproducibles in my classroom because I want my students to create guides on their own and because I like designing projects without boxes. However, not all teachers work the same way. Teachers can repurpose the blank planning document in figure 8.1 (page 120) for any of the following projects.

I encourage you to steal any project that appeals to you. Teaching is a profession, and professionals share and borrow because coming up with entirely new strategies is exhausting. Because you are learning to become more design minded by reading this book, you should take these *ideas* and change them as best fits your classroom, your students, your school, and your needs. I never buy an idea. I test-drive it and make note of what parts I liked and what parts I didn't. My classroom is not your classroom; my students are not yours. In fact, my students this year won't be my students next year, and the way one of these projects works one year is not the exact same way it will work the next year. So, the descriptions are as specific as they need to be so that they are useful, while being as vague as possible to allow you to make the projects your own.

Sometimes, it feels like there are no new ideas in education. It seems like every project has been done, and at best, all teachers are doing is remixing old ideas. Rather than let the end of new ideas depress me, I embrace it. Baseball exists with basically three pitches: (1) fastball, (2) breaking ball, and (3) changeup. That's all. And yet every pitcher throws those pitches slightly differently. Every hitter reacts to those pitches differently,

Project name:

Final product overview:*

Main learning goals of construction and design:**

Main learning goals in general:***

Project introduction

Design process components

Define (approximate time: _____)

- What is the main problem? _____
- What are potential problems as we go? _____

Design (approximate time:_____)

Build (approximate time: _____)

- Include blueprints on a separate page.
- Important notes to remember during the build: _____
- Changes to design that occur during the build: _____

Test (approximate time: _____)

- Reminder of main problem to solve: _____
- Ways to test: _____
- Results of tests: _____

Revise (approximate time: _____)

- Issues noted during tests: _____
- Possible solutions: _____
- Positives noted during tests: _____
- Possible improvements: _____

Reflect (approximate time: _____)

1. What worked? _____
2. What could have worked better? _____
3. If I could change one thing about the final product right now, what would I change? _____
4. If I could change one thing about the process we used, what would I change? _____
5. What did I use in the process that I learned in this classroom? _____
6. Is something I learned from this process applicable elsewhere in school? _____
7. Any other thoughts? _____

Possible issues to keep in mind

* What is the Platonic ideal of this project when it is finished, keeping in mind that student creativity and flexibility will result in final products that reflect this only in the main aspects?

** What will students learn that they can translate to other building projects?

*** What is the main thing students will learn that they can generalize to anything else in school, keeping in mind peripheral learning will also take place?

FIGURE 8.1: Blank planning document.

Visit **go.SolutionTree.com/instruction** *for a free reproducible version of this figure.*

and every hitter has pitches they are strong against and pitches they struggle with. Every teacher has project ideas they can visualize and knock out of the park, and every teacher has project ideas they do not connect with at all and they cannot make work in their classrooms. Bad ideas are not a weakness; they just tell teachers what instruction skills they need to work on.

This chapter provides you with a wide range of project ideas; hopefully, some of them you will see immediately and want to rush off to try with your students. And some will give you a little knot of tension in your stomach the first few times you have your students swing at them. At this point, you'll remember some students will thrive while doing certain types of projects, while other students will struggle with them. There is both joy and growth potential in frustration. Design-minded students can be frustrated with a project and still work to find a way to at least get on base. Design-minded teachers will discover different ways to modify the project to help struggling students succeed. This, by the way, is where the metaphor falls apart because we teachers are trying to help students hit home runs and pitchers are *not* trying to help batters hit home runs. (That is, unless they pitch for the San Francisco Giants. Go Dodgers.)

I have done all these projects with fourth and fifth graders, except for the cardboard arcade, which I did with the entire school. Projects like these are not age or grade level dependent. A student in any grade could complete, to some degree of success, any of these projects. Will the car or movie or trebuchet of a kindergartner look the same as that of a fifth grader? No. But no fifth-grade student's work will look the same as that of any of the student's peers anyway. Design-minded teachers do not throw away ideas simply because they look too hard. Every project looks too hard if you look at it long enough. Every build seems too complicated if you let it get into your head. A design-minded teacher sees the difficulty as a challenge. A design-minded teacher knows their students and has confidence in them and their ability to learn from success and failure. A design-minded teacher accepts the arc of a school year and plays the long game, knowing what seems too hard in September is an important stepping-stone to what happens in May. These projects are not divided up by suggested ages because design-minded teachers would see the suggested ages listed and choose not to follow the instruction. "Don't tell me what my students can and can't do," they would say. "Watch them go."

A Closer Look at Grades K–2

Every time I present projects like these at a conference, in a training, or even among the teachers at my own school, some K–2 teachers come ask me something along the lines of "This is great for your big students, but what about my students?" This sidebar is dedicated to you, my K–2 friends. I say this with all the love and respect in my heart because I know how hard those lower grades can be: primary students can do this too. Some things might have to change for these students, like using cereal boxes instead of thick cardboard so their little fingers can more easily cut with safety scissors, but they can and do understand the basic concepts. Kindergartners can come up with some version of every single project presented in this book. Their versions will not be huge or complex, but the learning and the thinking will still take place. I believe in you as a teacher, and I know you believe in your students. If you can teach a five-year-old to go from zero to reading, you can do anything. If a five-year-old can go from zero to reading, *they* can do anything. Their stuff will absolutely fall down the first few times, sure. My big students' stuff falls too.

Note that some of these projects take place in my school's *MakerSpace*, and some of them take place in my own classroom. None needs to take place in one place or the other, but I will note the reasons why my students do the projects where they do. Our

MakerSpace is a classroom dedicated to making, building, and student exploration. It is filled with tools like tape, scissors, twine, and other objects too numerous to mention, all of which students could use to create things. It is also full of parent- and teacher-donated materials, like plastic building blocks, cardboard boxes, scrap cloth, sewing machines and thread, electronic tablets, various robotics materials, and more cardboard, tape, and scissors. My school is incredibly lucky to have a MakerSpace and a community willing and able to make it a reality and keep it up. Anything done in the MakerSpace could happen in a classroom, but it is nice to have a space specifically dedicated to creation with all the tools there for any class to use.

If you do use these projects in your classroom, or if you break these projects into bits and use what you like from these versions of them, we (Doug and Jennifer) would love it if you visited us at https://cardboardclassroom.com, where you can share your ideas and final projects. Teaching works best as part of a collaborative effort, and by sharing these ideas (or any other projects you love), you can create a design-minded community and hopefully lighten the load with others.

The projects are:

- ▸ Wind-powered cars
- ▸ Trebuchets
- ▸ Cardboard arcade
- ▸ Stop-motion movies
- ▸ Cardboard city
- ▸ Rube Goldberg machine
- ▸ Marionettes

FIGURE 8.2: Sample wind-powered car.

Wind-Powered Cars

Students in small groups have one hour to design and build wind-powered cars (see figure 8.2).

As a way to introduce this project to students, you might say something like the following.

> *"You are going to get into these small groups, and you are going to design, build, test, and present wind-powered cars. 'What is a wind-powered car?' you ask. It's a car that moves using the wind. That is all I'm going to tell you. I trust you. Work smart. Get some paper out to start designing, find your groups, and go."*

This is an excellent starting project for a class. It should come almost immediately after your first lesson about the design process. This way, students can put what they are learning to use at once, which deepens its importance and increases its "stickiness."

Nothing about this build requires much extra knowledge. Everyone knows what a car is, and everyone knows what wind is. This does not mean it's easy to build one, but the appearance of ease will allow students to launch into the project with verve and a positive attitude.

Give students an hour (an hour-*ish*, to be honest) because it shows students they can create something of quality quickly. A project is like a gas; it will expand to fill the space it is in. You can use this as a quick way to collect data about students' baseline skills regarding working in a group, active listening, and being a member of a community.

What Will Students Accomplish?

As a result of this lesson (some of the learning goals), students will do the following.

▶ Demonstrate a beginning understanding of the design process.

- They will think about defining the problem, designing to solve the problem, building their design, testing their design, and revising their design, and then reflect on what they did.
- All these steps will be rudimentary, and that's OK.

▶ Understand basic engineering concepts like an axle, a sail, a body, cause and effect, and friction.

The Platonic ideal of a wind-powered car is a four-wheel model with a sail. The wheels should be parallel and allow the car to move straightish. The sail should catch air and be stable enough to push the car forward rather than spin or flop over. As long as it is stable and moves, it works.

What Are the Teacher Considerations?

The following sections describe two issues teachers might run into and what teachers can do about them as they embark on this project. These issues are wheels not spinning and sails not catching air.

Possible Issue 1: Free-Spinning Wheel

At least one group in your class will do this, based on my years of seeing it happen: They will find chopsticks or some other sticks. They will find something round or cut four circles out of cardboard. They will stick the circles to the ends of the sticks. They will glue the sticks to the bottom of their chosen car body. They will then push the car across the carpet to test it, and nothing will spin because everything is fixed in place.

▶ **How a teacher should address it:** Let it happen. The students can see what the problem is, and part of the process is letting them find the solution.

▸ **How students often address it:** Some students will widen the hole in the center of the wheel until the wheel spins (read: wobbles). At this point, they need to figure out how to keep it on the axle. The better choice is the students will find the straws, attach the straw to the body of their car, slide the axle through the straw, and fix the wheels to the axle. Then the whole axle spins within the straw.

Possible Issue 2: Decent Sail

This doesn't sound real, but it happens every year. Students will build the car body, get the wheels to spin, and lie on the floor behind the car to blow as hard as they can on it until either they pass out or the car budges slightly. Clearly, this is not the way we suggest creating wind for this project.

▸ **How a teacher should address it:** Step in at this point by saying, "No, no, that's not wind powered. Try to think of other wind-powered things." Students will first think of the propellers of an airplane. "No, an airplane is engine powered; the engine is driving the prop, not the wind. Something else?" Soon, they will land on sailboats. It's also handy to have a small electric fan in the room where students are likely to notice it. Don't point it out; let the students huff and puff until someone notices said fan and asks if they can use it instead. Then let them use it.

▸ **How students often address it:** Figuring out a sail is tricky because unless affixed properly, a sail wants to spin around or flop over rather than catch the wind. But students can figure out how to solve the problem with testing and revision.

At the end, groups line up on either side of a track (which is just tape you hastily threw down while they cleaned the room), and one by one, they come up, talk about their car as far as what they did, what they changed, and what they expect to happen, and the why of all those things. Then, using the fan, they demonstrate their car for the class.

Stress this important point loudly and clearly: *this is a demonstration, not a contest.* The goal is not to see whose car goes the farthest, the straightest, or the fastest. That was never part of the directive. The only thing students are testing is whether theirs is a wind-powered car.

After the demonstration, go back to class and let the formal reflection process begin.

Bring this project back in exactly the same form much later in the year just so students can see how much they've learned. A good option here is to make this second demonstration a contest. Figure 8.3 (page 126) provides the quick project guide to building wind-powered cars.

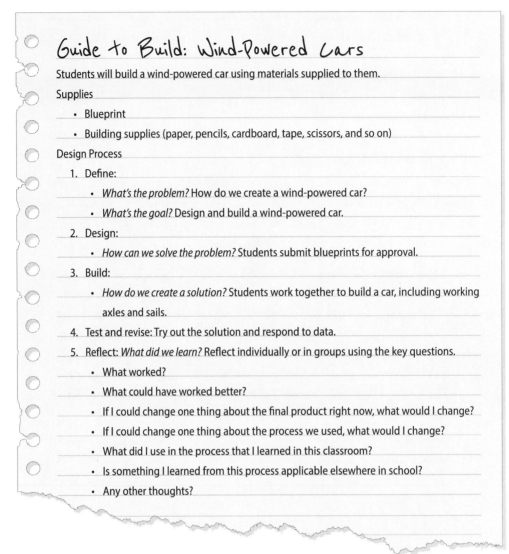

FIGURE 8.3: Guide to build wind-powered cars.

*Visit **go.SolutionTree.com/instruction** for a free reproducible version of this figure.*

Trebuchets

A trebuchet is a more complex version of a catapult. Instead of having one fixed end and one end that throws the projectile through the release of tension, a trebuchet uses a counterweight, a sling, and gravity to achieve a more powerful swing-and-throw motion. Students in groups use supplies given to build a trebuchet (see figure 8.4).

You may want to introduce this project by saying something like the following.

> *"You are going to make a trebuchet. I know you don't know what one is, so I'm going to spend ten minutes teaching you about finding trustworthy and reliable sources online, then give you ten minutes on the computer to research, and then an hour to design, build, and test."*

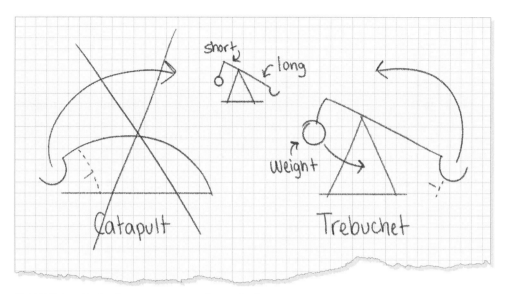

FIGURE 8.4: Trebuchet-versus-catapult simple design.

The project is difficult. All year, the teacher will be introducing concepts students have never heard of before. These include multiplying fractions, deconstructing texts, writing detailed research projects, and so many more. Students will be asked to build something they've never heard of to help them understand the teacher would never assign them something they can't do and to teach them to approach those new concepts with an open mind. Also, many students are going to fail to build a functional trebuchet, and this allows them to learn from failure safely.

The engineering skills the students will learn in this project are going to serve them well for every other project moving forward.

What Will Students Accomplish?

As a result of this lesson (some of the learning goals), students will do the following.

- Learn to fail and recover.
- Learn to use the computer to quickly research an unfamiliar topic and differentiate between trustworthy and reliable information and bad information.
- Effectively use my design process as a way to guide their process.

The final expectation of the project is students will have created a model that is able to throw small objects with some consistency and repeatability. Successful repetition means the model doesn't fall apart after working once. Students should also have some idea about where the projectile is going to go. Sometimes, students end up with projects that are more catapult than trebuchet, and that's fine only if students recognize the difference in their reflections. This is a difficult build, and there is a lot of failure, so you want to be able to see the thinking, the intent, and the possibility if given more time and better materials. This is often when students learn failure is an option and a learning opportunity.

What Are the Teacher Considerations?

I cannot say this enough: this is a difficult project. Building a catapult is much easier, which is why I don't assign catapults. The following sections describe four issues teachers might run into and what teachers can do about them as they embark on this project.

Possible Issue 1: The Pivot

Students have a tough time getting the crossbar holding the beam to sit on the frame because it has to turn freely without falling off. That part allowing the beam to swing through the frame of the trebuchet, called the *pivot point*, needs to be connected to move without falling off.

▸ **How a teacher should address it:** Step back, let them struggle, and step in or give hints only if students are reaching a frustration point stopping them from making further progress.

▸ **How students often address it:** Students will cover it in tape until it can't possibly fall-off, which solves the falling-off problem but worsens the not-pivoting problem. Eventually, they'll remember the axle from their wind-powered cars and find inspiration. Sometimes, they remember because their teacher mentions it, and sometimes, they remember because they see another group do it.

The pivot might also allow the beam to rotate too far, which will throw the payload into the ground. Teachers can tell students to imagine throwing a ball and checking the release point they have created.

Possible Issue 2: Stability

The frame should be stable because it needs to withstand the force of the counter-weight swinging through it. Unstable frames will tip, twist, or collapse under the strain.

▸ **How a teacher should address it:** The teacher can remind students excess tape does not equal strength and stability and they should use what they found on the internet as a guide. Consider saying to them, "Think in triangles and triangular prisms."

▸ **How students often address it:** Some groups will anchor their frame to the ground in some way, often with more tape than they need. Others will reinforce their frames by adding thickness to the struts. Avoid letting them cover the build in tape. More tape is almost never the right solution.

Possible Issue 3: Counterweight

This is what makes it a trebuchet and not a catapult. The counterweight goes on one end of the beam, and its falling energy is what makes the projectile get thrown. Students will often put things in the counterweight for size but will not take weight into account. This is a lesson in mass waiting to happen.

▸ **How a teacher should address it:** Only after multiple student failures should the teacher step in and emphasize the *weight* part of counterweight. Also, do not let students tape their items together into a bundle.

▸ **How students often address it:** Students will look for scraps and small items like marbles and LEGO blocks to make their counterweight. They will then try to bind their items together in some way. They should find a scrap of cloth or paper that they can use to securely hold the items.

Possible Issue 4: Sling

In a real trebuchet, the payload or projectile is in a sling on the long side of the beam, and then the sling whips around and releases the payload at the height of its arc.

▸ **How a teacher should address it:** This will feel like too much. It *is* too much. I've repeatedly said that I like how challenging this is, but the physics behind a successful sling are difficult, and I am totally OK with the students just using a cup to hold the payload instead. If they can figure out the sling, amazing. If not, I do not insist they bang their heads against this particular tree. We don't have the time, and I don't even understand how anyone can build a trebuchet simply. So as long as the sling has a place for the payload that is both sturdy and able to release the payload, let it slide.

▸ **How students often address it:** Some group will try to create a sling, and I let them while telling them it is OK to pass on that part. Other groups will go straight to a more catapult-like static payload holder.

The project ends similarly to the wind-powered car project. Students line up on either side of a taped aisle after cleaning the room, and group by group, they come up and show off what they made, why they made the choices they did, and how they expect the trebuchet to do. And just like during the wind-powered car project, remind students this is not a contest. No one is judged on how far or how accurately their trebuchet throws its payload. It just needs to swing and throw. And some groups' trebuchets won't swing or throw. Those groups point out why they think theirs won't. Then, students go back to class and write reflections. Figure 8.5 (page 130) is a quick project build guide for trebuchets.

Guide to Build: Trebuchets

Students will learn the difference between a catapult and a trebuchet, then design and build their own trebuchet with the supplies provided.

Supplies

- Computer for research
- Blueprint
- Building supplies (paper, pencils, cardboard, tape, scissors, and so on)

Design Process

1. Define:
   - *What's the problem?* A trebuchet uses many moving pieces to throw an object in a straight line.
   - *What's the goal?* Design and build a working trebuchet (not catapult).
2. Design:
   - *How can we solve the problem?* Students submit blueprints for approval.
3. Build:
   - *How do we create a solution?* Students work together to build a trebuchet.
4. Test and revise: Try out the solution and respond to data.
5. Reflect: *What did we learn?* Reflect individually or in groups using the key questions.
   - What worked?
   - What could have worked better?
   - If I could change one thing about the final product right now, what would I change?
   - If I could change one thing about the process we used, what would I change?
   - What did I use in the process that I learned in this classroom?
   - Is something I learned from this process applicable elsewhere in school?
   - Any other thoughts?

FIGURE 8.5: Guide to build trebuchets.

*Visit **go.SolutionTree.com/instruction** for a free reproducible version of this figure.*

Cardboard Arcade

The cardboard arcade (see figure 8.6) is a project done the week before winter break every year, and it is exactly what it sounds like: your class builds a functioning arcade out of cardboard.

First, show students the 2012 YouTube video "Caine's Arcade" (Mullick, 2012). Then, you might introduce the project with something like the following.

> *"Make groups of no more than four, no less than three. Together, you have five school days to design and create a cardboard arcade game. You must know what your game*

> *is, how it works, how you win, and why it's fun. You must also create fully detailed blueprints before you build. I want you to keep this idea in mind: complex to build, simple to play. I've invited a bunch of other classes to our arcade. We open on Friday."*

I schedule this project for my classroom during the week leading up to winter break because every teacher knows this week is one of the longest, hardest weeks of the year. By focusing the students on the cardboard arcade on Monday, I rarely have to answer questions like, "Are we having a party on Friday?" because Friday is full; we're opening. Every day until Friday is full because I expect these games to be big, complex, and awesome.

This project also allows the teacher to evaluate how well students are integrating being design minded into their thinking because it is so massive and involved. Think of it as a midyear assessment, if evaluating terms help you. But don't tell the students this is an assessment.

What Will Students Accomplish?

The learning goals here are huge and almost too numerous to name. As a result of this lesson, students will achieve the following learning goals.

- ▶ Collaborate.

- ▶ Have group discussions.

- ▶ Integrate ideas clearly.

FIGURE 8.6: Sample cardboard arcade game.

- ▶ Write about a topic in a way others can understand.

- ▶ Revise and edit the writing for clarity.

- ▶ Meet nearly every geometric standard you can think of.

- ▶ Prove a deep understanding of the design process and the ability to use it to create something brand new while following two specific guidelines.
    - The game must be complex to make but simple to play.
    - The game must be fun.

The final expectation of the project is each group will have created at least one detailed, thoughtful, functional, fun arcade game with at least one moving part. On Friday of the week before winter break starts, open the arcade to the school, and invite other teachers into the class to play. Games must hold up under the strain of repeated plays and be easily understood by kindergartners all the way to fifth graders.

Because games are teacher approved, there should be no repeated games. No two games are exactly the same. Some may be similar; for example, there are a lot of throwing-with-accuracy-style games, but some are Skee-Ball based, some are football themed or basketball themed, and some are something else altogether.

What Are the Teacher Considerations?

The following sections describe three issues teachers might run into and what teachers can do about them as they embark on this project. Because this is a longer project than the others in this chapter, I include a special breakdown by each day of the week this project is conducted.

Possible Issue 1: Time Intensiveness

I run this project for a full week, Monday to Friday, and I use as much time on it as I think I can get away with. The breakdown of the five days normally goes as follows.

- **Day one (Monday):** Introduce the project, watch the video, discuss, form groups, define, and design.
- **Day two (Tuesday):** Design deeply, thinking about blueprint angles and measurements, and answer the question, "Why will the game be fun?" Most plans will be approved today, and the build phase begins.
- **Day three (Wednesday):** Build, build, build. This is all work time.
- **Day four (Thursday):** Build, test, and revise. Games should be 90 percent ready to go by the end of Thursday. Playtesting rounds today are to check for stability, strength, and any flaws in the logic or rules of the game itself.
- **Day five (Friday):**
  - **Morning**—Sprint build. Finished groups help unfinished groups. Playtesting and revisions are finished.
  - **Afternoon**—Open for business, run multiple classes through, reflect, and break down games.

It's important to schedule weeklong projects ahead of time, as every single day is a risk factor for changing plans. Read on for tips on how to manage such a long-running project.

- **How a teacher should address it:** My students and I often fold mathematics and reading into arcade work time because we need them. I do not approve blueprints until they are almost perfect. That alone takes at least a day for most groups. And then the teacher cannot do much but get out of the way.

> ▸ **How students often address it:** Groups will often come to realizations through their build that they are reaching too high and need to pivot in the middle of the week. There is not time to start from zero, so have them reimagine their builds from where they got stuck. Not finishing a game is not an option.

Possible Issue 2: Interpersonal Issues

A group may try to splinter midbuild, as the result of some form of conflict, and form two smaller groups without telling the teacher. Sometimes students just have different enough ideas that they want to try them both and can't compromise.

> ▸ **How a teacher should address it:** Don't let group splintering happen unless the problem is very serious. Remind the group that they don't have to be friends, and there are tools they can use to make working together easier (like protocols and rubrics). Help students communicate with *I* statements instead of *you* statements (for example, "I think we should do *x*, and I do not feel heard").
>
> ▸ **How students often address it:** Most interpersonal issues happen because students don't clearly communicate their thoughts, or because students are so married to their own ideas they struggle to compromise. Mediate these problems and help groups find a solution everyone is at least OK with. This often involves taking a step back from the project and taking a short break when students feel the time crunch.

Possible Issue 3: Panic

I've done this project for years. Every year, it has worked and been awesome. On Wednesday of this week every year, I stand in the center of my room and tell myself everything will be OK. On Wednesday, no game looks like a game. No group looks like they are making enough progress. Nothing looks like it is going to work out. It will. I have to keep my hands as clean as possible and trust my students can make it happen. This is not my arcade; it's theirs.

> ▸ **How a teacher should address it:** Breathe. Trust. Breathe some more.
>
> ▸ **How students often address it:** They won't notice the teacher panicking unless the teacher lets them. They're too busy working. Let them work.

The project ends when other classes come in. There is nothing quite like having thirty-five fifth graders pile into your room and collectively go, "Ooh," as they see the carefully laid-out games around the room, each with a fourth grader standing beside it, beckoning them over. It's so very loud and overwhelming. My students have been practicing their pitch and explaining the rules over and over to each other. They know the game has to work no matter the size or age of the player, and they are ready. I cycle classes through every twenty minutes or so, depending on the class size, with a few minutes after each group for reset and minor repairs. I also invite my administration in because the students will want to show off.

Once the last class leaves, we all sit for about five minutes and enjoy the silence. Then we get out our journals and begin the reflection process, just like always. Time dictates whether we disassemble the games then or we wait until after we get back from break. Do not take time away from reflections for teardown. Then, go home and sleep for the first time in maybe a week.

Figure 8.7 is the quick project build guide to the cardboard arcade.

Guide to Build: A Cardboard Arcade

Students will conceive, design, and build a fully functioning arcade machine out of cardboard using the supplies provided.

Supplies

- "Caine's Arcade" YouTube video (Mullick, 2012)
- Blueprint
- Building supplies (paper, pencils, cardboard, tape, scissors, and so on)
- Even more cardboard

Design Process

1. Define:
    - *What's the problem?* How do we use what we know about design to create a challenging-to-build but simple-to-play arcade game?
    - *What's the goal?* Design and build a fun, straightforward cardboard arcade game.
2. Design:
    - *How can we solve the problem?* Students submit blueprints for approval.
3. Build:
    - *How do we create a solution?* Students work together to build a game.
4. Test and revise: Try out the solution and respond to data.
5. Reflect: *What did we learn?* Reflect individually or in groups using the key questions.
    - What worked?
    - What could have worked better?
    - If I could change one thing about the final product right now, what would I change?
    - If I could change one thing about the process we used, what would I change?
    - What did I use in the process that I learned in this classroom?
    - Is something I learned from this process applicable elsewhere in school?
    - Any other thoughts?

FIGURE 8.7: Guide to build a cardboard arcade.

*Visit **go.SolutionTree.com/instruction** for a free reproducible version of this figure.*

Stop-Motion Movies

Using a slideshow app like Google Slides or Microsoft PowerPoint, students will draw a frame-by-frame summary of their learning (see figure 8.8). Normally, this would be a summary of a story the class is reading, though you could use this project for anything. Students will then use a screen-capture tool to record their animation. If the screen-capture tool can record sound, students will also play the parts in their movie and supply sound effects as they quickly scroll through the slides. This will animate the movie.

A teacher can begin the project by showing a clip of a professionally made stop-motion movie like *Kubo and the Two Strings* (Knight, 2016) or *ParaNorman* (Fell & Butler, 2012). Even though the project is called "stop motion," students *create* motion, so the teacher

FIGURE 8.8: Example of a stop-motion movie slide.

could use a video about the early days of animation as an example too. The following is a way to introduce the project.

> *"Today, we are going to summarize the story we're reading, but you're going to summarize using the computers to make a movie. You're going to have settings and characters and action and do voices, and you're going to get very creative in doing all of this."*

Also, before introducing the project with an actual academic assignment, teachers might want to introduce the basics and then allow students one work session to familiarize themselves with no actual goal beyond "play around with the tools."

I introduce the project with a story called "Invasion From Mars," which is a selection from the *War of the Worlds* radio broadcast (Internet Archive, 2013). It is written as a play, so after our first read, I break the students into groups and challenge them to recreate the script as a stop-motion movie. I do not expect them to get all the way through the story; it takes a lot of work to make one of these movies good. Students will have invented a bunch of interpretations of the story by the time the project is over. A good interpretation means the students read the story very closely. Does the alien look how the story describes it? Does the ship? Are all the characters there? By the way, allow the students to gender-flip the characters. As written, the three main speaking parts are men, and I feel we should be modeling women and nonbinary people as main characters too. Also, teachers could easily use this project to have students summarize a historical event or a scientific process or even a word problem. Once students have the basic skill, they can take it anywhere.

This project exists because while many teachers love student plays and reader's theater, these are not easy to put on, and they leave out students or sort them into inactive rolls like "set painter" or "tree." Students can do stop-motion movies in small groups (the preferred group size is always three students), which means no one gets left out; there aren't enough people in the group to handle the project if someone is slacking. This project also exists because as good as it is to have students making things with their hands, making does not stop where keyboards start. The computer is a tool just like construction paper, cardboard, and scissors. Encourage students to see the computer as being for more than typing work and accessing a boring mathematics website. It's a place to *create*.

What Will Students Accomplish?

As a result of this lesson, students will achieve the following learning goals.

- ▸ Summarize their learning.
- ▸ Retell a story including main idea and details.
- ▸ Use technology to publish work in a variety of ways and become more familiar with specific tools.

The final product is a recorded stop-motion movie complete with narration, voices, and sound effects, which is then played for the class. Students do not present their slide-shows, just as when you see an animated film, the animators don't appear on screen and hold each frame up to the camera to describe, "OK, so here you can see the mouse is driving a boat. In this next frame, his hips move slightly to the right, and musical notes appear above his head, suggesting he is whistling."

What Are the Teacher Considerations?

The following sections describe three issues teachers might run into and what teachers can do about them as they embark on this project.

Possible Issue 1: Number of Slides

The higher the number of frames per second (FPS), the smoother animation looks.

- ▸ **How a teacher should address it:** Teach students a high number of slides with very slight movements between the slides results in smoother-looking movies. If you are using STEAM rather than STEM (and I am), you want art to be part of it, and a pretty project means that you have successfully incorporated the development of artistic skill into the STEAM-based project.
- ▸ **How students often address it:** With a higher frame or slide rate comes a slightly higher time commitment. Students who take the high-slide-count

directive to heart may end up with a hundred or more slides for something that takes only thirty seconds to complete. This is often self-correcting if your class does the project more than once because students who use a small number of slides, like twenty, will see the quality difference between their movie and the ones with five times as many slides (and they will also hear it wasn't much more work).

Possible Issue 2: Creation of Characters and Backgrounds

You can do this project with any slideshow program, like Microsoft PowerPoint. My students use Google Slides because my district runs on the Google Suite. We also use Google Slides because multiple students can share the slide project and work at the same time. Do not allow students to search for images with transparent backgrounds to add to their movie except for a simple, static background object like a car or a farmhouse. The Google Slides shape tool allows users to draw simple rectangles and circles, and my students use these to create anything dynamic in their movie. You can see that in figure 8.8 (page 135). It's not Pixar, but it does allow students to move and pose their characters in dynamic ways that fixed images do not afford. Creating characters takes the most time.

▸ **How a teacher should address it:** Teachers can tell their students they need to find a happy medium between stick person and Pixar. Their stop-motion movie is never going to look beautiful, but it can look good and be expressive. To illustrate this point, tell the class Pixar animators test their characters by playing a scene without sound or facial animations, and if they can still tell the main emotions of the scene, they know they've animated the scene well. (And yes, I keep using Pixar, because I use the best.)

▸ **How students often address it:** Some students will get deep into the character creation, but this often eats into the time they can use to do the real storytelling work. Often, this mistake happens once, and the second time those students do this kind of project, they are able to self-correct based on past experiences.

Possible Issue 3: Screen Capture

I am not going to tell you a specific screen-capture tool because these apps and extensions come and go so quickly, whatever I pick might be out of date by the time you read this. However, you should look for an app or extension with video-recording and audio screen-capture capabilities.

▸ **How a teacher should address it:** Be sure students know if they make a small mistake, it's OK, but if they make a big one or a lot of small ones, they should probably try again because the free screen-capture programs rarely have an edit feature.

▸ **How students often address it:** Students should rehearse multiple times before hitting record. This teaches them the value of practice and helps them see fixable problems. Rehearsal is the test-and-revise step in the real world.

The stop-motion movie project ends with a mini-film fest. Each group plugs their final movie into whatever kind of overhead screen the district has bequeathed to our classroom for the year, and away we go. We also add links to the stop-motion movies on the class website so parents can watch. Figure 8.9 is the quick project build guide for stop-motion movies.

Guide to Build: Stop-Motion Movies

Students will conceive, design, and create a stop-motion movie after writing a script and creating characters digitally.

Supplies

- Script
- Computer with slideshow creation program

Design Process

1. Define:
   - *What's the problem?* How do we turn a story or concept into a smooth, entertaining stop-motion movie?
   - *What's the goal?* Design and create a stop-motion movie.
2. Design:
   - *How can we solve the problem?* Students submit scripts for approval.
3. Build:
   - *How do we create a solution?* Students work together to create a stop-motion movie.
4. Test and revise: Students rehearse their movies and then record.
5. Reflect: *What did we learn?* Reflect individually or in groups using the key questions.
   - What worked?
   - What could have worked better?
   - If I could change one thing about the final product right now, what would I change?
   - If I could change one thing about the process we used, what would I change?
   - What did I use in the process that I learned in this classroom?
   - Is something I learned from this process applicable elsewhere in school?
   - Any other thoughts?

FIGURE 8.9: Guide to build stop-motion movies.

*Visit **go.SolutionTree.com/instruction** for a free reproducible version of this figure.*

Cardboard City

The cardboard city is a schoolwide project that takes place both in classrooms and during a massive parent and student Maker Night at Powell Valley Elementary School, where I have taught. On Maker Night, students and their families come to the school to visit rooms each representing an aspect of STEAM. In each room, the student and their family modify a small cardboard house in a way that aligns with the room's STEAM aspect. Completed houses are then placed on a giant map in the gym (see figure 8.10). While this is a deeply complex project, it is also *amazing* when finished. Because of the depth and complexity of this project—which is a *ton* of work—the cardboard city is two design-minded projects in one. The first is the work of designing how the Maker Night will go, because every school is different, and the second is the design work participants do during the Maker Night itself. Also, because the cardboard city is visualized as a whole-school project rather than a class project, the following project description sections explain it a bit differently.

This project exists because my school had organized a MakerFaire at the end of four school years and it was starting to get old. These events celebrate making and creativity and involve students creating some-thing on their own, or

FIGURE 8.10: 2019 Powell Valley Elementary School cardboard city.

in classrooms, and then coming together to share their creativity and learning. They take the idea of a science fair and expand it beyond science projects. Though the idea was initially a success, enthusiasm among students and staff had waned over the years, and we wanted to find a way to revitalize it. So, the MakerFaire committee members put their heads together and tried to narrow down exactly what the school wanted out of the event. The committee decided the best feature every year was the make-and-take corner, where families spent ten or fifteen minutes making a flashlight or little lightsaber from electrical components and with basic directions. If that was the most popular feature, how could the interactive concept be more central to the MakerFaire in future iterations?

At the same time, versions of the MakerFaire had drifted away from the central tenets of STEAM over the years, and the consensus solution became to drive STEAM home harder. These ideas formed the outline of the committee's needs: how could the MakerFaire involve families in exploring STEAM?

Once the MakerFaire committee had the idea in place, the principal gave the committee time during a staff meeting to explain it to the other teachers and get them on board. As this new approach reinvigorated the idea of a Faire, the staff were excited. We even made a short video commercial to play during a school assembly to hype the students up about the change.

The most important part of the STEAM idea is the de-siloing of subject areas so they all come together in an interdisciplinary way. At some point, someone on the MakerFaire committee hit upon making houses out of cardboard, and from there flowed the ideas for each room and how the whole project would eventually shake out. The end of this project is now a massive community event joining the staff together with student families to create something unique and amazing.

In class, every student in the school makes a small cardboard house using cereal box cardboard and one of three templates the MakerFaire committee found online. These are simple, undecorated starter houses, and just because a student makes one, it does not mean the student will use that home on the night.

On the night students and their families come into the school, they select one of the premade houses from a table and then visit, in any order they'd like, five rooms. Each room represents an aspect of STEAM and has a specific goal. The rooms are as follows.

- ▶ **Science:** In the earth science room, families can make plants and natural features to decorate the home. Students make trees, bushes, bodies of water, or even small animals from the resources available. They are then attached to or put in the house.

- ▶ **Technology:** Using tiny LED lights, copper tape, and watch batteries, students and their families follow instructions (in theory) to place a light somewhere on their house and make it light up.

- ▶ **Engineering:** Something on the house needs to move or be interactive. Students and families receive wooden craft sticks, straws, string, and other small building materials. Some will create a drawbridge or a functional garage door, a fancy porch, a rope swing to hang from their tree, or a boat dock.

- ▶ **Art:** The basic house is cereal-box brown. This room supplies materials to make the home beautiful and unique. This part deliberately provides almost no guidance; instead, it is left up to the students' and families' imagination.

- ▶ **Mathematics:** Before putting their completed home on the map, students and their families follow a series of prompts using a variety of measuring tools and formulas (some friendly for kindergartners, like, "What is the perimeter of your house with a ruler?" up through some for fifth graders, like, "What is the volume of your home?") and record their findings on a big chart.

What Will Students Accomplish?

As a result of this lesson, families will understand the interdisciplinary but separate elements of STEAM, and adults will see what students are capable of when creating and problem solving. All the directions are on posters on walls, and one or two volunteers will station themselves in each room to provide coaching or just-in-time teaching when needed. Adults and students are working together to make a thing. Everyone does a lot of learning, but everyone's learning is unique.

A teacher will make a giant map and place it on the floor somewhere in the school. The map should have roads crossing it, lots of green space, and a long river running down the center. Someone (wearing socks to avoid ripping the map) should always be at the map to help students put down their finished houses.

The final project is incredible. It can have almost more houses than space, the lights work beautifully, the houses are wonderful and so creative, and it makes all the hours and stress worth it. Look at figure 8.10 (page 139). It is amazing.

What Are the Teacher Considerations?

Teachers can do this project alone in their class. It would be awesome. But it's a thousand times more awesome as a school night event. There's a lot to do. Teachers and administrators have to prepare the base houses, plan and organize the rooms, come up with a better mathematics idea than the MakerFaire committee did, and recruit a bunch of volunteers. The following sections describe four issues teachers might run into and what teachers can do about them as they embark on this project.

Possible Issue 1: Preparing Base Houses

To prepare the houses, collect approximately a metric ton of cereal boxes from students for a few weeks. Cereal box cardboard is lighter and easier to work with than regular cardboard, making it ideal. Give the older classes (third grade and above) the templates to cut, fold, and tape the houses by themselves. The younger classes (kindergarten through second grade) find an older buddy class, and the big students help the little ones through the tracing, cutting, folding, and taping.

Possible Issue 2: Organizing and Planning Rooms

The trick with each room is to give ideas without telling people what to do. There is no right way to do the engineering room. The science room has no expected product. And this freedom with suggestions yields impressive results. For example, I stopped a third-grade student walking out of the science room with his family because I couldn't see any plants or animals on his build. I was curious and asked him why he hadn't added plants to his home. "I have plants. Look, a greenhouse," he said. And sure enough, he'd made a little dome of construction paper and put a whole bunch of tiny plants inside it. I looked at the parents with wide eyes, and the mom said, "His idea. We are just as impressed as you."

Each room only has two posters listing instructions (four for the first project, because the committee printed each poster in English and Spanish), supplies, and a volunteer or two.

Having a blank map helps make the whole thing feel real and exciting. You aren't making a bunch of cardboard houses. Those houses all come together and form a city. A fifth-grade teacher at my school, who is often my partner in crime in big ideas like this and is the person with whom I'd initially worked to create the MakerSpace and MakerFaire at my school, had his class build big buildings like a theater, a McDonald's, and a 7-Eleven to decorate the map. It gave the cardboard city a realism it didn't have before.

Possible Issue 3: Rethinking Mathematics

The mathematics room idea was easy to come up with but hard to execute and fell flat. Having students and their families measure their homes and record their measurements seemed like an excellent idea, but when placed next to the much more active and engaging rooms, it lacked interactivity. The whole committee agreed on that. We knew that the theme for the following year was the undersea world and we'd need to come up with something better for mathematics to do that theme justice. That was put off until the following year, though, because after the project, we all were exhausted and didn't want to talk about it for a while. Then COVID-19 happened in 2020, before we could address it. I think one solution would be to make mathematics a running idea in each room rather than a room of its own.

Possible Issue 4: Gathering Volunteers

Teachers and administrators cannot do this alone. Volunteers must have an idea of what is happening in their room. I work with smart people, so it's not like I have to train them in things like, "This is how they should make a tree." But if the volunteers don't know what the room is for and don't understand the concept, the people coming to the room won't either.

Often, the volunteers who have the most trouble are the ones in the technology room. Those tiny LED lights and batteries and copper tape pieces are fussy. I knew this going in for my school's project, so before the night, I grabbed two of my sharpest students; gave them a bag with an LED light, a battery, and copper tape in it; and told them to figure out the best way to explain how to make it all work. Once they thought they had it, both created a step-by-step guide and made a short video showing the process. Then, two other students followed those directions to check how clear they were. They seemed clear. If teachers do this in their own iteration of the project, they should print copies of the directions and set up a half-dozen computers with the video queued up.

Here's the thing: some students don't listen to directions when they're excited and just start. The students who never grow out of that turn into adults with the same habit. So, the technology room volunteers have to do quite a bit more helping and supply rationing than expected because some families will just grab and go without asking questions and then get confused, which is fine. Families learning what it's like to use STEAM is part of the goal for the night. But it does add an element of stress to those helping there.

Powell Valley Makes: A Cardboard City was a two-hour event at the end of which the community had dozens of unique and wonderful tiny homes. We scheduled the night for a Tuesday because we have assemblies on Wednesday. So, on Wednesday, we were able to show off the completed city to the entire school. Teachers carefully walked their classes around the perimeter of the map so students could see their house, their friend's house, and everyone else's houses. It felt like a real community effort. On Friday, teachers sent students to the gym to grab their house to take home if they wanted it. For me, the project ended with me going home that night exhausted but too jazzed to sleep. When I look at pictures of what we made, I'm still blown away. For our school, the project ended when the city was finally taken apart and all the homes found their students and were taken home. My class and I reflected one last time on the whole process using our reflection questions, and even students who could not attend the night were able to reflect on the work done in class to make the night a success. Figure 8.11 features a quick project build guide for your own cardboard city.

Guide to Build: A Cardboard City

Students will build a cardboard home with elements representing every subject of STEAM.

Supplies

- Cereal boxes
- Home templates
- Building supplies (paper, pencils, cardboard, tape, scissors, LED lights, copper tape, small batteries, and so on)

Design Process

1. Define:
   - *What's the problem?* How do we create community in our school while also learning about the essence of STEAM?
   - *What's the goal?* Design and build cardboard houses using STEAM and collect them into a giant city.
2. Design:
   - *How can we solve the problem?* Students travel from room to room designing each piece of STEAM.
3. Build:
   - *How do we create a solution?* Students and families work in each STEAM room to build their home.
4. Test and revise: Try out the solution and respond to data from room to room.
   - For example: Does the light work?

FIGURE 8.11: Guide to build a cardboard city.   continued →

5. Reflect: *What did we learn?* Reflect individually or in groups using the key questions.
    - What worked?
    - What could have worked better?
    - If I could change one thing about the final product right now, what would I change?
    - If I could change one thing about the process we used, what would I change?
    - What did I use in the process that I learned in this classroom?
    - Is something I learned from this process applicable elsewhere in school?
    - Any other thoughts?

Visit **go.SolutionTree.com/instruction** for a free reproducible version of this figure.

Rube Goldberg Machine

A Rube Goldberg machine is an overly complicated chain reaction with the goal of completing a simple act. For example, a marble bumps into a toy monkey with cymbals in its hands; the cymbals open to release a string, which lowers a bucket; and so forth. These machines get their name from artist Rube Goldberg, who drew cartoons of such machines. Rather than draw them, as Goldberg did, students break into groups of three or four and build sections that will be combined into a classwide machine. Figure 8.12 shows an example of what it looks like to design one of these machines.

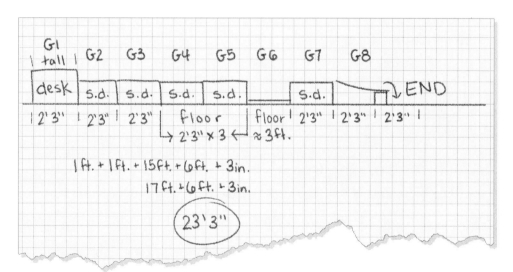

FIGURE 8.12: Sample Rube Goldberg machine layout.

There are many examples of Rube Goldberg machines on the internet. One example encompassing music, silliness, and a fantastically wide range of energy transfers is the "This Too Shall Pass" music video by the band OK Go (2010). A teacher can show this first to pique student interest. The video is such a fitting example of a Rube Goldberg machine in action, all a teacher needs to say after showing it to a design-minded classroom is "We're going to do that!" You can include a goal for the machine to "work for," too, for added excitement and to add a sense of direction. When I do this project in my class, my goal at the end of the project is for the Rube Goldberg machine to somehow pull away a curtain or pull up a cover to reveal a portrait of the class.

Teachers should use this project because it is a difficult project near the scale of the cardboard arcade, but more challenging. This can occur near the end of the year as a final assessment of how students have grown accustomed to the design-minded classroom. This project has an added level of difficulty because students need to think about their section and take into account what groups are doing before and after them; those groups are directly impacting the students' work, and the students' work is directly impacting the group following them. This is the reason the Rube Goldberg machine is an excellent choice for the final big project of the year. This is design thinking as a universal whole. It helps students *see the matrix*, if you will.

What Will Students Accomplish?

As a result of this lesson, students will achieve the following learning goals.

- ▶ Students will learn engineering concepts like simple machines that use the following.
  - Pulleys
  - Inclined planes
  - Wheels
  - Wedge
- ▶ Students will learn scientific concepts, such as the following.
  - Friction
  - Gravity
  - Inertia
  - Kinetic and potential energy

  The students have to know these things because they need to be able to communicate clearly within their own groups and with the groups that their choices will impact. And the expectation is those conversations are more academic than "Then this thing is going to hit that thing and it's going to fall, but it'll also make the next thing go because *look*."
- ▶ You can help students create figurative or metaphorical Rube Goldberg machines by doing the following.
  - If applicable to the curriculum, have students plot out the entire story of *Romeo and Juliet* and how one action causes another action until, at the end, a cup of "poison" pours into the waiting mouth of the heartbroken hero and a knife plunges into the chest of the very confused heroine. You can do this with any story heavily featuring a cause-and-effect plot structure.

- Use a Rube Goldberg machine to teach complicated chemical reactions, especially the kind that might be frowned upon if done for real.
- Have one student say one gossip-based thing to another, and all of a sudden, fake Instagram accounts appear all over the place and cyberbullying steps in to blow the rumor out of proportion. This is a perfect way to talk about how the rumor mill works in school, where students may bully each other using social media.

▸ Learn communication and teamwork, such as by asking and answering the question, "How are the choices you are making impacting those with whom you share this classroom and the world?"

Expect each group's section to involve two or three reactions. For example, a marble will roll down a ramp and impact a toy car that is being gently held in place in some way. The impact of the marble jostles the car loose (reaction one), and the car begins to roll down the ramp. A string is attached to the car, and once the car reaches the end of the ramp and falls to the floor, this string will pull loose another car set on a higher ramp (reaction two), and that car will move on to the next group's section.

The groups will need to make sure their reactions work with each other and are repeatable and easily reset. The groups will also all have to communicate to the groups on either side of their section of the machine to be sure the prior group's reaction will trigger theirs and theirs will trigger the following group's.

The final expectation of the project is a massive Rube Goldberg machine successfully completes its cycle with zero student intervention after the first reaction is triggered.

There are a lot of moving parts in this project. Yes, that was a pun.

What Are the Teacher Considerations?

The following sections describe three issues teachers might run into and what teachers can do about them as they embark on this project.

Possible Issue 1: Confidence

Much like the cardboard arcade, this project doesn't look like anything until it suddenly looks like what it is. There's not really a better way to explain it.

▸ **How a teacher should address it:** On Wednesday morning, the teacher will probably stand in the middle of their room while nursing a stress headache because these students' ideas aren't working and might not be any good. Their blueprint was good, though, so there's hope. On Wednesday afternoon or Thursday morning, when 80 percent of the groups are ready to start the second testing phase (which in this case is linking pieces together), it starts to look like a real machine. It's a complicated, slightly messy, possibly wobbly machine held together with tape and held breaths, but a machine nonetheless.

▸ **How students often address it:** They will do the work until it is done. This is the end of the year. It will come together. Get out of the way, hold back on commentary, and let the students work.

Possible Issue 2: Gravity

Everyone's first instinct is to use an inclined plane as the way to generate and transfer energy—all the marbles roll downhill, all the cars roll downhill, everything falls onto the next thing. But if, for example, seven groups each needed a distance drop of six inches for their reactions to carry the requisite energy, and they each had two reactions requiring a six-inch drop, the machine would end up with a foot of drop per group and seven feet of drop total. The starting point would need to be much too high up, and the energy transfers would be boring, linear, and simple.

▸ **How a teacher should address it:** Ask for volunteer groups that are willing to have their final energy transfer (the one that triggers the next group) somehow go up instead of down. This could involve the falling car pulling the string above it or a stick slowly swinging like a baseball bat to start the next section.

▸ **How students often address it:** Students are flexible, and since the teacher has drawn out the potential level changes (seen in figure 8.12, page 144), they understand the limitations they are working under. Those limitations force creativity and make the transfers more interesting.

Possible Issue 3: Failure

It is hard to make Rube Goldberg machines work. If every energy-transfer point is 90 percent reliable, and there are seven groups with three energy-transfer points each (totaling twenty-one transfer points), the chances of all those points not failing at the same time are 0.9 to the twenty-first power. That total is 0.109, which is 11 percent when you round up. An 11 percent success rate means that out of one hundred tries, your Rube Goldberg machine will work eleven times.

▸ **How a teacher should address it:** Accept the mathematics. Tell the students the mathematics in simple terms they'll understand, and then add something like, "This will not be easy, and it will not go quickly. But if we're exact with our designs, and if we communicate well, we can make it work."

▸ **How students often address it:** Students need to test vigorously and repeatedly to get their transfers as close to 100 percent reliable as they can. The machine won't work most times, even if everything was well built and tested. This is also why each student section needs to be easy to reset for another test. Students can make small adjustments once the entire machine is together, and eventually, things will work out. Sometimes, all a ramp needs is a better wall.

This project ends with a lot of failure. It ends with conversations about patience and perseverance. It ends as an amazing amount of tension builds in the classroom. But if it's built well, it will work. Each transfer will trigger the next exactly as students imagined it would, until finally, the machine pulls off the napkin and reveals the class portrait. When everything works, the entire room explodes into cheers. It's beautiful. Figure 8.13 is a quick project build guide for implementing the Rube Goldberg machine project in your classroom.

Guide to Build: A Rube Goldberg Machine

In this project, student groups will collaboratively build a fully functioning Rube Goldberg machine.

Supplies

- Example videos of Rube Goldberg machines in action (like OK Go's [2010] music video "This Too Shall Pass")
- Blueprint
- Building supplies (paper, pencils, cardboard, tape, scissors, and so on)

Design Process

1. Define:
   - *What's the problem?* We want to reveal a picture of the class in the most roundabout way possible.
   - *What's the goal?* Design and build a clever, classwide, multistep Rube Goldberg machine.
2. Design:
   - *How can we solve the problem?* Students submit blueprints for approval.
3. Build:
   - *How do we create a solution?* Students work together to build their section of the machine and link it to every other section.
4. Test and revise: Try out the solution and respond to data.
5. Reflect: *What did we learn?* Reflect individually or in groups using the key questions.
   - What worked?
   - What could have worked better?
   - If I could change one thing about the final product right now, what would I change?
   - If I could change one thing about the process we used, what would I change?
   - What did I use in the process that I learned in this classroom?
   - Is something I learned from this process applicable elsewhere in school?
   - Any other thoughts?

FIGURE 8.13: Guide to build a Rube Goldberg machine.

Visit go.SolutionTree.com/instruction for a free reproducible version of this figure.

Marionettes

The marionette project is what it sounds like. Having the simplest-possible project names saves time. Build a puppet, specifically a marionette, which is a puppet controlled by strings from above (see figure 8.14). Note that this project has *never* been completed in my classroom. The Great Stay Home (the COVID-19 pandemic) derailed this project before we finished it. As such, part of your teacher brain is thinking this could be the one to fail on all levels. I have included this project in this book for two reasons. First, it has value and there's a way to do it right. Second, even if it failed for me, that doesn't mean it would fail for someone else. This book can't mention the value of failure throughout and *not* include something that might have ended up failing in the classroom.

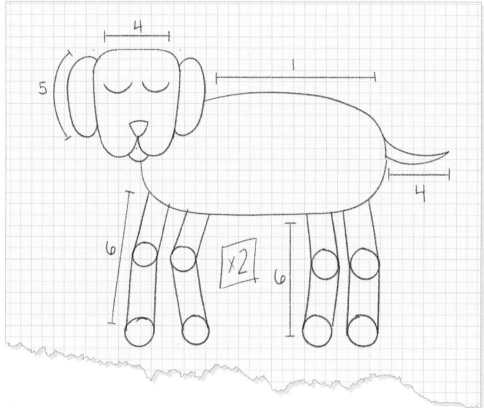

FIGURE 8.14: Sample design for a marionette.

The final project expectation is a simple marionette puppet with three or four string connection points and maybe twice as many pivot points that a student can control. The students design their marionette, they choose how it should move, and they design to solve the problem of how to make it move.

I will be completely honest here. We made marionettes because I wanted to see whether we could. I bought one at a state fair, put it in my classroom, and left it up until I could puzzle out a reason it would be in my classroom. The students gave me a clue by asking if they could make their own. A student-driven idea? Sounded great to me.

What Will Students Accomplish?

The biggest learning goal is simply "Can we make working marionettes?" A justification for this project arrived when I learned a story in our reading textbook was a play, and it talked about puppetry and puppet performance in plays. Justification for the project and the learning goals to share with students and the administration was the class would build puppets, then write scripts around the puppets, and then perform those scripts as plays starring the puppets. But really, the project exists just to see if the class can do it.

What Are the Teacher Considerations?

The following sections describe two issues teachers might run into and what teachers can do about them as they embark on this project. These may not be the most pertinent problems that come up during this project, because I was only able to run it once. If you run into any problems conducting this project in your classroom, I want to hear about it!

Possible Issue 1: String Control

Marionettes are *way* harder to build than people might think they are. Even simple ones with few pivot points and string connections tend to move with their own minds. I underestimated the ease with which the controls could be strung.

▸ **How a teacher should address it:** I did not give my students enough time to research marionettes before we started, which resulted in us having to stop after a very frustrating day and a half, go back to the drawing board, research deeper, design more thoughtfully, and start again. That's not a bad thing; it's an important lesson for the students to learn. Give your students plenty of time to research marionettes, and have at least one on hand as an example.

▸ **How students often address it:** My students were pushing through and experimenting, as well as asking for a chance to go back to their research.

Possible Issue 2: Creation of a Three-Dimensional Figure

I noted that my students were making flat objects. So, the group that was making a dog was using only one piece of cardboard for the body of the dog and only one for the head. Those students had forgotten, in their excitement to get to the build (and in my misunderstanding of the difficulty of the project), to include depth in their blueprints.

▸ **How a teacher should address it:** I should have stepped back and had everyone look again at their blueprints, then redraw them with depth measurements.

▸ **How students often address it:** At some point, the students would have realized their error and brought it to my attention if they beat me to it, and then we would have gone back to the drawing board.

My planned ending for the project was to have groups of students write and perform scripts using their marionettes as the characters in the stories. The performance part of the project would work. Unfortunately, all marionettes from the inaugural attempt are in the garbage somewhere because students put them down one day, and the next day, the school was closed on account of the 2020 global pandemic. I kept the marionettes around in hopes that we would really be back after a few weeks, as we were all initially told, but in the end, they had to be scrapped.

I believe in this project; I believe in its difficulty and its layers and the multitude of ways I could find to use student-made, complex puppets in the classroom. That's why it's in this book. I'm a working teacher, and every single project described in this chapter changes every year. This is a good project that hasn't yet found completion in a classroom.

If you do try this project and are successful, please share it with me at the *Cardboard Classroom* website (https://cardboardclassroom.com). I would be excited to see how the marionettes came to life for you. Otherwise, please find the quick project build guide for marionettes in figure 8.15.

Guide to Build: Marionettes

Students will design and construct functioning marionettes on strings.

Supplies

- At least one working marionette as an example
- Blueprint
- Building supplies (paper, pencils, cardboard, tape, scissors, and so on)

Design Process

1. Define:
   - *What's the problem?* How do we use what we know to make a working marionette?
   - *What's the goal?* Design and build a marionette.

2. Design:
   - *How can we solve the problem?* Students submit blueprints for approval.

3. Build:
   - *How do we create a solution?* Students work together to build a marionette.

4. Test and revise: Try out the solution and respond to data.

5. Reflect: *What did we learn?* Reflect individually or in groups using the key questions.
   - What worked?
   - What could have worked better?
   - If I could change one thing about the final product right now, what would I change?
   - If I could change one thing about the process we used, what would I change?
   - What did I use in the process that I learned in this classroom?
   - Is something I learned from this process applicable elsewhere in school?
   - Any other thoughts?

FIGURE 8.15: Guide to build marionettes.

Visit go.SolutionTree.com/instruction for a free reproducible version of this figure.

The Joy of Specific Designs

I conceived of these seven projects in my design-minded classroom, but they perfectly embody the goals and spirit of project-based learning and are applicable in most classrooms (although maybe with some details or curricular source materials changed). They inspire creativity, fully follow the design process, and connect to most standard curricula. As often as I encourage you to create your own projects (because it's so much fun, in addition to all the actual, practical benefits of inventing design projects), I include these as base models for you to test-drive in your classroom when you feel ready. It'll be up to you to assess whether your students are ready for these projects. The next chapter will show you how making learning assessments and preparing for tests aren't obstructive to creating a design-minded classroom; rather, assessment and design mindedness belong together and enrich each other in some ways, even if assessment in a design-minded classroom might look different from anything you've seen before.

CHAPTER 9

Assessment in the Design-Minded Classroom

The trial never ends. We wanted to see if you had the ability to expand your mind to new horizons. And for one brief moment, you did.

—*Q in* Star Trek: The Next Generation

Of all the things distinguishing a nondesign-minded classroom from a design-minded classroom, assessment is likely the most noticeable. Well, assessment and cardboard. This chapter gets into the details of what it looks like to assess student learning. First, it considers teacher evaluation and data-driven instruction, as they are the most frequent topics of conversation when design-minded teachers talk with other teachers. One question in particular always comes up during these teacher-to-teacher conversations, whether they occur in a workshop or in the hallway between classes. Sometimes, teachers ask it bluntly. Sometimes, they whisper it following a professional development session or send it in a private direct message. That question is, "What does your principal think?"

A routine part of being a teacher is the self-evaluation meeting with a building or district administrator. Before the meeting, teachers usually rank themselves in multiple aspects of their job, from professionalism to student rapport to subject-matter knowledge. Usually, they do this on a five-point scale, with one being far below expectations, two being approaching expectations, three being meeting expectations, four being above expectations, and five being well above expectations, though some such tools use a four-point scale or even a check mark–based scale (✓–, ✓, and ✓+). Opinions on the effectiveness of such assessment tools vary, but even if they're useful, most teachers—most *humans*—generally have a hard time marking themselves low on the scale (Darling-Hammond, 2013; Stiggins, 2014). The results often show lots of threes and fours. Being a design-minded teacher means accepting threes, even twos, in two categories: (1) organization and (2) assessment (or their equivalents).

By this point in the book, it's probably clear why being design minded presents challenges around organization. This isn't to say being design minded necessitates mess and disorder, but such classrooms will inevitably look different. Student work products will naturally accumulate. Boards and notes will look different. These classrooms have a different kind of organization. In my (Doug's) classroom, I have a routine of explicitly teaching students where to find things they might need at any time, how to get access to things needing adult supervision, and where to store things. Teachers know where everything is. Students know where everything is. It's just that where it is might include "that pile of stuff, halfway down." That sort of organization tends to break rubrics (and cause stress for some students, while feeling more comfortable for others). In this chapter, we get into how evaluation works in a design-minded classroom. Despite personal reservations about standardized testing, it's still vital to consider how teachers evaluate themselves (or are evaluated), how they prepare the class for tests, and how they use checklists and rubrics to keep learning consistent.

Teacher Evaluation

Even the most open-minded, flexible, and design-minded school principals and assistant principals are under strictures. The district administration, superintendent, or board has expectations of them. The state has expectations of them. The federal government has expectations of them. The parents have expectations of them. And right in the middle of the sea of expectations is the brave school principal, the admiral of it all. Surrounding every principal is a fleet of teachers, each seeking to achieve the same grade-level expectations but nevertheless captaining their ship of students in their own way. All ships are mostly doing the same thing, many of them working with practiced crews following routines with well-oiled smoothness. And then maybe a little ahead, maybe a little behind, always off to the left a little more than the admiral might want, there's the design-minded ship. Its crew members are resewing the sails again, trying out a different rigging, and taking apart pieces of the deck because someone had a better idea for the crew quarters. *And they're doing this over and over again, all the time.*

What is an admiral to do? How does the admiral (the principal) evaluate a teacher when it seems so very much happening on the ship is nonstandard? The answer lies in a different book we're not qualified to write. However, my (Doug's) experiences as a design-minded teacher in different schools can provide some insight for such teachers and administrators who encounter design-minded teachers. Taken together, these experiences shed light on what can work and what likely won't—how a design-minded teacher and an administrator who doesn't practice design-minded thinking can build a successful relationship, and how without that work, they're likely to crash and smash against rocky shoals. The following two sections examine experiences at two schools, with names, places, and identifying details changed for this book.

Administrative Experience at Rockaway Elementary School

The staff at Rockaway Elementary School, like at most schools in the United States, were predominantly white women. The school had few students of color and no teachers of color. Some of the teachers were the daughters of women who'd taught there before, and they'd inherited their mothers' bulletin board decorations and classroom knickknacks. These details were not unique to Rockaway Elementary, and are part of a larger pattern of schools, especially elementary schools, coded as traditional, feminine spaces (Borgioli Binis, 2018a).

The administrator tasked with teacher evaluation was the assistant principal, Ms. Anderson. She had a clear sense of what a classroom should look like, the way it should be run, the way lesson plans should be written, and the way grades and evaluations should be done. She was an efficient administrator who took pride in managing a staff of professional educators who were consistently on the same page and consistently moving their students forward.

It would be unfair to Ms. Anderson, or others with a similar leadership style, to claim the tensions between me and her were solely related to gender dynamics. I probably had an easier time experimenting with design-minded teaching because I was one of the few men on the faculty, and there likely was an expectation my classroom would be different (Smith, 2012). But in terms of teacher observation and her goals for the teachers in her charge, Ms. Anderson concluded my classroom was too different, too messy, too loud, and too much. She raised concerns about the amount of cardboard used for lessons and struggled with my explanations, likely because I struggled to provide concise answers—I hadn't yet fully developed my design-minded teaching.

Conversations about curriculum had the same tensions. In one instance, Ms. Anderson stopped by for an informal visit, and when a student told her the class was writing plays, she asked me about the disconnect between what the students were doing and the pacing plan's expectations. I explained, "The play is a summary. See, the students are having to carefully reread the story and then rewrite it in their own words but as action and dialogue. Then they'll perform it. So really, they are summarizing it twice, because first is the script and second is the performance."

She replied something to the effect of "The standard is students learn to write essays where they summarize things. You are wasting time doing all this other stuff and falling off the pacing guide." Repeatedly, we found ourselves at an impasse. Soon after, I made a decision I would *not* recommend to new design-minded teachers: I went to the principal with my concerns. It didn't go well. I started the following year in a different school, having been up-front in interviews about my design-minded pedagogy.

From my experiences at Rockaway Elementary, I took away two lessons.

1. **Be prepared:** Teachers are obligated to answer administrators' and parents' questions about student learning, standards, and activities, and to do so clearly, concisely, and correctly. It's also obligatory that teachers make sure

students can answer questions about not just what they're doing but what they're learning—and students can answer not just because an administrator asked but because they understand how designing a Skee-Ball game connects to angles and measurement.

2. **Fit matters:** Honesty is a great way to find a fitting school community. When applying to work at Rockaway Elementary, I didn't tell the interview committee about my developing design-minded identity. It simply didn't occur to me to mention it because it was still in an embryonic form at the time; I didn't know what it was or whether it was important. Administrators should know as soon as possible if teachers plan on deviating from the standard methods of teaching, as it builds trust between the two and avoids mismatched expectations in the future. Being honest about the intention to create a design-minded classroom creates an opportunity to sell the idea of your pedagogy.

I was fortunate and privileged to be able to leave an ill-suited school and interview until I found a more fitting school. If you are considering adopting a design-minded approach to the classroom, start the conversation with an administrator today. Be honest about what you want to accomplish and why you're experimenting.

Administrative Experience at Goldfield Elementary School

My relationship with the administrator at Goldfield Elementary School was different from the beginning. Instead of giving answers reflecting what I thought the administrator wanted to hear, I was honest: I said I was a design-minded teacher who planned on structuring my classroom as a design space where students would build, fail, iterate, and explore. On a tour of the building during the interview process, the principal, Ms. Zine, explained her approach to lesson plans, curriculum, and data. Ms. Zine went on to explain data were more than quantitative values like numbers; they were qualitative measures like student work samples, parent perception surveys, and more. She also shared her identity as an administrator: she was an art-minded leader. She specifically said the words, "I believe teaching is an art." She shared she saw teaching as an art informed but not dictated by science. Her job was to ensure all students in the school were learning, and she would look to me for evidence to confirm students were learning.

It's difficult to stress how important and impactful those early candid conversations were. I would eventually learn I wasn't special; the principal had similar conversations with every new teacher. In effect, she collected the data she needed from all her teachers to meet them where they were. Her faculty included anti-racist teachers, traditional teachers, teachers with maker spaces, teachers who did service-learning projects with their students, and teachers who likely taught the way they were taught. Because of her leadership style, Ms. Zine actively supported individual teacher identity and pedagogical practice with the goal of continuous improvement.

In addition to actively supporting teachers' pedagogical practice tied to their identity, the principal kept a close watch for evidence of student learning. She was incredibly organized and knew the standards and expectations of every grade level and classroom. But she also started from a place of trust her teachers would do right by their students. As part of the trust agreement, she taught her teachers her expectations and boundaries. These involved meeting informally with me to discuss instructional end goals and instructional detours. That allowed me to *re*fine my practice instead of feeling compelled to *de*fine it. When something went wrong, her door was open; she expected teachers would walk in, discuss, plan, and make sure it didn't happen again. When things went well, she was first to admire students' finished products and celebrate updates from teachers. She helped educators change what didn't work and increase the efficiency of what did.

This isn't to say everything was smooth sailing all the time. I consistently scored low on organization during teacher evaluations because a design-minded classroom can be messy and it's often hard to contain the multitudes of what's happening in the neat and tidy boxes required for lesson and unit plans. My classroom is a work in progress. And then there's the tension around the large-scale, state-mandated standardized tests. Oh, *yes*. The state tests.

Test Preparation in the Design-Minded Classroom

There is likely no classroom magic like the magic of a design-minded classroom when everything is humming along. Every group is working well together, failure is met with laughter and a flurry of solutions, and students are doing well on formative assessment measures, proving they're not just doing stuff; they're learning stuff too. These moments seem to be most common in the late autumn and early spring when everyone has settled into routines and structures and knows what they are doing. But, alas, springtime also brings the large-scale, state-mandated tests required of public school students in grades 3–8 in the United States. No matter how smooth the ocean was before, the arrival of these tests is akin to a hurricane—lots of water, stress, noise, and fury, and then a disconcerting stillness somewhere in the middle.

There are lots of different ways to approach how to prepare students for such tests, and before we get into what teachers can or should do, we're going to spend a moment on what teachers *shouldn't* do. Basically, don't do what I did in my early years of being a design-minded teacher who had to prepare my students for large-scale tests. As in my interactions with the vice principal at Rockaway Elementary, I made a mistake. I mistakenly assumed my students could handle anything because they could think around corners, adapt their learning, and be flexible. As if expert yachters could handle a warship. They can't. Not unless someone teaches them how to transfer their skills to a different format.

State assessments fall into the *must-do* category for nearly all public school teachers, regardless of their identity or pedagogical approach. Ignoring them doesn't work.

Wishing them away doesn't work either. In a design-minded classroom, the problem of externally mandated tests becomes just one of the many problems the teacher tasks students to solve. You can harness, tame, and manage the hurricane. The following sections offer a few ways to handle test preparations in a design-minded way.

Test Prep Approach 1: Ignore the Tests

In the beginning of my transition from a more traditional teacher to a design-minded one, I was so wrapped up in the beauty of teaching students to be design minded, so focused on seeing how big and creative we could get, I forgot to teach the students some of the more basic things they needed to know to do well on tests. My scores were lower than those of my colleagues. My students didn't show the growth other students in their grade did.

It made for a serious conversation with my principal at Goldfield Elementary, but not an awkward one, as she'd laid the groundwork for her expectations, and I'd kept her informed of my pedagogical decisions and goals. I detailed the growth I was seeing and expressed frustration that said growth wasn't showing up on the assessments. She'd been in my classroom, and she understood. She had firsthand experience with what I was saying.

THINKING LIKE A DESIGNER

This is a secret to being a successful design-minded teacher: invite admins into the room. Administrators, for the most part, love being asked to come into classrooms to watch lessons. Teachers rarely ask a principal to come in; they usually have to schedule a visit as part of an evaluation or observation. Design-minded classrooms are fun, and nothing will get a good administrator on a teacher's side like seeing students enjoying being at school. It also gives teachers a common framework through which they can discuss their class.

In our planning conversation, Ms. Zine and I looked at how I could couple her expectations with my teaching mindset. Because she was open and honest with me about her expectations, while also being open to my ideas and accepting of my unconventional way of teaching, we were able to strike a balance that ultimately made me a better teacher.

As an example, she helped me restructure my reflection process so it required all students to author a full essay and bring in external sources. She helped me pace my projects more effectively so a traditional lesson came before and after each project, and minilessons appeared throughout based on the space between what I was seeing in my students' work and the identified learning targets. These lessons included explicit instruction from me on the concept of generalizing learning and asked students to name how they could generalize their learning, and the next week, students would put their words into action by completing something. By generalizing their learning, students would, for example, go from understanding that a small marble would not transfer enough energy to a heavy toy car to make it move, to understanding that mechanical energy transfer occurs when a moving object acts on a stationary object via work. The energy is moving but staying in the same form. They would also focus on the content they were learning and utilizing during the project. For example, if students were learning about energy transfer during their build, I would be sure to include focused lessons on potential and dynamic energy to scaffold the discoveries students were making on their own. Those experiences helped move me into a different, more design-minded approach to test prep.

Test Prep Approach 2: Do Design-Minded Test Prep

(Spoiler: this is the approach both authors recommend.) Teaching students who spend their year in a design-minded classroom how to take large-scale, state-mandated standardized tests makes for a flurry of mixed messages for students. After months of being encouraged to fail and iterate, they're told they get *one chance* to solve a problem. Days, sometimes hours, after debating and discussing with their classmates how to fix or do something, they're told they cannot ask for help or help each other. Because testing comes in many forms, they have to show their learning in this form in a different way from what their learning looked like the rest of the year. Helping students make a transition requires a thoughtful, systemic approach, and a design-minded worldview offers a powerful starting point.

The first tension at hand is answering the question, "What is the problem we're trying to solve?" The answer likely varies from design-minded teacher to design-minded teacher, but in all cases, it's probably not "The problem of low test scores." That reflects a traditional or inherited approach, an approach teachers take because they think they're supposed to take it, or because they saw other teachers take it. A commitment to being design minded isn't about the short term; it's about the long-term impact of combining background knowledge with application. Teachers can apply that same type of thinking to preparing students for large-scale, state-mandated standardized testing. Table 9.1 (page 160) compares a traditional approach to a design-minded approach.

To further envision what design-minded test prep looks like, consider what observers would see in design-minded classrooms: they would witness teachers focused on fostering the long-term application of skills, creating community, and ensuring students know they are supported above and beyond any test. If the teacher mentions scores or performance levels, they are framed as part of a bigger picture or series of data points. In a tangible

TABLE 9.1: Traditional Test Prep Versus Design-Minded Test Prep

Traditional or Inherited Approach *Test Prep Done by Rote*	Design-Minded Approach *Test Prep Done Right*
The focus is on: • Increasing students' scores • Decreasing reliance on individual thinking • Increasing right-answer thinking	The focus is on: • Extending skills beyond the day of the test • Decreasing student anxiety • Increasing students' sense of control and metacognition
The goal is finishing workbook activities, refining and improving proficiency in a skill.	The goal is transferring already-taught, already-learned skills and understandings to the test medium.
When teachers ask the students to share their thinking, the goal is to ensure all students are doing it the "right" way.	When teachers ask the students to share their thinking, the goal is to highlight individual student approaches and strategies.
Teachers model thinking around answering a given question with statements like, "This is how you should answer this question," and "Here's the right way to solve this problem."	Teachers model the skill-transfer concept with statements like, "This is what I'm thinking as I take this test," and "This is what the skill looks like in our classroom, but this is also what the skill looks like for the test."
Large school gatherings around the test focus on communicating a sense of personal responsibility. ("I know I can count on you to do your best.") A particular score (for example, level 3) is treated as a target for everyone.	Large school gatherings around the test focus on a sense of community and togetherness. ("We're in this together. We know how amazing you are.")
Administration takes a hands-off approach, leaving test prep up to individual teachers. The most frequent response to the students' concerns is "You're smart; don't worry about the test."	Administration takes the temperature of the school, classrooms, and individual students and answers all questions to respond to rumors and speculation.
The needs of students from historically marginalized groups are ignored or addressed in front of all students. Teachers of color may be tasked with addressing the needs of students of color.	The needs of students from stereotyped groups (such as students of color, students who experience poverty, and anxious students with high expectations for themselves) are addressed to reduce stereotype threat, not increase it.
Leaders talk the talk by reporting they are diminishing pressure, but there is a disconnect between their actions and their words. The state assessment scores drive many conversations, including local data-driven conversations.	Leaders walk the walk by making concerted efforts to diminish pressure or stress around the tests. They work to develop a culture in which the state assessments are only one of many data sources used to determine students' areas of strength and need.

Source: © 2020 by Learner-Centered Initiatives, Ltd. All rights reserved. Adapted with permission.

sense, this means celebrations for learning unrelated to state tests are as big as, or bigger than, those for the state tests. In contrast, in classrooms that aren't design minded, one is more likely to hear conversations focused on individual students doing their best or the implication students are expected to hit a minimum standard (for example, level 3 or proficiency), and it's a target or goal for all students.

Finally, and perhaps most importantly, a demarcation between schools that do test prep right and schools that do it by rote is how they attend to the needs of students from historically marginalized or underserved groups (like students of color or students who experience poverty) as well as anxious students with high expectations for themselves. The rote approach is to treat test prep as if one method works for *all* students regardless of their needs. When schools treat test prep as a design problem, teachers recognize they need to thoughtfully seek out resources on stereotype threat and engage with students and their families around their specific needs and concerns.

Stereotype threat is best understood as a theory about the baggage people carry into tests and situations that has less to do with their abilities than how they perceive their abilities (Inzlicht & Schmader, 2012). For example, there is a stereotype in the United States that girls are worse at mathematics than boys are. Research suggests that if girls are reminded of their gender moments before they take a science test, they are likely to perform worse than if they were not reminded of their gender (Inzlicht & Schmader, 2012). A design-minded teacher can help students understand and counteract those stereotypes to control their own story and manage their own stress. Watching short clips of women, especially women of color, such as Mae Jemison (2002) giving her TED Talk where she talks about her accomplishments and life as an astronaut can also help counteract these stereotypes.

Grades by Design

There's no point easing gently into this: being design minded does not make grading easier. If anything, grading becomes much more time consuming and complicated, especially at first, because there are so many moving parts. Here's a secret you shouldn't share with parents (because many of them were brought up thinking this word is important) or administrators (same reason; if you're an administrator, please forget this as soon as you finish reading): I never use the *g*-word in my classroom. Ever. I never mention grades. Instead, I use assessment tools (more on these in the following section) and detailed, high-quality feedback (Lalor, 2012). Generally speaking, when giving feedback, I follow the same structure for every student: "I like how you _____ here. Don't forget to _____. Otherwise, you're _____."

I use percentages when going over tests and quizzes because they help students think about growth and progress. For example:

> *"If you got ten right, then you got 75 percent of the questions correct. The goal is for you to be at or above 75 percent. That's the goal. Above 75 percent, and you know your stuff. The further below 75 percent you are, the harder you need to think about coming to me later and asking for help so we can bring the grade up if you*

> *decide to retake the test. I also want you to think about whether this score is better than the last mathematics test or not. Growth is growth, and growth is the goal."*

The only *g*-words related to assessment in my classroom are *goals* and *growth*.

The reason for this is simple: I don't want students reducing their learning to a single letter or number. During my September opening routines, I'll stress *growth*, *goals*, and *pride*. If students ask later in the year, they may use the *guardian test*, especially if they have expressed concern about their parents' or guardians' opinions, or if their parents or guardians share they routinely check their student's work. The guardian test is a simple question: "Would you be proud to show this to _____?" (where the blank is the student's parents or guardians).

To be sure, not all principals tolerate a classroom without grades. To revisit an earlier point, communication with administrators at the beginning of the design-minded process is *essential*. Start thinking about how to move away from letter or number grades, even if your school requires them, and then start thinking about alternatives. Teachers in a traditional grading environment may find it useful to start to think about transitioning to a standards-based reporting system (Guskey & Bailey, 2010) in which students receive not single grades for each content area but proficiency ratings based on specific curriculum standards. Those in a standards-based reporting system may want to start thinking about how to move to a system that dramatically reconsiders grading, usually called *ungrading* or *de-grading* (Stommel, 2018). Grades are complicated, and there is no easy answer (see table 9.2). They are, perhaps, the greatest design problem a design-minded teacher will face.

TABLE 9.2: Possible Responses to Frequent Student Questions About Grades

Student Question	Possible Teacher Answer
"How long does this have to be?"	"Until it's done."
"Is this good enough?"	"Is it? Did you check it against the checklist and rubric? Did you compare it to the examples?"
"Is this finished?"	"Are you happy with it? Does it fulfill the expectations?"
"I don't know if it's done, though. Really."	"Have you thought about _____?"
"How do I get an *A* on this?"	"How do you knock my socks off? Check the rubric. More importantly, make it good to *you*. Be honestly proud of it."
"Is my score good?"	"How well did you do on the last test? Growth is the goal."

The Classroom Assessment Toolbox

The absence of grades does not mean the absence of assessment. We thought about turning the previous line into a sea shanty or perhaps repeating it for this entire section because it's far and away the most important part of this chapter, but we thought better of it. Instead, we'll say the design-minded classroom is awash with assessment. My second principal (Ms. Zine) clarified data are more than numbers and percentages—data are quantitative and qualitative. Student work samples, videos of student discussions, and transcripts of student discussions are also rich sources of data.

To see their power as meaningful and useful data, it's helpful to reframe *assessment* as the strategic collection of student learning evidence (Lalor, 2017). If a teacher's goal is to understand what students have learned, the teacher has no need to turn evidence into a number. Instead, a design-minded teacher requires a clear sense of the learning goals, standards, and pacing plan. (If you've seen *Moana* [Musker & Clements, 2016], it's similar to Maui teaching Moana to check the stars and the water temperature to find her position in the ocean relative to the stars and land.)

In every design-minded classroom, usually buried under cardboard or sitting next to the stack of cardboard, there's a toolbox. The contents vary depending on the time of year and the level of adult supervision needed for the different tools, but the toolbox features a collection of things students need to accomplish their learning and design goals. A design-minded teacher can't ask students to do something without giving them the tools to do it. Day-to-day assessment in the design-minded classroom is about having a fully stocked, updated-as-needed assessment toolbox, which includes routines, checklists, and rubrics.

Routines

The first, and likely most important, feature of the toolbox is the classroom routines. In the beginning of the year, a design-minded teacher can best prepare students for the differences of the design-minded classroom by explicitly teaching them how to do the following.

- ▸ Work in groups.
- ▸ Find and put away tools and supplies (and assorted rulers from chapter 4, page 53).
- ▸ Get unstuck when stuck (asking for help from a classmate or the teacher).
- ▸ Take part in discussions.
- ▸ Resolve disagreements.
- ▸ Self-assess against short- and long-term learning goals.

You can teach these routines in the moment as needed, such as following the creation of the classroom rules, while teaching the design process, or in anticipation of an upcoming design activity. I document the degree to which students are following the routines I've taught them. I typically rely on verbal or written feedback to let students know what needs to stop, start, or change.

Checklists and Rubrics

Every teacher has experienced giving students a verbal direction, having them affirm they heard you, perhaps even repeat it back, and then watching them go and do the exact opposite of that direction. Relying more on tools like rubrics and checklists than on verbal feedback can avoid that happening on the regular. The key difference between the two types of tools is what the document describes: checklists are about counting while rubrics are about describing. Imagine a teacher asks students to cut a cardboard circle approximately four inches in diameter. Give a ruler to a hundred people who know how to use a ruler, and they'll all be able to say, "Yes, the circle is approximately four inches in diameter," or "No, it's not." Ask those same hundred people whether the cuts are clean, and there will likely be fifty different answers. "Is it four inches in diameter?" is a yes-or-no, zero-or-one question. That's what goes on a checklist (Gawande, 2010). The quality of cuts slides on a scale from messy to sharp. That's what goes on a rubric. When it comes to assessment, teachers can communicate their expectations before, while, or after students work. Table 9.3 describes the different kinds of checklists and when they're most useful.

TABLE 9.3: Different Types of Checklists

Tool	Purpose
Read-Do Checklist	I want to: • Prime students for success before working on a task • Develop a shared language with my students • Provide students with explicit criteria
Do-Confirm Checklist	I want to: • Remind students of things to check after working on a task • Develop a shared language with my students • Provide students with explicit criteria
Self-Assessment Checklist	I want to: • Provide students a way to self-assess before, during, and after their work • Help break down a larger task and support a rubric • Develop a shared language with my students • Provide students with explicit criteria

Rubrics require a little more unpacking. To start with, it's helpful to identify what distinguishes rubrics from other assessment tools. The following are three general attributes of rubrics.

1. **Rubrics are about the quality of work:** *Work* is a general term describing a product students create, a performance they put on, or even the process they follow to do a task. The language of a rubric describes the quality of a piece of work rather than the quantity. If you want to count items in a student's work, you could just create a checklist.

2. **Not all tasks are worthy of a rubric:** Generally speaking, rubrics are used for authentic tasks—tasks you do outside of school (in the "real world"). Frameworks of quality exist in nearly every aspect of life. From professional trades and sports to writing and television, the concept of quality is one people regularly explore and articulate. Rubrics are best for answering questions like the following.

   - "What does quality look like for this task or process?"
   - "What does *better* look like so I can self-assess and revise my work without waiting for your feedback?"
   - "What does it look like when a beginner does this type of project or task? What about when a master does it?"
   - "What does it look like to break the rules or be creative for this type of work? How will I know if I'm *breaking the rules* or doing it wrong?"

3. **The purpose of rubrics is to make intangible concepts of quality accessible to learners:** If a teacher elects to draft out a rubric of any variety, students can help in revising, refining, or establishing examples that support or explain the text (also known as *anchors* or *models*). If students are part of the rubric-development process, they will better understand what quality looks like for the product, process, or performance they will be working on. If a teacher hasn't checked a rubric against student work, developed it with students, or gotten student feedback, it should be considered a draft. Some rubrics, even quality ones, may stay in draft form over a project's duration for revising content or adding or removing anchors and exemplars.

Once you understand what makes a rubric a rubric, the next step is to articulate what makes a rubric worthy of the design-minded classroom, or what you might think of as a *quality rubric*. A quality rubric is the result of defining and communicating expectations. The piece of paper a quality rubric is written or printed on is the product created from the process of articulating expectations for student learning and work. This is to say the document itself is the least important part of the process. It enables and supports conversation between assessor and learner, self-reflection by the learner, or peer review by fellow learners.

Quality rubrics give students a way to reflect on and then improve their work. Telling students what they did wrong doesn't help them do what's right. Meanwhile, the language in quality rubrics focuses on what is present, not just what is absent. In a quality rubric, students should be able to identify where their work falls behind and see what they need to do to improve their work's quality (adding one source won't make the research better unless the source is accurate, high quality, and legitimate). Teachers may create a rubric to support their grading efforts, save time, or quickly convey feedback. They may create a quality rubric with students to do the following.

- Communicate expectations.
- Prompt student learning through self-assessment.
- Help with grading, save time, and improve feedback.

A quality rubric is *not* meant to stifle students' creativity or to embarrass a student who hasn't yet obtained mastery. In a quality rubric, the highest level describes what exceeds the standard or expectation and may include language about transcending rules, or clarifying a new, innovative, or unexpected approach to a task. Meanwhile, the lower levels describe what someone new to a project may do. The example rubric in figure 9.1 was created for a fifth-grade design-minded classroom where students were tasked with researching a topic and pitching an idea. Early drafts from students revealed many were just cutting and pasting sentences and paragraphs they found on the internet. So, after noticing this and explaining it, the teacher developed a rubric with students for academic honesty.

Cover Song	Mixtape	Honest Original	Exemplar
The work is mostly cobbled together from other people's work, and I'm trying to pass it off as my own. I need to reflect and rewrite before submitting.	The work is mostly other people's, but I tried to make it my own by rearranging their work or by using different words that mean basically the same thing. I need to reflect and revise before submitting.	I've read a variety of sources and combined their thoughts, words, and ideas into new ones that reflect my thinking. Every time I use someone else's work, I let the reader know by using quotes and citations. I am ready to submit my work.	I combined a variety of diverse sources into new thinking. Every time I use someone else's work, I let the reader know by using quotes and endnotes or footnotes. My citation list includes a brief annotation of each text and my opinion. I am ready to submit my work and share it with others.

Source: Borgioli Binis, 2018b.

FIGURE 9.1: Academic honesty rubric to assess potential plagiarism.
*Visit **go.SolutionTree.com/instruction** for a free reproducible version of this figure.*

Keep in mind that rubrics are not the goal; student understanding of levels of quality is the goal. Before working with students to construct a rubric, consider these guiding questions.

- ▶ Is the task worthy of a rubric? Will students have sufficient time to revise and get feedback?
- ▶ Is the primary goal in designing the rubric to support student self-reflection or to communicate any expectations for grading purposes? If it's the latter, consider using a checklist.
- ▶ What will the students focus on? Product or process? Content or delivery?

In a design-minded classroom, where iteration is the name of the game, students will be constantly giving and receiving feedback. However, without tools like checklists and rubrics, that feedback can often be overwhelming or disconnected from learning targets or instructional goals. In figure 9.2 (page 168), we describe how to design a rubric with your students and involve them in the process of evaluating work examples by conducting a whole-class discussion.

As you conduct your first rubric design with your class, keep in mind the following tips. Consider using real-world examples such as literature, advertisements, video clips, students' work, or projects. Present at least three examples of good-quality work and three examples of bad-quality work. During the discussion, focus the students' attention on the quality of the piece (like mechanics or nice lines), rather than the quantity of what they see. If they provide the same evidence of quality for multiple pieces, put a star or asterisk on the strip. Additionally, if students name an especially good trait or characteristic, consider coding it for use at the highest rubric level.

Consider providing students with dramatically different versions of quality. Before moving on, ask students to generate examples of quality work from their own experiences. How do they know they are good or bad quality? For older students, consider exploring the role of personal opinion in determining quality. How can one person's quality be another person's junk? How do they reconcile this?

This is a good opportunity to instill good constructive-critique practices in the way students think about evaluating the quality of work. As the students talk, remind them to describe what *is* present. You can support this by avoiding the words *not* and *didn't* and restating students' comments into the positive. For example, a student's note, "The author doesn't mention the main character," is more productive if phrased as, "The author focuses on secondary or supporting characters." In the same way, "The bridge fell down" is more helpful as "The support structures gave out under the weight of the bridge." The goal is to create categories describing what is occurring so students can identify their own or their group's work. It's difficult, if not impossible, to prove something doesn't exist. It is much easier to report on what one sees.

Guide to Build: A Collaborative Rubric Design

Supplies

- At least three examples of high-quality work
- At least three examples of lesser-quality work
- Examples of work at a variety of levels for small-group work
- Sentence strips (lined strips of paper about four or five inches high and a foot or so long), and a means of posting them for students to see
- Markers

Steps to Facilitate a Large-Group Discussion

Step 1:

Present students with an example of high-quality work. Pose guiding questions such as the following.

- "How do you know this is good?"
- "What makes it quality?"
- "What about this piece do you like?"

Script student responses on sentence strips, and post them on the whiteboard so students can see. Ask students to generate examples of quality work from their own experiences. Ask, "How do you know they are quality?"

Step 2:

Present the students with an example of low-quality work. Pose guiding questions such as the following.

- "How do you know this isn't good?"
- "What makes it less than quality?"
- "What about this piece do you not like?"

An important note about negative statements: have students focus on what they can see needs work, not what they think the work is missing or doesn't do. Script student responses on sentence strips, and post them on the whiteboard so students can see.

Step 3:

Ask students to look for patterns among both high-quality and lower-quality traits. Have students cluster the sentence strips into possible groups or categories by physically rearranging them. Label each cluster of sentence strips with a heading. Write a definition for the heading in the form of a question the students can use to reflect, such as, "How well did you support your ideas?"

Step 4:

Have the class prioritize each group in terms of importance or value. Create a rubric with these groups, and place the most important dimensions (according to student input) first in the rubric.

Step 5:

Use the traits found in step 1 to begin to flesh out the level below the highest one for each of the identified dimensions. As much as possible, use the students' own wording and examples.

Step 6:

Use the traits found in step 2 to begin to flesh out the lowest level for each of the identified dimensions. As much as possible, use the students' own wording and examples.

Step 7:

Use the traits found in step 1 to begin to flesh out the highest level for each of the identified dimensions. As much as possible, use the students' own wording and examples. The highest level should be above the expected standard of excellence.

Step 8:

Write the descriptors for the second level of the rubric. Remind students the rubric is a draft, and placeholder language at this point is common. The teacher may have to do all the scripting for students who are not yet independent readers.

Step 9:

Ensure all students can see the rubric on a screen or via distributed copies, and break the class into five groups, or one more group than the number of levels in the rubric. Distribute work samples for each level to four of the groups without telling them which level the work stands for. Ask students to use the rubric to match their pieces to a corresponding level.

Step 10:

Make any necessary edits to the rubric, and then distribute the rubric to students with its corresponding activity. Consider a second round of feedback on the rubric after students have an opportunity to work with and reflect on the tool.

FIGURE 9.2: Guide to building a collaborative rubric.

*Visit **go.SolutionTree.com/instruction** for a free reproducible version of this figure.*

As a class, prioritize each category in terms of importance or value. Create a rubric (either on chart paper or on the whiteboard), and place the most important dimension first in the rubric. This generally includes the traits students first notice when they talk about quality unless they've become trained to focus on mechanics. In this case, encourage them to name what makes a product compelling beyond presentation.

By the time students are writing the descriptors for the second level of the rubric in step 8, they will generally be comfortable brainstorming the language. They will probably no longer need support stating evidence in the positive but may need support describing what is "almost there." Remind students the rubric is a draft, and placeholder language at this point is common. The teacher may have to do all the scripting for students who are not yet independent readers.

The Joy of Assessment in the Design-Minded Classroom

Creating assessment tools with students is remarkably like designing anything else. The problem at hand is closing the gap between students' mental models of quality and the teacher's mental model of quality (based on learning targets, standards, or the curriculum plan). Gather evidence of a student-teacher quality-expectations gap by taking anecdotal notes and reviewing the work students produce and how students do during routines and lessons. Students will find the right words and tools for closing the quality-expectations gap during the build phase. Test and revise as needed.

As for grappling with administrative experiences and test preparation, this is where adaptability and flexibility are crucial. Talk to your administrator as soon as you know you have a plan or intent to start adding to your curriculum. Be prepared to accept only partial approval from the administration, but don't hesitate to push back if their concerns are about the impact on student learning. Share your plan for data collection and how you'll use formative assessment data to test and revise. If you decide to incorporate design-minded teaching into your classroom, be prepared for long and frequent conversations with colleagues, principals, parents, and even students about your plans and your goals for learning. In the next chapter, we'll address some common issues and misconceptions that come up when deciding to become a design-minded teacher and how trust and a realistic outlook work together to make the previously mentioned conversations easier and more productive.

CHAPTER 10

Cure-Alls, Buy-In, and Trust

> The best formula for failure is thinking you've
> got the formula for success.
>
> —*Adam Savage*

I (Doug) have been in the classroom since 2003, teaching across three states, four districts, and four school buildings. I have taught in third, fourth, fifth, and sixth grades in teams of two and teams of six and have been responsible for class sizes ranging from twenty-one students to a bursting thirty-seven. I've lost track of how many principals I've had and how many parent conferences I've held. Similarly, Jennifer has worked with thousands of teachers across the East Coast in the United States, helped design hundreds of assessments and curriculum units, and been a visitor in dozens of classrooms. Even with so much experience, we know there is only one truth to teaching: there is no one best way to teach.

Teaching is a study in tensions between the collective responsibility of a profession and the choices every adult must make about the role they want to play in a student's life. Saying to teachers they must teach a particular way because it's what's *best* for students inevitably leads to confusion. Who gets to say what's best? We're advocates of helping teachers realize their pedagogical identity with the guidance of those who are going alongside and those who have gone before. There are best practices and recommended strategies to help fleets get across the pond, but armadas function best when they're composed of disparate ships, including those piloted by captains who are constantly evolving. Good captains are always keeping an eye on designing a faster sail, a more effective desalination system, and a more comfortable hold. This is to say teachers will and do constantly adjust to meet the needs of the students in front of them.

Over the course of K–12 education, students travel from shore to shore dozens of times under the guidance of dozens of captains. They likely experience everything from tightly locked-down battleships to their own one-person canoe in which they feel adrift. Meanwhile, the resources available to their captain vary wildly because of decisions adults not in schools make. Some students cross each year in well-resourced, ultramodern yachts, while others experience leaky galleons held together by donations and the captain's sheer force of will. Design-minded teaching can't fix those problems, but there are those working to use design thinking to solve larger problems, such as improving sanitation in communities with limited access to water and connecting children who live far from other children to their peers (Parker, Cruz, Gachago, & Morkel, 2021), and we're optimistic.

Even though the impact of an individual teacher adopting a design-minded approach is limited by the classroom walls, there is incredible potential and power in a critical mass of design-minded teachers changing the public's belief about classroom dynamics. To work toward changing public belief, I talk to student teachers at every available opportunity and invite them to consider pushing against the limits they may encounter in a teacher prep program. To be clear, this isn't about branding, selling, or insisting this is *the way* to be a teacher. It's a request that anyone who is responsible for student learning consider their identity and the space they create for students in their classroom. It's less a demand and more an offer. It's also not a magic bullet. In this chapter, as we review ways to push against the status quo and make more room for design-minded thinking in the classroom, we'll explore the misguided search for teaching cure-alls, the importance of community buy-in, and the cornerstone of becoming a design-minded teacher: trust.

Cure-Alls

Becoming a design-minded teacher will not make student behavior troubles fade away. It won't end state-mandated tests or make the school library more culturally responsive. It won't restock science kits. But it *can* help teachers think differently about those tests, how they engage with the class library, and how they use those kits. Even if teachers become fully dedicated to design-minded teaching, their students will still probably have to read terribly boring stories because they're in the pacing guide. Nothing can fix everything.

Becoming and staying a design-minded teacher means constant work and regular failure. It means opening the mind to all possibilities and then trying to grasp them before they fade away when confronted with the realities of pacing guides, state tests, budgets, and that one group of students who mean well but haven't let the teacher finish a sentence without interrupting. Things will go wrong. Adopting a design-minded worldview is exciting because when one is oriented toward learning from failure, fixes become more obvious and solutions more accessible.

To be sure, it's a good thing design-minded teaching isn't a cure-all. Most cure-alls end up being nothing more than snake oil or temporary fixes. Someone who adopts a design-minded approach with the expectation it will fix all the things has forgotten a foundational truth of teaching: teachers must teach. Play is great. Spending six hours a day playing with cardboard isn't likely to end well for anyone, which is to say teaching is hard work. There are many reasons it's so hard, but the most relevant reason for this book is classrooms can be simultaneously boring and unpredictable, and students are simultaneously boring and unpredictable in the best of ways.

Negotiating those tensions requires thoughtfulness, systemic awareness, and plans. Design-minded teaching supports the creation of routines and novelty for students and helps teachers better attend to the short-term and long-term goals. Adopting a design-minded approach makes it easier to see how pieces fit together while fundamentally understanding those pieces are structurally integral to students' lived experiences, which shapes the story they will tell about themselves as leaders and people. Teachers don't do magic. We teach.

Buy-In

I (Doug) consider myself a fiercely independent teacher committed to design-minded teaching. I love working in groups and collaborating with colleagues, and it took me a long time to come to terms with the reality that many of my colleagues are just as committed to their approach to teaching as I am to mine. My door is always open to other teachers, though, and I don't shy away from questions. When asked at department or faculty meetings, in passing in the hallway, or when someone stops by, I try to model what I do in my classroom and honor questions from other teachers by treating them as part of the teachers' data collection process as they design their own classrooms. In my experience, buy-in comes slowly—so slowly, in fact, I often didn't realize it was happening. Even though teachers collaborate, they do the majority of the work alone in the classroom. A faculty with multiple design-minded teachers is wonderful. An entire school organized around design principles is even more so. On the way there, though, two groups' buy-in is essential for a design-minded classroom to work: (1) administration and (2) students.

Administration

Chapter 9 (page 153) recounted how two different administrators responded to my approach to teaching. One stayed firmly planted in her comfort zone. The other one compromised with me. When an administrator says, "At 10:25, every third-grade class will be in the vocabulary section of the same story, and the students will have learned the ten vocabulary words by exactly 10:35, at which point every third-grade teacher will move on to reading comprehension," things go poorly. I know they go poorly because I once taught under such conditions. It was a nightmare for everyone involved.

Teachers can barely breathe, much less develop their teacher identity, under excessive control, to say nothing of being design minded. The same goes for students. A principal is deeply influential for setting the tone of a school. This includes how a teacher approaches the variety of needs involved in student learning. If you are considering trying to go design minded and worry the admin might be hesitant, consider asking them for a few months to give it a try. I once made a deal with one of my principals, which was essentially "If scores drop or goals aren't met over an agreed time period, I'll change. But trust me first. Please." I then invited the principal into the classroom to watch and talk to the students. Often, hesitant administrators need to see design-minded teaching and learning to understand them. Once they see the enthusiasm of the students, once they feel the electricity in the classroom, they usually come around.

Be sure to stay focused on your pedagogical obligations around content and make formative assessment a routine part of the day. The ideal demonstration of administrator buy-in is the simple statement, "I trust you. I want to see the students enjoying learning." Trust is all teachers are asking for (that, and some money to buy supplies).

Teachers who are designers must have their administrators' trust and respect to truly implement these processes. Administrators who are reading this right now: hi, thanks for buying this book. I'm looking at you. Please give your teachers time, trust, and flexibility so they can do this work bravely. But also, as the cliché goes, don't hesitate to trust but verify. Hold design-minded teachers accountable to the promises we make.

Generally speaking, when an administrator comes into a design-minded teacher's room midproject for the first time, the same thing happens. The administrator walks in, stops in the doorway, and takes it in. The teacher does not notice the administrator has come in because they're on the floor with a group or under a table with a group or on top of a table with a group. Or they're standing in the center of the room remembering it's normal to panic about the process at this point because this happens every time and everything will be fine, just be cool. The administrator will go to the teacher, stepping gingerly over students and projects in various stages of construction.

After the administrator picks their way to the teacher and gets their attention, they (hopefully) smile with their mouth if not fully with their eyes. They ask the teacher the question, "So, what are your students learning today?" I hope this is the first question an administrator will ask, instead of "What on earth is happening here?" Asking this first suggests they trust the teacher that something academic is happening (or even see it for themselves). An administrator who is uncomfortable with design thinking can still trust the teacher to be doing their job well. However, the administrator might decide to get more detailed and ask, for example, "It's the reading block right now. Why aren't the students reading?" If the project happening in the room is curriculum motivated, then the teacher would be able to point to any group with books out and say they are actively reading, but they are also deepening their reading through a project. This should be enough to cause the administrator to circle back to "What are your students learning today?"

This is where teachers have the following two choices. The choice they make will reinforce for them and their students how much confidence and trust they have in the process and in the students, and how high their expectations are for the quality of learning of whatever project students are doing.

1. **Play it safe:** Tell the administrator what the students should be learning. After students read a book, this choice might sound like a verbal *I can* statement (Moss & Brookhart, 2012). Here's an example: "At the end of this lesson, students will be able to compare and contrast characters using details and inferences from the text, as well as compare these characters to characters in the previous story." Use simple, observation-friendly, standards-ready, and academically approved professional teacher language.

   This is the simpler, safer choice and the one I do *not* want you to make unless your administrator insists.

2. **Take a risk:** This is the choice I urge you to make. Say to the administrator, "Ask the students what they are learning. And ask them why. They know." Then hold your breath, and send a silent prayer to *Instructus*, the goddess of education. Because this choice is a bigger risk, you must warn your students ahead of time that you will do this every single time a visitor comes to the classroom and asks questions about their learning. Talk to your class in detail about this choice so they know what's coming and why.

Thinking Like a Designer

Teach students about learning targets, and about why adults ask what they're learning and why it matters. Tell students, "If you want to keep doing this kind of learning, you must know what you're learning and why you're learning it."

The first choice is clear and obvious, so let's explore why the second is secretly better. Telling principals to ask students what they are learning and why is a massive risk because, even though we teachers all love and trust each one of our students, there are students we'd prefer not be asked this question. The principals know who those students are too. The students know what they are learning, but can they explain it? Are they on track?

Your confidence students will be able to answer the question is not a magic spell that makes all students completely engaged in the learning and fills their heads with everything they need to know. But it clearly communicates to every learner in the room, including you as the teacher and your school administrator, that students *can* know. Students would miss an opportunity for organic learning if they were laser focused on only what they are supposed to learn. The teacher must be there to guide and clarify and sharpen. But the students learn they can learn from doing on their own as well. And when students reflect out loud with teacher-directed questions and in their writing on their learning, they can share those organic moments and make everyone stronger.

For example, a student once learned the Pythagorean theorem while making a Skee-Ball game. (Remember, from chapter 3, page 37?) That was a total accident. I wish I could claim I had it all planned out and I knew someone would make a Skee-Ball game, so they'd need special measurements, and then I could say, "Look how clever I am for thinking this out." No. It was an accident. It was a pure, organic learning moment that stuck in the student's brain, and it was beautiful to behold. The student mentioned it in their reflection.

I also once had a group of students who were making a wind-powered car but spent 90 percent of their time decorating said car to look like a sloth (sloths were a thing that year for whatever reason). The car ended up being a very pretty but very stationary box. Each time I checked in with the group's members, they insisted they were almost done decorating. They just had to add one more thing. *Just one more, Mr. Robertson.* After the third time, I chose to ride it out, and as expected, they did not have time to start from scratch, so their revision process was focused on fixing anything they could to make their beautifully decorated sloth box into a moving car. They failed the challenge in the end, but they learned an important lesson, and they were willing to let me use it as an example for the whole class for the rest of the year.

To be clear, I did not pick up the sloth box, turn to my class dramatically, and say, "Behold! Look upon what they have wrought, and despair for them! See their failure and learn from it, my younglings!" No, I quietly asked the group in question what they learned from it, and they said, "We learned to get the work done right first, then make it pretty." And I said, "Is it OK if you share with the whole class, not to make fun but because this is a good learning experience for everyone?" They agreed. Reflection does not need to be painful, and it does not need to be individual—not if there's respect for each other and the process. That sloth box is still sitting on top of a shelf in my classroom in a place of honor as a reminder to focus on the work first, then make it pretty.

Students

Supporting student buy-in is often a lot easier than people think. The novelty of the design-minded classroom can go a long way toward capturing students' curiosity, and thus, their interest (Ostroff, 2016). Achieving buy-in requires being consistent and following through on projects and ideas. Students buy into being design minded when both the classroom around them and the teacher communicate, "We're in this together, and this is your class too. I want you to feel ownership." Often, this means giving up things teachers normally control, like seating charts, job charts, exact expectations for final products, and inflexible due dates.

One way to build student buy-in is to start the year, semester, or month with a design activity seemingly disconnected from anything too academic with a capital *A*. I'm fond of the wind-powered cars quick build (see page 123) to start things off. It's fun. The students

get to be in their own groups, and they get to puzzle out something only mildly complicated but still challenging. They get to do something that doesn't feel like regular school.

Buy-in for students can happen within the first thirty seconds or not for weeks.
Some students may never fully engage in design-minded classroom activities. It can also
look different for different students. Some students may take leadership roles. Others
may ask for worksheets to do instead of working with more cardboard. The hard work
of being a design-minded teacher is helping leaders learn to follow and helping the
worksheet fans find the same comfort in the routine of construction and destruction.
Teachers will know their students have bought in because they'll offer alternatives when
given a task. They'll ask for wiggle room or wonder, "What's next?" That can be enough
if the students believe something interesting is coming soon. This may sometimes make
a design-minded teacher feel like Mr. Incredible (from the movie *The Incredibles* [Bird,
2004]) when a child in his neighborhood is watching him closely from the driveway of
Mr. Incredible's home:

> Mr. Incredible: "What are you waiting for?"
> Kid: "I dunno. Something amazing, I guess."

But that means students are still watching. They have bought into the new way of teaching.

Trust

Becoming design minded is less hard than it is scary. It's scary to let go; it's scary to
give over power and control. There's more comfort in teaching the way teachers learned
to teach and the way they think a teacher is supposed to be. It's hard to take a step back
when so much external pressure is telling teachers to step closer, pick up any lost learning, and teach harder, louder, and faster to make up for lost time. And even if a teacher
makes the choice to adopt a design-minded approach, what makes it work? What's the
secret to keeping the ship watertight? Trust.

The sentiment we want to convey sits somewhere between the idea of belief and
confidence and can likely best be described as *relational trust*, which is a collaborative,
dedicated, and intentional effort on the part of the community to improve its school,
achieved through values like respect, personal regard for others, competence, and integ-
rity (Bryk & Schneider, 2002). Instilling these shared values builds relational trust, but
keeping relational trust means the administration has to recognize the vulnerabilities of
teachers and students and authentically engage parents in the learning process whenever possible. A small school size helps build relational trust too (Bryk & Schneider,
2002). While the pandemic has shaken bonds between families and schools, teachers
and administrators, and students and teachers, a design-minded approach can go a long
way toward rebuilding them (Dorn, 2021). All of this is to say put more trust in people. The students can do it if their community lets them. No matter their age, grade, or

individualized education program (IEP) status, trust them. Teachers can do this whether this is their first year or thirty-first. Teachers should trust themselves. Teachers probably already have design-minded elements in themselves and their teaching philosophy. Give them the space to grow.

Part of the trust of being a design-minded teacher is acceptance. There will be struggles and hard times and dips. A design-minded teacher is much like Prince Herbert's father, the king of Swamp Castle, in *Monty Python and the Holy Grail* (Gilliam & Jones, 1975). You build a castle, and it sinks into the swamp. You build a second castle. That one sinks into the swamp. You build a third castle. That one burns down, falls over, and sinks into the swamp. But the fourth castle stays up, built with the knowledge gained from three failed castles and supported by the three failed castles below it. That is the strongest castle. It is a castle built on trust, confidence, and failure.

We believe in the design-minded approach to the elementary classroom. Doug's confidence comes from years of work and experience. Jennifer's comes from being in design-minded classrooms and bearing witness to the mess, the energy, and the learning. She recognizes for many students, a design-minded classroom might be one of the few opportunities that can make them feel like they truly belong in the place called *school*. And so, we trust in your ability to captain a ship you design with your students. We trust you can take these ideas, put them into your own operating system, and change the way you and your students see school. It's impossible to be design minded and pessimistic, and because of that, we are confident in you and your students.

A design-minded teacher trusts the process.

We trust you.

Frequently Asked Questions (FAQs)

If you build it, [they] will come.

—Field of Dreams

In the following sections, you'll find questions commonly asked by those considering implementing design thinking into their classroom, along with responses from Doug based on his teaching experience. Please visit www.cardboardclassroom.com to access extra materials beyond this book.

? Does Being Design Minded Mean My Students Never Do Worksheets, Take Tests, or Do Homework?

A central tenet of being design minded is the only thing a teacher should be hardline about is never being hardline about anything. Being design minded is not just about building things; it's about rebuilding how you, the teacher, see your classroom. Nothing is wasted. If something does not work, then design-minded teachers can ask themselves, "How can I break this so I can make it work?" or tell themselves, "I can't see any use for this *yet*, so I'm going to put it over here and wait for the seed to sprout."

Your students will do worksheets, but rarely will they be worksheets you've gotten from a website, nor will they be worksheets from the prescribed curriculum unless you've found a way to modify said worksheets to work for your students. You will not throw those things away, but you might not use them the way their designer intended either. You will sometimes use part of a worksheet or take a section to use for a different assignment. You should use worksheets when you have your students organize their thinking by writing down their design steps or their reflections on replicated forms. For a design-minded teacher, the problem is not the worksheet itself but the way it's used. Viewing worksheets as just another tool to support the design-minded classroom will help you see them as adaptable materials for your own unique plans.

As far as homework goes, design-minded students rarely do homework. This wasn't the case when I first started teaching, and I would guess that goes for you as well. My thinking about students' time out of school evolved concurrently to my own philosophy. Homework, as we all learned because this reality was practically lit up in neon over the course of the Great Stay Home of 2020–2021, is deeply inequitable. You will routinely send students out the door at the end of the day with a reminder to think about their projects. You can encourage them to write or draw if they want to, but know building or project completion rarely happens at home.

The homework philosophy of a design-minded teacher is as holistic as anything else. You might tell your students to read every night for at least twenty-five minutes. Why twenty-five? Because it's a memorable number. But don't require a reading log for this assignment. Tell your students you'll know they're reading at home if you can see them getting better at reading. Practice matters. At the beginning of the year, you might routinely say, "A few weeks into the year, and you'll know where you're strong and where you need work. If your times tables aren't strong, you should work on those at home. I won't send home worksheets unless you ask. But I will know if you're working on your times tables because I'll see you getting better at mathematics." Teach your students about the idea of growth, and encourage them to share all the ways they've grown or changed in your time together.

You will give tests because, out of all of the above, tests are the most expected by the system we're operating within. You'll routinely give quizzes and mathematics tests as a form of retrieval practice (Agarwal & Bain, 2019) because they are the quickest ways to figure out if students have learned the background knowledge they'll need, which is the knowledge we're responsible for teaching. Retrieval practice is when students practice bringing previously learned information back to the forefront of their minds. But the projects are where the students show how they synthesize and use the concepts. As for reading, don't give spelling tests. Teach ways of figuring out how to spell words they don't know how to spell. Spoiler: the answer to that riddle is to have many conversations about patterns and quirks of the English language. Meanwhile, offer students multiple ways to show their understanding of a story that don't rely on written assignments.

? How Do I Apply Design-Minded Thinking to Curriculum I'm Required to Teach?

Design-minded thinking is not something applied to something else. Curriculum does not become design minded. Curriculum is a tool. The *teacher* becomes design minded. The teacher is the active agent in the mix of student and curriculum. You will rarely create something brand new, because after all, who has the time? Trying to create a brand-new project, assessment, and process for every single concept taught throughout the school year is a recipe for burnout. Instead, you'll consider the possibilities inherent in the required curriculum. When mapping out plans for the week or month (I'll plead the Fifth on lesson plans), don't edit your ideas right away. You should consider any possibility, even if it seems like a stupid idea. Murphy's Laws of Combat state, "If it's stupid and it works, then it's not stupid." Turn the idea this way and that, and if you can find a way to make it work with your students, the curriculum, and your long-term pedagogical goals, then it's not stupid.

As an example, I think it would be great for my students to take part in building a functional cardboard chandelier to suspend over their desks. I love the idea of them working together to create a statement piece for our classroom as an analogy for learning. Sadly, it is still just an idea because I can't make it work with the instructional goals. Building a cardboard chandelier is a ridiculous idea that, on its surface, has no educational value. Even I know doing a project for the sake of doing it, with no pedagogical purpose, is taking design mindedness too far and creating a contrived pseudo-context (Spencer & Juliani, 2017). No one wants to do these projects more than I do, and if I can't find a way to justify them within the curriculum and standards, that means I am reaching much too far and creating a false connection, or context, with which to excuse the projects. Being design minded requires honestly looking at yourself and your ideas. To go back to the analogy from the very first chapter (page 11), while the classroom is a ship at sea, district- and school-mandated curricula represent hoops. I, an avowed design-minded teacher, look at them and think, *Those hoops would look great on the side of my ship. I bet I could catch fish with those.*

❓ How Do I Respond When a Parent Is Uncomfortable With My Classroom Structure?

This probably happens more than we are aware of. Many parents are too polite to say, "Uh, what's going on in here?" I should qualify the previous statement with a disclaimer; they are likely too polite to say that to *me*, a white cisgender man with visible tattoos who some might see as intimidating, and others might just read as an authority figure. Female, nonbinary, or transgender design-minded teachers likely have different experiences. In my experience, parents will stand up to cisgender women teachers and question them and their expertise more readily than they will mine. For example, if the female-presenting special education teacher has a suggestion, the parents might push back, but if I have the same suggestion, they won't. This is part of that glass escalator we mentioned in the introduction (page 1). Men in women-dominated professions are more likely to be seen as voices of authority. While we teachers can't presently do anything about that on a systemic level, we can try to dissuade this line of thinking in our own communities, one conversation at a time. The following are a few things a design-minded teacher will find successful when parents express concerns.

Give the parents as much of your time as you reasonably can to help them feel comfortable. We have all had multiple phone calls or in-person meetings to answer questions. You might need to walk a parent through your seating and homework policies and everything else you might take from this book. If a parent asks a question you can't answer, it means you haven't spent enough time thinking through something. On the occasion when an adult related to one of your students asks you something you can't answer to both of your satisfactions, make changes or adjustments. There are times, though, when you give an answer that satisfies you but doesn't satisfy the parent.

In those cases, turn to the student's work and actions. Even with all the attendant impostor syndromes and doubts and bad days that come with being a teacher, you will hopefully be able to confidently say students love your class. When a student's grown-up remains unsure, the student's love for your class can be a tipping point. If the student goes home and talks about what they built in class, how fun it was, what they learned, how it all happened, and that "Mr. Robertson almost fell off a desk; it was so funny," parents will generally accept most of what you do.

I hold one parent conference close to my heart and remember it on *those days* when I need something to anchor me. A father told me he had a hard time getting his daughter to come to school during the previous year. She never wanted to get out of bed, and getting anything done was always a fight. She really hated school. A few weeks into my class, she got angry when he made her stay home because she had a 101-degree fever. I will not, and cannot, promise following the philosophy laid out in this book will lead to the same scenario for you, but trust there are parents out there who will celebrate their child's experience learning in the design-minded classroom.

? In What Way Does the Design-Minded Approach Shape My Classroom Rules and Routines?

Design mindedness touches every single piece of the classroom. Don't make a seating chart unless the year is going extremely poorly and you need to prove just how much the class as a whole is struggling. When students come into your class on day one, greet them and then tell them they can find a desk. Any desk. And all the while, make observations and take notes. Who sits where? Who sits next to who? Watch your students' parents and guardians. Which parents laugh nervously when they hear you say that? Which guardians look to see what other students are doing before they send their child off to pick a desk? These details go down in your notes. In effect, you're modeling design-minded teaching as you've presented a problem: find a place to sit. You make it clear it's *our* classroom, not *yours*. Give them choice, and not a small choice. Where a student sits is a *big-C Choice* for any student in any classroom. This simple activity communicates, "I trust you. You will be taking control, which also means you will be taking responsibility."

Don't give students rules; rather, make the rules with them. After everyone has found a desk and you've gone through the required routines, ask the class, "You've been in school for years now. What rules does a classroom need to run well and help everyone learn the best, based on your experience?" Let the students go for as long as they can while you write down their comments. Cover the whiteboards at the front of your room with their notes. Write on chart paper, and hang it on every flat surface. It's amazing what they come up with: "Don't run in the classroom," "Don't talk while the teacher is talking," and "Don't put gum in anyone's hair." After they've shared all their ideas, adopt a teacherly affect and say in your best teacherly voice, "OK, here are your class rules. Memorize them, please. No, no, you must memorize all of them so when you get in trouble, you know why. That's fair." Without fail, a student will look around at their classmates, look at you, raise their hand to the level of their shoulder, and suggest something like, "Well, can't *no running with scissors* and *be safe* be the same rule?"

"Of course, they can!" you say. "Any others we can combine?" And every year, without fail, you'll get down to four rules: (1) be safe, (2) be responsible, (3) be respectful, and (4) make good choices. Then describe to the students what you did. You drafted the rules, put them to the test, and revised. Tell them that's how you're going to be approaching problems in your classroom all year long. Your colleagues set similar rules and discuss them. They end up at the same place as your class, but the journeys are very different.

If there is a way you can take a decision off your hands and put it in the hands of the class, do it. At the same time, don't have class jobs, and don't expect your students to create them. Who's a line leader? Whoever is in the front of the line when the class lines up. It doesn't take long for students to realize the rule "be respectful" means not pushing others out of the way to be at the head of the line. When the class cleans the room, it's never "pick up *your* trash." It's always "pick up *our* trash." Who is getting books for the group? You don't care; students get books for their group. Have them work it out.

Everything you do is to build communication and community. You put decisions in the students' hands. And soon, they stop looking to you for answers because they know they can solve the problem on their own and you trust them to do so. You will occasionally remind them asking for help isn't a weakness, and if you stop to help a group, it's not because they're in trouble. It only means you suspect they're experiencing strong winds, and you want to make sure everyone is safe.

? Will My Colleagues Ever Complain or Worry About My Students Being Ahead or Behind Theirs?

I have been so lucky when it comes to grade-level teams. I honestly could not ask for more open-minded, helpful, rough-and-ready teachers to work directly with. Everyone understands we are all doing what we think will be best for our class. Let that mindset forge a collaborative, not competitive, colleague culture at your school. We all know theft is good, for example, so share, "Please steal my ideas because I'll steal yours." The people who worry about students being in front of or behind others are mostly administrators and parents.

This worry will happen most for parents on the rare occasion when two students from the same family are in the same grade level but split between two teachers. Those teachers will need to touch base frequently. Their parent meetings will include a question like, "In the other class, my son is doing *x*, *y*, or *z*, and in here, my daughter isn't. Why is that?" And both teachers will answer, "The other teacher is an excellent teacher, and we work together closely. So, while the action your son is doing might be different, the learning is not." They will use the same basic answer with administrators.

To be sure, there are teachers who simply don't agree with the design-minded philosophy. Some teachers who see what you're doing can't get past the mess, the building, or whatever else isn't traditional in their eyes. I'm sure their worry is not so much about your students falling behind theirs as it is about your students having a "weird" teacher who they don't think is doing the best by them. I've come to terms with being weird in a way best summarized via an exchange between Commander Lock and Morpheus at the end of *The Matrix Reloaded* (Wachowski & Wachowski, 2003):

> Commander Lock: "Dammit, Morpheus, not everyone believes what you believe."
>
> Morpheus: "My beliefs do not require them to."

Doubt from others should not stop you from doing work you believe in.

? How Do I Respond When a Student Is Uncomfortable With My Classroom Structure?

Student comfort is a priority in a design-minded class. It is awfully hard for people to learn new information when they are uncomfortable. This isn't to say students are always comfortable in your class. Sometimes, the content itself is uncomfortable. It's uncomfortable to repeatedly experience failure during the designing and testing, but if your classroom's structure is what makes them uncomfortable, do your best to work with the students and their families to solve the problem.

The most common source of discomfort in a design-minded class is the cognitive dissonance students experience when they compare your classroom to the "game of school." The students who usually express this cognitive dissonance are organized, find comfort in structure, and need well-defined parameters and guidance to succeed. Frankly, I'm impressed by the students who know themselves this well in elementary school. They can articulate that the flexibility of your class throws off their stability, and they can call out your tendency to put things back on the students by asking open-ended questions like, "Is this done?" or "I dunno, is it?" as stressful for them. They are used to the teacher telling them what they need to do, and then they do that very well, and then they get praise. With such students, you may need to have a firmer touch and give them more specific guidance than others to start. The problem is finding a comfort level where learning is possible. A lack of structure doesn't work for them. So, go back to the drawing board, collect more data with the student, and adjust. That's part of being a design-minded teacher: you're designing your classroom environment. With some students, you can say, "Make a thing. Go." And they will. Some need more detail, which is where you find how few direct steps you can give while still giving the students what they need.

In most cases, as students learn to trust you and each other, they get more comfortable with being uncomfortable. They come to realize on this ship, you walk around with a backpack full of nets, ready to catch someone before they fall into the water or scoop them up if they do fall in and can't find their own way back onto the boat. Your goal is for them to be able to sit with discomfort but feel confident in their ability to find a way through.

? Will There Be Moments When I Worry About Being a Design-Minded Teacher?

Only every day. Many teachers will tell you constant worrying about doing the best you can do for students is a normal part of education. (An analysis of teachers' constant anxiety and doubt as a bad thing is a whole different book.) You will worry all the time. You'll worry when you don't think your students have gotten far enough in their book because you spent a week building traps. You'll worry when you see certain evaluations come back lower than you know they are supposed to be, even though out loud, you say you don't care about those evaluations because they don't measure learning in a real, reliable way. You will get a permanent crick in your neck from listening to the little teacher on your shoulder who repeats, "What if I'm wrong?"

This is the only way I know how to be a teacher. My entire classroom is built on being design minded. Being design minded means being flexible, evolving, failing, and coming back better. Still, right around the end of winter break every year, I feel confident I'm doing right by my students but unsure I'm doing the *best* right. Failure in a design-minded classroom is very visible. When a big project goes badly, it does not go badly quietly, and it takes hard work to salvage. My students and I learn from failure. That doesn't stop me from mournfully staring at the ceiling tiles after everyone has left while heavy metal blasts from my speakers. But I continue to trust the process. I trust my students and I trust myself because every year, all my students successfully make it to the far shore on a ship we steered together.

It is in the self-questioning that lightning can strike. *Self-questioning* is where confidence in students' abilities comes in and you can find the ways to trust yourself and your students. And the more you engage in self-questioning, the more you will trust yourself.

Failure is not bad. Not adjusting to failure is bad. Doubts are not bad. Not confronting doubts is bad. If you feel that being design minded will be good for you and good for your students, you hold to that because it has value and it will bear fruit. Plus, you will be experiencing and modeling the process your students will go through. How often do we, as teachers, truly identify with what is happening to our students in our classrooms? How often is that learning experience shared? Being design minded allows you to share the growth.

? What's Your Favorite Design-Minded Memory?

The first big project of the year, called the *hobby project*, tasks students with learning something new. In only three weeks, they have to choose a topic, research it, teach themselves, and prepare to share their new hobby. The project timeline is long enough to go from zero to something, but not long enough to go from zero to expert. The purpose of the project is for students to experience making a choice, starting something by being bad at it, and then getting better at it. My favorite memory comes from the first year I tried this project with my class, which was early in my design-minded journey.

A student who had been making a questionable name for himself in my class chose to learn magic. To this point, he had barely turned anything in, and what he had turned in was lackluster both in effort and in final product. I wasn't sure what to expect, but I admit to being more pessimistic about the magic trick than a teacher should have been.

Come the day of his presentation, he asked for a volunteer and pulled up his best friend. The class preemptively giggled, likely expecting some nonsense like the things he'd done for laughs earlier in the year. The student then went into a seemingly well-rehearsed "Is this your card?" trick that, even during its early stages, I thought may have been making fun of his friend, the class, me, or magicians in general. The gist of the trick was he quickly cut cards from the deck that were not *the card* until he was down to ten.

Then he went through those ten cards, asking with each card reveal, "Is this your card?" to which his friend responded no every time. He did it again with the same ten cards. *No. No. No.* Finally, he had his friend grip one corner of the ten cards, which were facedown. Suddenly, he smacked the cards out of his friend's hand. Cards scattered all over the floor. The class gasped and looked at me. I looked at them and then back at the student and finally at his assistant, who was left holding only one card facedown. It hadn't fallen with the rest of the cards somehow. The boy again asked his question, "Is this your card?" and this time, there was something just a little different in his voice.

Keep in mind we'd seen each of these ten cards three times. His friend flipped the card over, and I watched his mind explode. That was his card! I know you're thinking the two of them planned it, but trust me; the friend wasn't that good of an actor. His mind was well and truly blown. The class *exploded*. I exploded. The magician held up his hands and loudly proclaimed, "Wait!" With all eyeballs watching him, he collected the final card as well as every card on the ground and quickly counted them out for us to see. There were still only ten cards.

I do not know how the student did the trick. I don't want to know. In that moment, to every student in my class, he went from one of *those* students who are in trouble all the time to a wizard. I marched him over to the teacher next door, interrupted her class, and announced, "You have to see this." I tried to send him to the office to show the office staff and the principal, but he wouldn't go because he'd never been to the office for something good and didn't trust it.

The sound my class made in that moment will echo in my mind forever (mostly because I made the same sound). It wasn't like I hadn't believed in him before this project. I had. But in one moment, we all realized how wrong we had been about this boy. He wasn't who we had thought he was. He showed me I could push students, and if we trusted each other, we could go big.

It was a turning point for this student too because up until that point, he had never felt successful like that in class. He hadn't been publicly praised, cheered for, or told that what he did was better than decent. I brought this back throughout the whole year. When he would struggle or doubt himself, I could talk about the magic trick. He could remember his reflection about the project and how his hard work had brought him excellent results. The hobby project happens at the beginning of the year because I can use it for the rest of the year as a reminder that dedication to improving a skill and learning something brings great benefits.

? What Will Be the Hardest Lesson to Learn About Being Design Minded?

Balance. You might love working in public school even with all the issues that go along with it. You might do nothing but build stuff and go crazy with big projects all year if you could. You can't do *only* big projects because that's not good teaching. Parents trust public education to educate their children, not just keep them amused all day.

Students need to do certain things to succeed in their learning. They need to do things maybe not as fun as building cars and Rube Goldberg machines. They need to learn and practice their times tables because number fluency is just as important as sound fluency. They need to understand the rules of writing so they can subvert them when they get better at it. They need to do the basics, which are not flashy or big but will benefit them on the big, flashy things as much as they will benefit them on the tests, in their next school year, and in the year after that. The principal I had during my first year of teaching was great at talking with me about needing balance and about keeping my ideas but remembering why I was in the classroom. Those conversations are why there isn't a cardboard chandelier in my classroom. Yet.

Being design minded does not mean you're always making things and doing cool stuff. From the outside, though, it might look like that. I have had more than one teacher tell me my classroom looks like fun and games and cardboard and craziness, and not in a good way. Students may often be excited to have you as their teacher because they have looked into your room from the hallway, and they have seen puppets and builds and who knows what else. And then when they get to you, they will be a little bit confused and let down when they still have to get out their reading books and define vocabulary words. But you teach standard subjects like vocabulary because they are important, and the more words or concepts students know, the more colors they have on their palettes to paint with.

So, your instinct to go big (such as by making a working cardboard chandelier) because it'll be cool will always be fighting against your more formal teacher instinct to ask, "Yes, but what are students learning?" ("What's the point of a cardboard chandelier if it's *only* cool? You've seen *The Phantom of the Opera* too many times. Be a teacher!") Being design minded is not a thing you do; it's what you are. And it must be liquid, changing to fit your needs, the needs of the students, and the needs of the school.

In the end, every design-minded teacher's journey is different. That's the point of being design minded. No two classrooms will look the same, but at the same time, the big ideas—the design process, the struggle, the lightning—will be present in all of them. Expect to question yourself, and prepare to be reflective, possibly in ways you've never had to reflect before. By preparing for discomfort, we are better able to move with it and use it.

Trust in the process, in the struggle, in the students, and in yourself. Be flexible in all things except your willingness to be flexible, but at the same time, be strong and firm in your journey. In the design-minded classroom, there is no ending because every answer, every question, builds to something new, something better.

REFERENCES AND RESOURCES

Adam Savage's Tested. (2021, January 10). *Ask Adam Savage: Would you have changed anything about MythBusters?* [Video file]. Accessed at www.youtube.com/watch?v=IkawOT_Cg-s on September 15, 2021.

Administrative Office of the U.S. Courts. (n.d.). *Glossary of legal terms.* United States Courts. Accessed at www.uscourts.gov/glossary on January 7, 2022.

Agarwal, P. K., & Bain, P. M. (2019). *Powerful teaching: Unleash the science of learning.* San Francisco: Jossey-Bass.

Ahmed, S. (2017). *Living a feminist life.* Durham, NC: Duke University Press.

Ahmed, S. K. (2018). *Being the change: Lessons and strategies to teach social comprehension.* Portsmouth, NH: Heinemann.

Allowitz, M. (Director). (2017, May 16). *Infantino street* (Season 2017, Episode 22) [TV series episode]. In D. Nutter, G. Stanton, S. Schechter, A. Helbing, T. Helbing, A. Kreisberg, et al. (Executive producers), The Flash. Bonanza Productions.

American Psychiatric Association. (2022). *Diagnostic and statistical manual of mental disorders: DSM-5-TR* (5th ed.). Washington, DC: Author.

Apple, M. W., & Beane, J. A. (Eds.). (1995). *Democratic schools.* Alexandria, VA: Association for Supervision and Curriculum Development.

Apple, M. W., & Beane, J. A. (Eds.). (2007). *Democratic schools: Lessons in powerful education* (2nd ed.). Portsmouth, NH: Heinemann.

Barker, J. E., Semenov, A. D., Michaelson, L., Provan, L. S., Snyder, H. R., & Munakata, Y. (2014). Less-structured time in children's daily lives predicts self-directed executive functioning. *Frontiers in Psychology, 5*(593). Accessed at https://doi.org/10.3389fpsyg.2014.00593 on September 13, 2021.

Berger, R., Rugen, L., & Woodfin, L. (2014). *Leaders of their own learning: Transforming schools through student-engaged assessment.* San Francisco: Jossey-Bass.

Bird, B. (Director). (2004). *The Incredibles* [Film]. Pixar Animation Studios.

Blackburn, B. R. (2018). Productive struggle is a learner's sweet spot. *ASCD Express, 14*(11).

Borgioli Binis, J. (2016, March 25). *The intersection of women and leadership.* Accessed at www.edweek.org /teaching-learning/opinion-the-intersection-of-women-and-leadership/2016/03 on January 5, 2022.

Borgioli Binis, J. (2018a, May 3). *Prison cells and pretty walls: Gender coding and American schools.* Accessed at https://nursingclio.org/2018/05/03/prison-cells-and-pretty-walls-gender-coding-and-american-schools on September 13, 2021.

Borgioli Binis, J. (2018b, February 1). *Three moves for assessment-system success.* Accessed at www.ascd.org/el /articles/three-moves-for-assessment-system-success on January 31, 2022.

Borgioli Binis, J. (2019, August 21). *What women "want": Wordsmithing education reform rhetoric.* Accessed at https://nursingclio.org/2019/08/21/what-women-want-wordsmithing-education-reform-rhetoric on January 7, 2022.

Boss, S. (2018). *Project based teaching: How to create rigorous and engaging learning experiences.* Alexandria, VA: Association for Supervision and Curriculum Development.

BrainyQuote. (n.d.). *Guillermo del Toro quotes.* Accessed at www.brainyquote.com/quotes/guillermo _del_toro_872928 on September 15, 2021.

Bryk, A. S., & Schneider, B. (2002). *Trust in schools: A core resource for improvement.* New York: Russell Sage Foundation.

Burvall, A., & Ryder, D. (2017). *Intention: Critical creativity in the classroom.* Irvine, CA: EdTechTeam Press.

Carpenter, T. P., Fennema, E., Franke, M. L., Levi, L., & Empson, S. B. (2015). *Children's mathematics: Cognitively guided instruction* (2nd ed.). Portsmouth, NH: Heinemann.

Cohen, E. G., & Lotan, R. A. (2014). *Designing groupwork: Strategies for the heterogeneous classroom* (3rd ed.). New York: Teachers College Press.

Common Core of Data (CCD). (2020). *Table 2. Number of operating public schools and districts, student membership, teachers, and pupil/teacher ratio, by state or jurisdiction: School year 2019–20.* Accessed at https://nces.ed.gov/ccd/tables/201920_summary_2.asp on February 28, 2022.

Csikszentmihalyi, M. (2014). *Applications of flow in human development and education.* New York: Springer.

Darling-Hammond, L. (2013). *Getting teacher evaluation right: What really matters for effectiveness and improvement.* New York: Teachers College Press.

del Toro, G. (Director). (2013). *Pacific rim* [Film]. Legendary Pictures.

del Toro, G. (Director). (2015). *Crimson peak* [Film]. Legendary Pictures.

del Toro, G. (Director). (2017). *The shape of water* [Film]. Fox Searchlight Pictures.

Denton, P. (2013). *The power of our words: Teacher language that helps children learn* (2nd ed.). Turners Falls, MA: Northeast Foundation for Children.

Donovan, F. R. (1938). *The schoolma'am.* New York: Stokes.

Dorn, S. (2021, February 28). *Transmission chains broke trust chains* [Blog post]. Accessed at https:// shermandorn.com/wordpress/?p=9090 on September 14, 2021.

Drapeau, P. (2014). *Sparking student creativity: Practical ways to promote innovative thinking and problem solving.* Alexandria, VA: Association for Supervision and Curriculum Development.

Duckworth, A. (2016). *Grit: The power of passion and perseverance.* New York: Scribner.

Dweck, C. S. (2016). *Mindset: The new psychology of success* (Updated ed.). New York: Random House.

Fell, S., & Butler, C. (Directors). (2012). *ParaNorman* [Film]. LAIKA Studios.

Fisher, D., & Frey, N. (2014). Speaking and listening in content area learning. *The Reading Teacher, 68*(1), 64–69.

Fisher, D., & Frey, N. (2015). *Unstoppable learning: Seven essential elements to unleash student potential.* Bloomington, IN: Solution Tree Press.

Gawande, A. (2010). *The checklist manifesto: How to get things right.* New York: Metropolitan Books.

Gilliam, T., & Jones, T. (Directors). (1975). *Monty Python and the holy grail* [Film]. Python Pictures.

Goodreads. (n.d.). *Heinrich Heine quotes.* Accessed at https://www.goodreads.com/quotes/616583-christianity---and-that-is-its-greatest-merit---has on September 15, 2021.

Green, E. (2014). *Building a better teacher: How teaching works (and how to teach it to everyone).* New York: Norton.

Greene, A. H., & Melton, G. D. (2007). *Test talk: Integrating test preparation into reading workshop.* Portland, ME: Stenhouse.

Gregory, G., & Kaufeldt, M. (2015). *The motivated brain: Improving student attention, engagement, and perseverance*. Alexandria, VA: Association for Supervision and Curriculum Development.

Griffiths, A. (2013). *The 13-story treehouse*. New York: Feiwel and Friends.

Guskey, T. R., & Bailey, J. M. (2010). *Developing standards-based report cards*. Thousand Oaks, CA: Corwin.

Hammond, Z. (2015). *Culturally responsive teaching and the brain: Promoting authentic engagement and rigor among culturally and linguistically diverse students*. Thousand Oaks, CA: Corwin.

Harris, T. L., & Hodges, R. E. (Eds.). (1995). *The literacy dictionary: The vocabulary of reading and writing*. Newark, DE: International Literacy Association.

Hatch, M. (2014). *The maker movement manifesto: Rules for innovation in the new world of crafters, hackers, and tinkerers*. New York: McGraw-Hill Education.

Henriksen, D., & Mishra, P. (2015). We teach who we are: Creativity in the lives and practices of accomplished teachers. *Teachers College Record, 117*(7), 1–46.

Henriksen, D., Richardson, C., & Mehta, R. (2017). Design thinking: A creative approach to educational problems of practice. *Thinking Skills and Creativity, 26*, 140–153.

IDEO. (2012). *Design thinking for educators* (2nd ed.). Accessed at https://page.ideo.com/design-thinking -edu-toolkit on September 14, 2021.

Internet Archive. (2013). *Mercury theatre on the air 38-10-30: War of the worlds*. Accessed at https://archive .org/details/MercuryTheatreOnTheAir381030WarOfTheWorlds on April 26, 2022.

Inzlicht, M., & Schmader, T. (Eds.). (2012). *Stereotype threat: Theory, process, and application*. New York: Oxford University Press.

Jemison, M. (2002, February). *Teach arts and sciences together* [Video file]. TED Conferences. Accessed at https://www.ted.com/talks/mae_jemison_teach_arts_and_sciences_together on September 16, 2021.

Johnston, P. H. (2012). *Opening minds: Using language to change lives*. Portland, ME: Stenhouse.

Kaiser, A. (2020). *Designing the future: How engineering builds creative critical thinkers in the classroom*. Bloomington, IN: Solution Tree Press.

Katz, J., Heisterkamp, H. A., & Fleming, W. M. (2011). The social justice roots of the Mentors in Violence Prevention model and its application in a high school setting. *Violence Against Women, 17*(6), 684–702.

Kleinrock, L. (2021). *Start here, start now: A guide to antibias and antiracist work in your school community*. Portsmouth, NH: Heinemann.

Knight, T. (Director). (2016). *Kubo and the two strings* [Film]. LAIKA Studios.

Krebs, D., & Zvi, G. (2016). *The genius hour guidebook: Fostering passion, wonder, and inquiry in the classroom*. New York: Routledge.

Lalor, A. D. M. (2012). Keeping the destination in mind. *Educational Leadership, 70*(1), 75–78.

Lalor, A. D. M. (2017). *Ensuring high-quality curriculum: How to design, revise, or adopt curriculum aligned to student success*. Alexandria, VA: Association for Supervision and Curriculum Development.

Learner-Centered Initiatives. (n.d.). *Learner-centered test prep: Research, tools, and professional development support*. Accessed at https://lciltd.org/resources/learner-centered-test-prep on April 27, 2022.

Lenz, B., Wells, J., & Kingston, S. (2015). *Transforming schools using project-based deeper learning, performance assessment, and Common Core standards*. San Francisco: Jossey-Bass.

Lortie, D. C. (1975). *Schoolteacher: A sociological study*. Chicago: University of Chicago Press.

Lyon, H. (2020). *Engagement is not a unicorn (it's a narwhal): Mind-changing theory and strategies that will create real engagement*. Alexandria, VA: EduMatch.

Malkovsky, E., Merrifield, C., Goldberg, Y., & Danckert, J. (2012). Exploring the relationship between boredom and sustained attention. *Experimental Brain Research*, *221*(1), 59–67.

Mann, S., & Cadman, R. (2014). Does being bored make us more creative? *Creativity Research Journal*, *26*(2), 165–173.

Marshall, J. C. (2016). *The highly effective teacher: 7 classroom-tested practices that foster student success.* Alexandria, VA: Association for Supervision and Curriculum Development.

Martin-Kniep, G. O. (2000). *Becoming a better teacher: Eight innovations that work.* Alexandria, VA: Association for Supervision and Curriculum Development.

Martin-Kniep, G. O., & Picone-Zocchia, J. (2009). *Changing the way you teach, improving the way students learn.* Alexandria, VA: Association for Supervision and Curriculum Development.

Marzano, R. J., & Marzano, J. S. (2015). *Managing the inner world of teaching: Emotions, interpretations, and actions.* Bloomington, IN: Marzano Resources.

Mehta, J. (2014, June 20). *Deeper learning has a race problem.* Accessed at www.edweek.org/leadership /opinion-deeper-learning-has-a-race-problem/2014/06 on September 14, 2021.

Merriam-Webster. (n.d.). *Merriam-Webster medical dictionary.* Accessed at www.merriam-webster.com /medical on January 7, 2022.

Merritt, J. (n.d.). *What are mental models?* Accessed at https://thesystemsthinker.com/What-Are-Mental -Models/ on September 14, 2021.

Montgomery, S. (2006). *Quest for the tree kangaroo: An expedition to the cloud forest of New Guinea.* Boston: Houghton Mifflin.

Moss, C. M., & Brookhart, S. M. (2012). *Learning targets: Helping students aim for understanding in today's lesson.* Alexandria, VA: Association for Supervision and Curriculum Development.

MrWilliamsD8. (2016, September 9). *Put your two cents in: CLR discussion protocol* [Video file]. Accessed at www.youtube.com/watch?v=VTpa0eWQfko on April 8, 2022.

Mullick, N. (2012, April 9). *Caine's arcade* [Video file]. Accessed at https://www.youtube.com/watch ?v=faIFNkdq96U on September 16, 2021.

Musker, J., & Clements, R. (Directors). (2016). *Moana* [Film]. Walt Disney Pictures.

National Governors Association Center for Best Practices & Council of Chief State School Officers. (2010). *Common Core State Standards for English language arts and literacy in history/social studies, science, and technical subjects.* Washington, DC: Authors. Accessed at www.corestandards.org/assets/CCSSI_ELA %20Standards.pdf on September 14, 2021.

OK Go. (2010, March 2). *OK Go—This too shall pass—Rube Goldberg machine—Official video* [Video file]. Accessed at https://www.youtube.com/watch?v=qybUFnY7Y8w on September 16, 2021.

Ostroff, W. L. (2016). *Cultivating curiosity in K–12 classrooms: How to promote and sustain deep learning.* Alexandria, VA: Association for Supervision and Curriculum Development.

Parker, M., Cruz, L., Gachago, D., & Morkel, J. (2021). Design thinking for challenges and change in K–12 and teacher education. *Journal of Cases in Educational Leadership*, *24*(1), 3–14.

Parrish, N. (2022). *The independent learner: Metacognitive exercises to help K–12 students focus, self-regulate, and persevere.* Bloomington, IN: Solution Tree Press.

Pete, B., & Fogarty, R. (2018). *Everyday problem-based learning: Quick projects to build problem-solving fluency.* Alexandria, VA: Association for Supervision and Curriculum Development.

Physicians' Desk Reference Staff. (2017). *Physicians' desk reference* (71st ed.). Montvale, NJ: PDR Network.

Posey, A., & Novak, K. (2020). *Unlearning: Changing your beliefs and your classroom with UDL.* Wakefield, MA: CAST.

Robinson, P. A. (Director). (1989). *Field of dreams* [Film]. Gordon Company.

Roddenberry, G., Moore, R. D., Braga, B. (Writers), & Kolbe, W. (Director). (1994, May 23). All good things . . . (Season 7, Episodes 25 and 26) [TV series episodes]. In R. Berman, M. Piller, & J. Taylor (Executive Producers), *Star trek: The next generation*. Paramount Domestic Television.

Rosso, B. D. (2014). Creativity and constraints: Exploring the role of constraints in the creative processes of research and development teams. *Organization Studies, 35*(4), 551–585.

Savage, A. (2019). *Every tool's a hammer: Life is what you make it.* New York: Simon & Schuster.

Schlechty, P. C. (2002). *Working on the work: An action plan for teachers, principals, and superintendents.* San Francisco: Jossey-Bass.

Seidel, S. (2016, December 20). *Deeper learning has a race problem—and it may have the solution.* Accessed at www.edweek.org/leadership/opinion-deeper-learning-has-a-race-problem-and-it-may-have-the -solution/2016/12 on September 14, 2021.

Senge, P. (2002). *Schools that learn: A fifth discipline fieldbook for educators, parents, and everyone who cares about education.* New York: Doubleday.

Senge, P., Cambron-McCabe, N., Lucas, T., Smith, B., Dutton, J., & Kleiner, A. (2012). *Schools that learn: A fifth discipline fieldbook for educators, parents, and everyone who cares about education* (Updated and revised ed.). New York: Currency.

Shelley, M. (2003). *Frankenstein; or, the modern Prometheus* (Rev. ed.). London: Penguin.

Shulman, L. S. (2004). *The wisdom of practice: Essays on teaching, learning, and learning to teach.* San Francisco: Jossey-Bass.

Smith, R. A. (2012). Money, benefits, and power: A test of the glass ceiling and glass escalator hypotheses. *The ANNALS of the American Academy of Political and Social Science, 639*(1), 149–172.

Spencer, J., & Juliani, A. J. (2016). *Launch: Using design thinking to boost creativity and bring out the maker in every student.* San Diego, CA: Dave Burgess Consulting.

Spencer, J., & Juliani, A. J. (2017). *Empower: What happens when students own their learning.* San Diego, CA: IMpress.

Sprenger, M. (2020). *Social-emotional learning and the brain: Strategies to help your students thrive.* Alexandria, VA: Association for Supervision and Curriculum Development.

Stiggins, R. (2014). *Defensible teacher evaluation: Student growth through classroom assessment.* Thousand Oaks, CA: Corwin.

Stitzlein, S. M. (2008). *Breaking bad habits of race and gender: Transforming identity in schools.* Lanham, MD: Rowman & Littlefield.

Stitzlein, S. M. (2012). *Teaching for dissent: Citizenship education and political activism.* Boulder, CO: Paradigm.

Stockman, A. (2016). *Make writing: 5 teaching strategies that turn writer's workshop into a maker space.* Cleveland, OH: Times 10.

Stommel, J. (2018, March 11). *How to ungrade.* Accessed at www.jessestommel.com/how-to-ungrade on April 26, 2022.

Stromberg, J. (2012, February 22). Teller speaks on the enduring appeal of magic. *Smithsonian Magazine.* Accessed at https://www.smithsonianmag.com/arts-culture/teller-speaks-on-the-enduring-appeal-of -magic-97842264 on September 14, 2021.

Tolisano, S. R., & Hale, J. A. (2018). *A guide to documenting learning: Making thinking visible, meaningful, shareable, and amplified.* Thousand Oaks, CA: Corwin.

Tollefson, K., & Osborn, M. K. (2008). *Cultivating the learner-centered classroom: From theory to practice.* Thousand Oaks, CA: Corwin Press.

Truong, G. (2014, July 2). *Educators can combat the deeper-learning race problem.* Accessed at https://www.edweek.org/leadership/opinion-educators-can-combat-the-deeper-learning-race-problem/2014/07 on September 14, 2021.

Tyack, D., & Cuban, L. (1995). *Tinkering toward utopia: A century of public school reform.* Cambridge, MA: Harvard University Press.

Venet, A. S. (2021). *Equity-centered trauma-informed education.* New York: Norton.

Verbinski, G. (Director). (2003). *Pirates of the Caribbean: The curse of the Black Pearl* [Film]. Walt Disney Pictures.

Wachowski, L., & Wachowski, L. (Directors). (2003). *The matrix reloaded* [Film]. Village Roadshow Pictures.

Walsh, E. (1995). *Schoolmarms: Women in America's schools.* San Francisco: Caddo Gap Press.

Wiliam, D. (2011). *Embedded formative assessment.* Bloomington, IN: Solution Tree Press.

Wiliam, D. (2018). *Embedded formative assessment* (2nd ed.). Bloomington, IN: Solution Tree Press.

Will, M. (2020, April 14). *Still mostly white and female: New federal data on the teaching profession.* Accessed at https://www.edweek.org/leadership/still-mostly-white-and-female-new-federal-data-on-the-teaching-profession/2020/04 on September 14, 2021.

Williams, C. L. (2013). The glass escalator, revisited: Gender inequality in neoliberal times, SWS feminist lecturer. *Gender & Society, 27*(5), 609–629.

Williams, D. J., Escobedo, N., & Vadnais, S. (2019). Using think-aloud to strengthen inquiry and research pedagogy. *Collegial Exchange, 85*(4), 24–26.

Willingham, D. T. (2009). *Why don't students like school? A cognitive scientist answers questions about how the mind works and what it means for the classroom.* San Francisco: Jossey-Bass.

Willingham, D. T. (2021, February 28). Op-ed: Twitter condemns dad who let daughter struggle to open a can. What should he have done? *Los Angeles Times.* Accessed at www.latimes.com/opinion/story/2021-02-28/can-opener-problem-twitter-roderick-parent-child on September 15, 2021.

Wilson, L. W. (2017). *What every teacher needs to know about assessment* (2nd ed.). New York: Routledge.

Wong, H. K., & Wong, R. T. (2018). *The classroom management book* (2nd ed.). Mountain View, CA: Harry K. Wong Publications.

Zemeckis, R. (Director). (1985). *Back to the future* [Film]. Universal Pictures.

INDEX

Remaking Literacy
Jacie Maslyk

Maker education—an instructional approach that emphasizes hands-on learning—empowers students to become passionate, creative thinkers and problem solvers. With *Remaking Literacy*, you will learn how to transform literacy teaching and learning by integrating maker education into K–5 classrooms.
BKF890

Designing the Future
Ann Kaiser

No matter the subject or grade, giving students engineering design challenges encourages creativity, communication, innovation, and collaboration. Throughout the book, you will find more than 25 easy-entry, low-risk engineering activities and projects you can begin immediately incorporating into existing classwork.
BKF853

Sustainable Project-Based Learning
Brad Sever

Learn how to design, implement, and assess engaging sustainable project-based learning (SPBL) units while ensuring students gain surface-, deep-, and transfer-level knowledge. Author Brad Sever offers a five-step process that partners academic growth with social-emotional skill development.
BKG012

Bringing Innovation to School
Suzie Boss

Activate your students' creativity and problem-solving potential with breakthrough learning projects. Across all grades and content areas, student-driven, collaborative projects will teach students how to generate innovative ideas and then put them into action.
BKF546

Solution Tree | Press   *a division of* Solution Tree

Visit SolutionTree.com or call 800.733.6786 to order.